T0382247

THE FIVE PERCENT

PETER T. COLEMAN, PhD

DIRECTOR OF COLUMBIA UNIVERSITY'S INTERNATIONAL CENTER FOR COOPERATION AND CONFLICT RESOLUTION

*with major contributions from Robin Vallacher, PhD,
Andrzej Nowak, PhD, Lan Bui-Wrzosinska, PhD,
Andrea Bartoli, PhD, Larry Liebovitch, PhD,
Naira Musallam, PhD, and Katharina Kugler, PhD,
of the Project on Conflict and Complexity*

finding solutions
to seemingly
impossible conflicts

THE FIVE PERCENT

PublicAffairs
New York

Published in the United States by PublicAffairs™,
a member of the Perseus Books Group

PublicAffairs books are available at special discounts for bulk purchases in the U.S. by corporations, institutions, and other organizations. For more information, please contact the Special Markets Department at the Perseus Books Group, 2300 Chestnut Street, Suite 200, Philadelphia, PA 19103, call (800) 810-4145, ext. 5000, or e-mail special.markets@perseusbooks.com.

Library of Congress Cataloging-in-Publication Data
Coleman, Peter T., 1959–
The five percent : finding solutions to seemingly impossible conflicts / Peter T. Coleman. —
1st ed.
p. cm.
Includes bibliographical references and index.
ISBN 978-1-58648-921-2 (hardback) — ISBN 978-1-58648-922-9 (e-Book)
1. Conflict management. 2. Conflict (Psychology) I. Title.
HM1126.C57 2011
303.6'9—dc22

2010050947

Editorial production by *Marra*thon Production Services. www.marrathon.net

BOOK DESIGN BY JANE RAESE
Text set in 12-point Bulmer

FIRST EDITION

For Mort Deutsch and Leah Doyle,
the coauthors of the best chapters of my life

contents

acknowledgments

THIS BOOK BEGAN WITH THE SIMPLE QUESTION, Why are some conflicts impossible to solve and what can we do to resolve them? This is a question I have been working on with my colleagues and students at Columbia University for over fifteen years. The answer is both complex and simple. The research that went into answering this question has been very complex. It involved in-depth case studies of impossible conflicts, expert interviews, lab experiments, mathematical formalisms, computer simulations, and a thorough review of the scholarly literature. This led to an elaborate and nuanced understanding of these types of conflicts. But the ideas and methods for addressing these problems that came from this research, and from extensive interviews and conversations with conflict mediators and peacemakers of all stripes, are simple, basic, practical, and straightforward. These practices are the main focus of *The Five Percent.*

This book is the product of our team. We are a motley crew: an unlikely mix of social psychologists, an anthropologist, an astrophysicist, complexity scientists, conflict specialists, and peacemakers. We were brought together by a deep, shared commitment to addressing the misery and mystery of impossible, destructive conflicts. Our Dynamical Systems Team is composed of Robin Vallacher, Andrzej Nowak, Lan Bui-Wrzosinska, Andrea Bartoli, Larry Liebovitch, Naira Musallam, Katharina Kugler, and myself, Peter T. Coleman. Our work together is never easy, always fruitful, and has thus far been the highlight of my career.

But let me be clear: the insights shared in this book were born out of the confusion, conflict, and nonlinearity that come only from working with such a talented, opinionated, multidisciplinary team as ours. None of us could have accomplished this feat alone. Consequently, the ideas and methods outlined here often go against conventional wisdom in the field of conflict resolution. In fact, they tend to challenge it directly. This is part of our mad method: to create enough tension in our field to break through the current frames of understanding in order to begin a new conversation where we must all *think different* about the possibility of resolving impossible conflicts. Fortunately, our work has been generously supported by the visionary James S. McDonnell Foundation and the Community Foundation of Boulder. It has also been enlightened and supported by a host of extraordinary PhD students, including Christine Chung, Lukasz Jochemczyk, Wieslaw Bartkowski, and Ryszard Praszkier. We are greatly indebted to them all.

We also want to thank all the eminent scholars and practitioners whose work has served as a foundation and inspiration for ours. They include Mary Parker Follett, Kurt Lewin, Morton Deutsch, Dean Pruitt, Herb Kelman, Chris Mitchell, Ronald Fisher, Louis Kriesberg, John Paul Lederach, David Johnson, Dean Tjosvold, Bill Ury, Roger Fisher, Heidi and Guy Burgess, John Gottman, Philip Tetlock, Dietrick Dorner, Gareth Morgan, Laura Chasin, Bernard Pearce, Stephen Littlejohn, Paul Diehl, Gary Goertz, William Zartman, Jacob Bercovitch, and Stephen Cohen. Also, we wish to thank the incredibly supportive staff of our center, the International Center for Cooperation and Conflict Resolution at Teachers College, Columbia University, including Beth Fisher-Yoshida, Claudia Cohen, Molly Clark, Juliette De Wolfe, Jeff Schiffer, and Manpreet Sadhal.

Finally, I want to personally thank my family for their patience, care, support, and fun before, during, and after the writing of this book. My love, Leah, my children, Hannah and Adlai, and my infamous siblings, Bob, Cookie, Bob H., Michelle, and Patrick. They keep me happy, humble, and sane in an often seemingly intractable world.

introduction

THE IRRESISTIBLE POWER OF THE PAST

It began with a single act of hubris. Tantalus, the ruler of an ancient city in Greece and a favorite of the gods, decided one day to test the gods' omniscience by chopping up and cooking his own son, Pelops, and serving him to them as a meal. Although the gods were on to this deceit from the beginning, one of them, Demeter, was distracted by her troubles with Hades. She feasted on the boy's shoulder before realizing what was happening.

Furious with this deception, the gods banished Tantalus to the deepest part of the underworld, starved and tortured ("tantalized") him for eternity, and cursed his entire family. So began the protracted misfortunes of the House of Atreus (Tantalus's descendants), which have served as the primary source of all tragedy from Homer and the great Greek dramatists to Shakespeare and O'Neill.

Life went downhill in the House of Atreus after Tantalus. His daughter, Niobe, whose fourteen children were slain by the gods, was turned to stone. The gods brought Pelops back to life, but he ended up killing his father-in-law (who coveted his own daughter) in order to marry his bride. Pelops then had two sons, Atreus and Thyestes, who murdered their half-brother (the illegitimate son of Pelops) to please their mother. Later, Thyestes seduced Atreus's wife and stole his golden fleece before fleeing into exile. Believing himself forgiven, he later returned to enjoy a meal at his brother's table that turned out to be Thyestes's own children.

Then things got complicated. Atreus's two sons Menelaus and Agamemnon married two sisters, Helen of Troy and Clytemnestra. Helen's kidnapping started the Trojan War. Then, to appease the gods in order to set sail for war, Agamemnon sacrificed his own daughter, Iphigenia. He came home from the war ten years later only to be murdered by his wife, Clytemnestra, before she was dutifully executed in turn by her own son Orestes. He later was driven mad by the Furies who of course were obligated to punish matricide.

So it went in the House of Atreus for generation after generation. Tragedy begot unspeakable suffering and sparked more tragedy for all who followed: Iphigenia, Electra, Orestes, you name it. As this ancient legend goes, all of it—the murder, incest, cannibalism, betrayal, seduction, matricide, patricide, war—sprang from the deeds of one man. His one act set in motion a chain of events that no human could stop. The curse of the House of Atreus was simply too powerful to resist. Time and again, the members of this misbegotten family, often against their own will and better judgment, were "driven into evil by the irresistible power of the past."[1]

Some problems never go away.

Experts estimate that about 5 percent of our more difficult conflicts become *intractable:* highly destructive, never ending, and virtually impossible to solve.[2] They occur in families, between friends, at work, among neighbors, and in the geopolitical arena. Like the gods' curse on the House of Atreus, they seem to have a power of their own that is inexplicable and total, driving people and groups to act in ways that go against their best interests and that sow the seeds of their ruin.

Intractable conflicts are grueling. They tend to worsen over time and rarely just go away. Despite all the progress that has been made over the past seventy years in understanding and negotiating most types of conflict, this 5 percent has remained unworkable.

The research on intractable conflicts tells a bleak tale. They tend to enrage us, trap us, frustrate us, drain us of energy and other critical resources, and seem to never go away no matter what we do. They, in fact, *attract* us, pulling us in and dragging us away with them. We often think we understand these conflicts and can choose how to react to them, that we have options. We are usually mistaken, however. The 5 percent rule us. Once we are drawn in, they take control. Like this.

WORLD WAR II REDUX

A few years back, a small group of friends and colleagues gathered for dinner one night at an apartment in the West Village in New York City. They were all members of an elite research and development team at a top international consulting firm, each from a different country: Korea, Scotland, Israel, Germany, the United States, and Poland. Having all joined the firm at around the same time, they had become very close, bonding over their demanding workload, the late nights, the high cost of living in New York City, and being strangers in a particularly strange land. They were an outstanding team at their firm, collectively nicknamed the "Alpha Dogs."

That night, the Israeli host of the party had prepared a tasty Middle Eastern supper, which they all enjoyed along with several bottles of red wine. As often happened, at some point in the evening the conversation veered into politics. The Israeli mentioned that she and several of her close friends had recently traveled to Poland to participate in the March to Silence. This was an increasingly popular pilgrimage that Israeli Jews made to visit sites of atrocities in Poland related to the Holocaust, as a way to silence deniers of the Nazi campaign of genocide against Jews. She shared in some detail how powerful and transformative the experience had been for her.

After a long silence, her Polish colleague spoke up. He said he resented the fact that the march took place *only* in Poland. He explained that because the Nazis had successfully destroyed most of the camps in Germany by the end of World War II, there were few German sites left to visit and memorialize. Since the Nazis had left the sites intact in Poland, his was the primary country where the world went to remember the terror and shame of the Holocaust. After all, he stressed, it was the *Germans* who had built the camps, and millions of Poles had perished in them as well.

It was at that point that World War II broke out again in that living room in New York City. The conversation immediately became heated as the past became present, and latent wounds, shame, and rage came rushing to the surface. How could the Poles possibly deny their complicity in the Nazi atrocities after centuries of pogroms and other forms of anti-Semitism had so flourished in Poland? How could the Germans speak such nonsense, given their unprecedented history of fascism and heinous crimes against humanity? How dare either of them take those positions, particularly in the company of someone whose Jewish ancestors had perished in the camps? A couple of the friends (Scottish and Korean) attempted to help calm the others, but this simply inflamed things. The audacity of them trying to minimize these issues!

Didn't they realize what was at stake here? After an hour or so of mounting tensions verging on threats, the dinner broke up. And after that night, the group was never the same.

The firm's management attempted to address the group's tensions, as this team had been exceptionally creative and productive and represented a considerable training investment by the company. They brought in two sets of consultants, including a conflict mediation firm, and each worked with the team over several months. But they failed to mend the divide. At the end of one particularly intense session, one of the members smashed a computer monitor in fury.

No matter what happened, every time the triggering issues came up the colleagues found themselves instantly back where they started—enraged. A few of them did go on to work together again, but the bond they had once all shared was shattered, and what had been a very talented R&D group collapsed.

Five percent conflicts are everywhere. They happen to all of us at some point in our personal or professional lives. For although 5 percent sounds uncommon, consider all the actual and potential conflicts you experience on a daily basis, from minor disagreements or frustrations in your immediate relationships (siblings, friends, coworkers) to more major disputes with, say, estranged ex-spouses, petulant neighbors, or abusive authority figures. When you think about how ubiquitous conflict is in our lives, the 5 percent rule starts adding up. Sooner or later, you too will be affected.

When they happen, the 5 percent can trap us for what seems like an eternity and, like Orestes, leave us exhausted and in despair. They may even have little to do with us *directly.* They can be long-standing conflicts between our friends or our loved ones, or between other people or groups at work and in the community. (Imagine the dilemma faced by the other members of the Alpha Dogs after the team imploded, split, and polarized.) But that does not matter. They suck us in and bring us down with them anyway.

Much of the research on these conflicts comes from the international domain, from places like the Middle East, Colombia, Cyprus, Sudan,

Angola, Northern Ireland, Kashmir, and Mozambique. But although the differences between geopolitical and personal or work conflicts are great, the study of intractable international disputes has important and direct implications for addressing some of the more difficult conflicts found in people's day-to-day lives. Conflicts need not be violent and large scale to be intractable. Many lives have been destroyed by personal conflicts where no blood was shed.

But there is also another and far more important (and unnerving) reason to be concerned about intractable conflicts: it is almost impossible to know whether any given conflict will degenerate to intractability. Under "perfect storm" conditions, even a trivial incident over something minor can evolve to an averse state of affairs that feels unstoppable. I once mediated a community dispute where a minor altercation between neighbors over how tree sap from one neighbor's trees stained the paint job on the other neighbor's car escalated into a protracted series of increasingly violent encounters. On the other hand, what might strike you as a particularly serious conflict between people might prove to be resolvable in a reasonable amount of time, without bringing about toxic feelings and long-term hostilities.

It is important to understand that the surface features of a conflict—the seriousness of the issues that provoked it, the personalities of the antagonists, the level of violence it invokes, whatever—do not necessarily predict whether it will turn bad and remain that way for a long time. To understand intractable conflicts, we must understand the underlying and often invisible dynamics at work. We must understand their curse. So, although you are most likely a reasonable person with good social skills and intuition, you probably have limited insight into the opaque forces that can generate these destructive forms of conflict—conflicts that can control your life.

I remember vividly my experiences in the minutes, hours, and days immediately following the attacks on the World Trade Center on 9/11. I was in New York City at the time, living on the Upper West Side of Manhattan with my wife and two small children. I had just begun teaching my first course of the fall term at Columbia University at nine o'clock that morning, when the news about the planes hitting the towers started coming in. My wife, Leah, had just dropped off our children at their school downtown. My son, Adlai, was in pre-kindergarten and my daughter, Hannah, in the fourth grade. The cell phone lines were jammed making communication impossible, so I ran, literally, sixty blocks south to my children's school. We eventually found each other and walked home through the streets with hundreds of debris-covered survivors. We spent the next several days huddled together, immersed in the swirling confusion of the events and the information and misinformation coming through the media. We soon learned that some of the parents of my children's friends had perished in the attack.

I remember perfectly the overwhelming feelings of anxiety, confusion, frustration, bitterness, and rage that stayed with me for weeks. These emotions combined with another powerful pull—to clarify for myself who had done this, who was responsible, who had committed these atrocities—and an urgent need to respond, somehow. It almost didn't matter how.

Teaching my theory of conflict resolution course at Columbia that fall term was trying. The 9/11 attacks, the role U.S. policies may have played in fostering them, and the hunt for those responsible were frequent topics of class discussion. Almost immediately, the class split into two camps: a large pro-American camp ("We are victims, blindsided by these unspeakable acts, hold no responsibility for them whatsoever, and should move to annihilate this enemy!") and a small but very vocal camp critical of America's role ("The U.S.'s addiction to oil and its policies and covert/overt practices in the Middle East brought on the attacks. We are largely responsible for the increasing divide between Islam and the Western world and should therefore take responsibility for these tensions!").

The ensuing conversations were painful and demanding. Holding the center was exceptionally challenging for me, a conflict-resolution expert whose family had been threatened by the attacks. Furthermore, the extraordinary complexity of the conversation was simply overwhelming. It included the history of relations of the "parties": the United States, Al Qaeda, bin Laden, the Taliban, the Afghanistan government, Israel, Saddam Hussein and the Iraqi government, etc.; the many relevant governmental policies and covert acts implicated; the role of America's endless thirst for energy; the part played by multinational oil corporations; the differences between terrorism and heroism, and many, many unknowns.

Those experiences have been on my mind these days, as I listen to the national debate over the Islamic community center and mosque to be built near "ground zero." The polarizing rhetoric of this debate forces people to choose sides. Are you for or against the victims of 9/11? For or against terrorism? For or against tolerance and peace? Perhaps this is inevitable while the wounds of 9/11 are so raw. But when rhetoric leads to overly simplistic gut reactions to complex problems and relationships, it often has the unintended consequences of further perpetuating the very problems we face.

These are what we call *conflict traps:* situations where people's reactions to conflicts make the very conditions that instigated them worse. We see this all the time. It happened in South Africa in the 1960s, when the apartheid Afrikaner government responded to nonviolent "stay-at-home" work stoppages by black Africans with brutal force. That contributed to another thirty years of conflict. It happened in France in 2005 and 2007, when the French minister of the interior reacted to antigovernment riots and car-burnings by immigrant community members in a manner that ultimately increased alienation and inflamed more conflict. It happens in Israel-Palestine, on both sides, all too often. And it happens in our homes. Virtually every time parents respond autocratically and punitively to an adolescent's attempts at independence by "trying out new behaviors," they simply increase the probability that such behaviors (talking back, breaking curfew, dying his or her hair) will continue and become more extreme. These conflict traps feed on themselves and can become self-sustaining, pervasive, and virtually impervious to outside influence. They can become the House of Atreus.

Worse, when these dynamics become self-perpetuating, people lose any sense of agency in the conflict, which typically leads to feelings of hopelessness, helplessness, and despair.

But do not despair!

The ideas and research presented in this book will help you to make sense of these seemingly impossible conflicts and discover new strategies for managing them constructively. At the heart of the book is the idea that there are powerful forces at work in these types of situations shaping what people see, feel, think, and do. In other words, when you find yourself in the grip of one of these conflicts, *do not trust your senses.* There is much more to the story than meets the eye. We are learning that human psychological and group processes—how people feel, think, and behave together in the midst of intractable conflicts—resemble the way complex systems throughout the universe behave. Based on decades of scientific research on complex systems, it has become possible to model the way these conflicts develop strong patterns, stabilize, and resist change. Most important to understanding these patterns is a phenomenon called *attractors,* organized patterns in the behavior of systems that emerge, endure, and of course attract.

Picture how a whirlpool organizes in a river current, a tornado in a summer storm system, or a violent maelstrom out at sea. All are strong, attracting structures formed by the dynamics of their surrounding conditions. Or, better yet, think of how people's heart rates stabilize around a certain beat pattern, or how their blood pressure seeks a particular level, or even how their weight has a specific set point. These, too, are attractors. They are all ongoing processes affected by many things that stabilize into particular patterns. And even though they may change temporarily (we may lose seven pounds on a crash diet), odds are they will soon return to their set point or original pattern, their attractor. Attractors can be seen in patterns found in microbiological cell life in the sea, in traffic patterns in cities, in planetary orbits in space, and in the psychosocial dynamics of thinking, feeling, and acting within groups and societies in conflict.

If you look at the geographic breakdown of Democratic-versus-Republican voting within each of the fifty states in the United States over the last three presidential elections, you see a fascinating pattern. The world has been changed dramatically since 2000, by 9/11, Al Qaeda, a world financial crisis, the rise of China and India, innovations in communications technologies, the spread of H1N1 virus, the worst environmental catastrophe in U.S. history (BP oil spill), and so much more. Yet despite this, the Blue-versus-Red voting breakdown within every state has barely budged. Our country and the world around us are transmuting. They are being buffeted by extraordinary forces from every direction, but U.S. citizens keep voting the same way in the same places. This is an attractor. This is an illustration of patterns of behavior that people feel drawn to reenact repeatedly and often automatically, even when they may at times prefer not to.

The study of attractors provides us with new perspectives and insights into how the many different aspects of complex problems assemble themselves into tightly coupled systems that resist change. This is critical. More manageable conflicts may be complicated, may be destructive, may even cause violence and misery. But this does not make them intractable. Intractability happens when the many different components of a conflict collapse together into one mass, into one very simple "us versus them" story that effectively resists change.

In this book we apply this idea of intractable conflicts as attractors to understanding and addressing life's most difficult conflicts. Of course, not all the physical and social systems that complexity scientists study are the same. However, research is showing that the *logic of their basic dynamics* is the same. That slime molds and weather patterns and cancerous growths and some conflicts in families, at work, and in the geopolitical realm in fact function the same way.

These ideas are new and can be very powerful and useful, but they are also demanding. They require us to suspend what we think we know about the more difficult conflicts in our lives, to be wary of our gut instincts, to doubt our own eyes, and to try to see these situations anew. This is *not* easy, but it can make for a much better life for those of us trapped in, even attracted to, the 5 percent.

THIS BOOK DESCRIBES THE 5 PERCENT PROBLEM and what can be done to address intractable conflict. I have no doubt that expert peacemakers working with difficult conflicts in all types of settings around the world have developed a variety of useful insights, intuitions, and methods for addressing these conflicts constructively. However, this book presents the first systematic, integrated, evidence-based model for understanding the 5 percent, and offers a coherent set of principles and practices for resolving them. Its four sections include various illustrations and examples of (seemingly) impossible personal, professional, and geopolitical conflicts.

In the first section we lay out our sense of the *problem* of the 5 percent: why mainstream approaches to resolving conflicts do not seem to help and why they are so intractable. In the second section we describe our *approach:* what we have learned from psychology and recent advances in complexity science that can help to address these types of conflicts. In the third we detail and illustrate our *method:* three basic practices gleaned from our approach for addressing impossible conflicts. The concluding section provides a summary of the *5 percent solution* by illustrating the main ideas and methods through a case description of the intractable sixteen-year conflict and unlikely outbreak of peace in Mozambique in 1992. We then extrapolate from this case and from the model to offer a few thoughts about employing these ideas and tools to increase the probabilities of peace in other daunting conflicts, such as in the Middle East. Finally, we outline the types of instruction and evidence-based training particularly useful for thinking and working with this approach. In the appendix, we provide an overview and link to a website that offers readers access to a computer simulation tool and tutorial for analyzing, visualizing, and resolving their own seemingly impossible conflicts.

For resolution, even of the 5 percent, can and does happen. Coincidentally, this month (November 2010) Britain and France, two nations that have spent centuries confronting each other on the battlefields of Agincourt, Trafalgar, and Waterloo, signed a landmark cooperative defense agreement. It included the creation of a joint expeditionary force, shared use of aircraft carriers, and combined efforts to improve the safety of their nuclear weapons, which commits the two nations to sharing some of their most carefully guarded secrets. Despite the deep-seated power of their bellicose histories, French president Nicolas Sarkozy proclaimed that the mutual security agreement displayed "a level of trust and confidence between our two nations which is unequalled in history."[3]

The impossible became possible. The curse was broken. How? Read on.

part one

THE PROBLEM

IMPOSSIBLE CONFLICTS

FEAR AND LOATHING IN BOSTON

They met together in hiding for six years. They had to. They moved their locations often, and spoke with few others about the meetings.

It felt hopeless. They all felt trapped by events. The horrible shootings that had occurred on Beacon Street had forced them to come together in secret to meet with the enemy. Now they were caught between a terrible dread of violence and retaliation on one side and their unshakable belief in what is right and true on the other.

Each despised the other group. They had all worked tirelessly for years to block and counter the other side's every move. They knew them as immoral, irrational people. Even meeting with them could easily taint their own reputations and cost them their careers, their standing in the community, and possibly even their lives. And yet here they were, face to face, in a small stuffy office in Watertown, Massachusetts, immobilized by shame, fear, and duty. Ordinary people captured by truly extraordinary events.

They were six women, all activists and local leaders from the Boston area who had been fighting for years on the front lines of the war over abortion. One was a lawyer, another a rector. One was a chemist, another a president and CEO, and two were executive directors of not-for-profits. Three were pro-life and three were pro-choice.

Before the first meeting, the pro-life activists prayed together in a booth at a nearby Friendly's. They had never before met directly with the others across this divide. But they knew them. They knew their rhetoric and their tactics. They knew how their minds worked, the hate they spewed, the wrongs they had committed, and the blood on their hands. They were clear on the *fact* that abortion was the murder of innocent children. They knew the research on what happens to a fetus during abortions and had seen graphic films of helpless unborn children being caught by the powerful vacuums of the abortionists. They knew stories by heart of women who, because of botched abortions, could never have children again.

The pro-choice women saw things differently. They knew that abortion was an extremely difficult and painful choice, *and* that the right to make that choice was a fundamental human right. The loss of this right was a slippery slope back toward the total control of women by men. They knew of too many cases where the lives of girls had been ruined by being forced to give birth to a child when they were too young. Wasn't it clearly better to let them wait until they were mature enough to love and care for a child? They had also known women forced to give birth despite the known dangers to their own health who had suffered serious consequences as a result. And they knew the science. They knew that in nature billions of sperm cells and millions of eggs were discarded from human bodies every day in a natural biological process. This was the *real* cycle of life. When women were denied control of their own bodies, of their own destinies, it was clearly a violation of their most basic human rights.

Both sides knew the facts. They knew they were *right*—it was unquestionable. But they also knew that the other side would stop at nothing to champion their cause and that their own group had to do everything in their power to stop them. That much was certain.

And then John C. Salvi III walked into the Planned Parenthood Clinic in Brookline, Massachusetts, that cold day in December 1994 and shot Shannon Lowney, the receptionist, to death. He then drove two miles down Beacon Street to the Preterm Health Services clinic and opened fire again, shooting Leanne Nichols, a volunteer, ten times with a rifle at point-blank range saying, "That's what you get. You should pray the rosary."[1] By the end of the day, two women were dead and five others were seriously wounded.

The quiet Boston suburb of Brookline was traumatized. The pro-choice community was devastated. Pro-life proponents across the country were ashamed and appalled. Fear of further violence reigned. The governor of Massachusetts, William F. Weld, and Cardinal Bernard Law of the Catholic archdiocese of Boston called for talks between the two camps. So when Laura Chasin of the Public Conversations Project reached out quietly to these six women and asked them to meet for a clandestine dialogue, they came. Despite their best judgment and despite the fact that every cell of their beings cried out to *stay away from them*, they came and met with the enemy.

It was hell at first. Despite agreeing at the onset to act in a respectful manner toward one another, tempers flared. They had to constantly fight their basic instincts to ridicule and condemn the other side, feeling driven by a searing combination of rage, disgust, and righteousness. Yet they returned. Month after month, year after year, they came together and spoke across the abyss. They slowly learned to work together in spite of their initial sense of the futility of such talks and their very real fears for their own personal safety.

And then something extraordinary happened. *The rift between the two groups became even greater.* After years of increasingly constructive dialogue—learning about the other women's personal lives, of their courage and integrity; working together to avoid further violence in the community and coming to respect each other deeply and to care about one another—they nevertheless found themselves even more polarized over the issue of abortion.

Ironically, by agreeing to drop their inflammatory rhetoric and to speak carefully and intimately about their concerns on the issues, they all found themselves even more deeply committed to their original cause. They had become both closer to one another and further apart. They wrote: "Since that first fear-filled meeting, we have experienced a paradox. While learning to treat each other with dignity and respect, we have all become firmer in our views about abortion. . . . . We saw that our differences on abortion reflect two world views that are irreconcilable."[2]

An impossible conflict? Perhaps. But there is more to this story.

chapter 1

CONFLICT RESOLUTION METHODS THAT WORK—AND WHY THEY DO NOT HELP WITH THE 5 PERCENT

TRY TO IMAGINE A WORLD WITHOUT CONFLICT. Can you see it? Even if it were possible, it would be so unbelievably tedious.

Conflict is everywhere in life. It is central to almost everything we do. That includes informed decision making, active learning, healthy relationships, careful parenting, thriving families, innovation at work, fruitful business negotiations, good governance, and important social movements like the women's, civil, gay, and human rights movements. And conflict makes everything more engaging. Imagine a novel, play, movie, or television show without conflict. Or an intimate relationship where you always get along. Or a day in your life without any conflict. Okay, you're right, that would be great. But go a week or a month without conflict—so boring.

Fortunately, we already know a lot about many types of conflict and how to manage them constructively. You might not know it from reading the morning newspapers or watching the evening news, but not all conflicts dissolve into crisis.

Decades of research, trial and error, and practical reflection have clued us into a host of strategies that can be immensely helpful in resolving our conflicts constructively. Popular books like *Getting to Yes, Getting Past No, Difficult Conversations, Critical Conversations,* and many others have outlined these tools. Whether we are negotiating with our boss for a raise in salary, problem solving with our families over household chores and curfews, mediating in schools and communities between violent gang members, or negotiating-persuading-cajoling-pleading with diplomats in the back halls of the UN General Assembly, there are useful tools out there that can make a big difference in resolving our conflicts effectively and enhancing the quality of our lives.

The issue is *not* that conflicts are bad and should be eliminated, as tempting as that might seem. That would not work for long. The issue is how, when, and why do conflicts result in good things: stimulate us, motivate us, excite us, and lead us to deeper understanding, better relationships, greater creativity, and a more just world. And how, when, and why do they go bad on us, make us miserable, and eventually trap us.

Here are a few simple rules of thumb about conflict and constructive conflict resolution gleaned from the current literature:[3]

- **Know what type of conflict you are in.** Some conflicts are win-lose (in order for me to win what I want you *must* lose something—money, property, political office, etc.), while others are purely win-win (we can both get exactly what we want if we're flexible and creative and work together to discover new solutions). But the vast majority of conflicts are a mix of both types (competing goals *and* shared or complementary goals), and all three types (win-lose, win-win, and mixed) require very different strategies and tactics to make them work. Learning how to identify these different types of conflict and how to respond appropriately is central to most conflict resolution training programs today.
- **Not all conflicts are bad.** Conflicts often make us anxious, and some can become quite painful and destructive, but these tend to be rare. More often, conflicts present us with opportunities to solve problems and bring about necessary changes, to learn more about ourselves and others, and to innovate—to go beyond what we already know and do. However, it is very easy to forget this because the conflicts that stand out in our memory tend to be the bad ones.
- **Whenever possible, cooperate.** Research has consistently shown that more collaborative approaches to resolving win-win or mixed-motive disputes (in other words, the majority of conflicts in our lives) work best. Therefore, we should try to approach conflicts

with others as mutually shared problems to be solved together. This may not always be possible, but it is often much more possible than we think. It also makes it more likely that everyone involved will get what they need, that any agreement reached will last, and that the conflict will not escalate or spread.

- **Be flexible.** Try to distinguish your position in a conflict (I want a 4 percent raise) from your underlying needs and interests in the relationship (I actually need more money, respect, parking, and time off). Your initial position may severely limit your options. Creativity and openness to exploration are essential to constructive solutions.
- **Do not personalize.** Try to keep the problems separate from the people when in conflict (do not make *them* the problem). When conflicts become personal, the rules tend to change, the stakes get higher, emotions spike, and the conflicts quickly become more unmanageable.
- **Listen carefully.** Work hard to listen to the other side in a conflict. Accurate information is critical to sound solutions, and careful listening communicates respect. This alone can move the conflict in a more friendly and constructive direction. And this is the only way to determine what is *really* at stake in a conflict: *divisibles* like money, time, and property, or something deeper and more meaningful (and loaded) like values, principles, or religious beliefs.
- **Be fair, firm, and friendly.** Always attempt to be reasonable, respectful, and persistent in conflict. (But do not cave in! Find a way to make sure your needs are met.) Research shows that the *process* of how conflicts are handled is usually more important than the *outcomes* of conflicts. It goes a long way in determining people's sense of justice or injustice in the situation.

These fine principles and guidelines can make a powerful difference in most of the conflicts in our lives. Together, they constitute the centerpiece of most approaches to developing and refining our basic skills in *integrative negotiation, creative problem solving, constructive controversy, mediation, town hall meetings, large-group consensus building,* and other practical methods of constructive conflict resolution. Applied correctly, these methods can go a long way toward moving *most* of our conflicts in a positive and satisfying direction, and enhancing our general health and well-being.

But not with the 5 percent.

The 5 percent seem immune to such strategies and tactics. Repeatedly, they have proven to be insufficient in dealing with deeply embedded intractable conflict. Just recall the myriad good-faith attempts at conflict resolution and peace making that have failed in Israel-Palestine, Sudan, Cyprus, Sri Lanka, the Democratic Republic of Congo, Colombia, Somalia, Lebanon, Afghanistan, Kashmir, North Korea, and other enduring conflicts across the globe. Research shows that mediation attempts in these situations often have little impact other than possibly delaying the onset of new spikes in violence. In fact, there is some evidence that mediation makes matters worse, as it is associated with a greater likelihood of war between long-standing rival states. (However, this might be due to the fact that it is the more difficult conflicts that require mediation).[4] Nevertheless, mediation appears to be, at the very least, ineffective in these settings.

The same can be said about many attempts to "resolve" polarizing community and family disputes closer to home. Often, when people try to negotiate or mediate particularly difficult issues—like building abortion clinics, hate speech on the radio, assisted suicide, or the right to wear religious garments when working for a private company—their interventions backfire, driving disputants further apart into more hardened positions. They do not seem to help at all.

Why don't these usually effective methods work with the 5 percent? The obvious answer is that the 5 percent are simply more difficult: more heated, entrenched, and complicated. But it is more than that. It also has to do with several interrelated challenges: the limitations of the scientific paradigm on which many of the current models and methods of conflict resolution are based, the unique nature of the 5 percent, and the fact that they are exceptionally difficult to comprehend. Each of these aspects is discussed below.

TOP TEN LIMITATIONS TO STANDARD APPROACHES TO SOCIAL-SCIENCE RESEARCH

Standard approaches to research in the social sciences are often based on a set of assumptions about science, intervention, and change that limits their applicability for addressing the unique, long-lasting challenges of the 5 percent. They include the following:

1. They compare fluid things to fixed things. Mary Parker Follett, one of the great unsung heroes of conflict resolution and management theory, said it first. Follett was a social worker and brilliant visionary who worked with labor-management conflicts in business and industry in the 1920s. She was an adviser to President Theodore Roosevelt and one of the first women invited to address the London School of Economics. She was also the first to recognize that the social sciences had a strange view of things such as leadership, worker relations, and human conflict: they saw them as static things. Science, commonly, looks to certain fixed attitudes, personality characteristics, reward systems, needs, opportunity structures, and so on and proposes that if people or situations have some quality, X (for instance a positive attitude or common interests), they will respond to conflict constructively. While rules derived from such correlations may sometimes hold true, this kind of thinking neglects the one thing we know to be constant in life: *change.*

All people, attitudes, personalities, goals, needs, and situations are fluid things that are constantly shifting and changing. Life is fluid. When we try to nail down some quality, X, as a stable entity (for instance that Rob is a contentious person), we are already violating what we know to be certain: that X does and will change. This of course is particularly true during the long course of a protracted conflict. Recognizing life's fluidity helps account for the fact that so much research on the effects of different personality variables (like authoritarianism, general trust levels, gender, and conscientiousness) on conflict resolution processes has proven to be largely inconclusive and confusing.[5] They are comparing fixed things to fluid things.

2. They think in straight lines. Most contemporary approaches to research on conflict resolution also tend to see events proceeding in straight lines. They will hypothesize, for instance, that if we *listen carefully* in a conflict, we will achieve a good solution. Again, this is much more likely to occur with more tractable, negotiable disputes and may even happen with the 5 percent. But it does not mean that listening carefully was responsible for the conflict ending well.

Whether difficult, sustained social conflicts are resolved effectively or not *rarely* depends on one thing causing another to happen. The resolution of these conflicts usually depend on many things: the people involved, their prior relationship, the issues, the situation, the processes employed, cultural norms, and any number of other background issues. In fact, what the future of these conflicts *really* depends on is how these many things interact and work together—that is, how the whole puzzle does or doesn't fit together.

Thinking in straight lines is part of Western science and society's long tradition of *linear causality,* the focus on how X causes or leads to Y. This focus has helped us understand how many of the pieces of the conflict puzzle influence other pieces. But it does not seem to help us understand how the many pieces of more difficult conflicts come together, or what will happen when they do. This is especially the case in complicated, long-term conflicts involving many people and many issues, in different situations, all of which keep changing over time. These conflicts require a different, *nonlinear* way of thinking. As science writer Kevin Kelly put it, in nonlinear systems 2 + 2 = apples. This simply means that we need to try to understand these conflicts, how they evolve, stabilize, change, and how they might be resolved, by looking beyond their linear connections.

3. They privilege the short term. Most of the research on negotiation, mediation, and other forms of conflict resolution today is short term. Studies tend to look at the immediate effects of different techniques or conditions for conflict resolution, leaving the long-term effects unexplored. As it happens, long-term studies are very hard to do and expensive. This means that most of our models of conflict resolution, if they are based on empirical research, are based on short-term laboratory or survey research. Short-term research is not necessarily bad, but it is an insufficient basis for developing and assessing the long-term practices necessary for the management of protracted conflict.

To a large degree, this short-term orientation has affected many of our standard practical approaches to conflict resolution as well. Today, the primary emphasis in most negotiation and mediation training programs is on prenegotiation analysis of conflicts, strategizing and planning for negotiations, creative problem solving during the process, and drafting agreements. In contrast, there is little focus on strategies for the effective implementation and long-term sustainability of agreements, or on techniques for assessing the longer-term outcomes of such interventions.

4. They focus on problems. The study of conflict, violence, and war has a long and impressive tradition in the social sciences and humanities. Today we know a great deal about these more destructive social processes—how they start, when and why they escalate, why they become violent, and when they lead to stalemate and to long periods of misery and strife. The trouble is that many conflict scholars have been so focused on understanding the pathologies of conflict and war that few have thought to turn around and look in the other direction and study *peace.* To date, very few scholars have studied the necessary and sufficient conditions for enduring peace.[6]

People often assume that if we understand a problem well enough, we will understand its solution. Peace is simply the opposite of war, right? Researchers have found this to be largely incorrect. In fact, it appears that there is a big difference between situations that lack destructive conflict and situations in which there are peaceful relations. Unfortunately, we currently know a lot more about the former than the latter.

5. They marginalize emotions. Pain, misery, loss, loyalty, rage, frustration, fear, anxiety, and despair are the fuel and lifeblood of intractable conflict. Yet decades of research on social conflict has paid little attention to emotions.[7] This has resulted in many practical techniques offering recommendations like "If you become emotional during conflict, wait until it passes before you act" or "Rise above your emotions and try to get a *rational* perspective on the situation." This advice may be useful when emotions are a passing anomaly or inconvenience as they are in many low-level a conflicts. But not with the 5 percent. Not when emotions are basic, not when they are enmeshed within the conflict, not when they *are* the rationale. To really comprehend the 5 percent, we need research models that place emotions at the center. We need models that not only see emotions as the energy behind the conflicts, but also recognize that they create the context through which we experience conflict.

6. They are overly simple. There is a value in science called *parsimony,* which means that we prefer the simplest possible explanations of phenomena whenever possible. As worthy as this value is, it has led many scholars to seek out "the simple and sovereign theory" to explain destructive conflict and related social problems in terms of one overarching factor or variable.[8] While this body of work has generated important insights about pieces of the 5 percent puzzle, the relative importance of these pieces is too often overstated, and the nature of the relationships *among* the many pieces that constitute such problems is poorly understood. As George Bernard Shaw once said, "For every complex problem there is a simple solution that is wrong."

7. They are overly complex. Responding to the consequences of oversimplification in science, a different camp of scholars set out to map the topography of conflict in all its immense complexity. Armed with the new perspective of *general systems theory,* they sought to identify all the variables relevant to conflict, its occurrence, escalation, and deescalation. This was an important next step because it began to provide some sense of the context of conflict processes and the forest that housed the trees. As useful as this development was, however, it soon hit a dead end.

The product of these efforts was often a series of extremely complex, multilevel models featuring a multitude of boxes and variables connected by a web of lines and arrows. These models did provide a sense of context, but it was hard to know what to take away from them other than the fact that everything is related to everything else.

Today, it has become increasingly clear that understanding difficult long-term conflicts requires a combination of simplicity and complexity. We need to recognize how a few central factors in conflict operate within a force field of many other variables, all pulling and pushing at the same time: *parsimony informed by complexity.*

This is no small matter. As Vaclav Havel once said, "Simple answers which lie on this side of life's complexities are cheap. However, simple truths which exist beyond this complexity, and are illuminated by it, are worthy of a lifetime's commitment." This is what it will take to contend with the 5 percent.

8. They miss the invisible. For humans, seeing is believing. Conflict scholars have the same tendency (most of us are human, after all). Consequently, most of our research has examined the implications of different conditions and techniques for dealing with current situations and tangible goals and outcomes, in the here and now. Important and necessary as this is in addressing destructive conflicts, the focus on the obvious and immediate can lead to neglect and misunderstanding of the more subtle undercurrents and longer-term trends unfolding in conflict.

When the pro-life and pro-choice leaders in Boston chose to wage contentious, inflammatory campaigns to vilify their out-groups and further their cause, it made complete sense to them—it was their duty and felt like an effective technique. But had they foreseen that their day-to-day choices would ultimately establish the conditions and climate in their community for catastrophic violence, might they have chosen differently? These invisible or *latent* possibilities in conflicts are critical to our understanding of 5 percent problems and must become better understood through research.

9. They feed the research-practice gap. A hundred years ago the field of medicine underwent a crisis. Up until then, many physicians happily plied their trade, paying little or no attention to the latest developments in science. Physicians had trained in schools and developed their skills with patients, and frankly didn't want to be bothered with whatever latest fads emerged from university laboratories. In 1910, the Carnegie

Foundation released the Flexner Report, which, among other shocks to the system, exposed the drift between science and practice. The report triggered a scandal in the field and led to significant changes in the education and licensing of physicians, as well as the requirements for their continued education. Even today, it is estimated that only 20 to 25 percent of medical practices are evidence based—that is, based on strong objective research evidence to support the treatment intervention.[9]

In the past several years there have been similar rumblings in such areas as education, psychology, organizational consulting, and, yes, the field of conflict resolution. A surge in activity and investment around negotiation, mediation, and other conflict resolution practices in the United States have brought the efficacy of these practices under increasing scrutiny. The increase in popularity of conflict resolution springs from various sources, including Supreme Court Justice Warren E. Burger's decision to institutionalize mediation within the U.S. justice system in the 1970s; the Quaker movement to introduce conflict resolution programs into schools (they are now in over five thousand American schools); and the use of mediation in both business and international affairs by such high-profile leaders as Jimmy Carter, George Mitchell, Kofi Anan, and Hillary Clinton.

However, an evaluation of the eighteen, mostly university-based, Hewlett Foundation–funded theory centers that conduct research in the area of conflict resolution found that the work of most practitioners surveyed had been largely unaffected by the important contributions (new theory, tactics, publications, etc.) generated by the various centers.[10] At the same time, much of the research conducted at these centers was found to be "removed from practice realities and constraints." Many practitioners of conflict resolution dismiss the contributions of theorists and researchers, especially when the research challenges their own opinions or methods. At the same time, scholars often fail to utilize the expertise of highly skilled practitioners in their development of theory, and research designs often fail to take into account what practitioners and policy makers want or need to know.

That means that too few of the theoretical models in the field are sufficiently informed by the practical realities of conflict. It also means that current practices employed in the field have been insufficiently informed by new research coming out of the lab—research that could help determine if they actually do what we think they do on the ground and could help explore how to make them most effective. This presents a serious challenge to the field as it stands today, particularly when it involves the high-stakes world of the 5 percent.

10. Finally, they too often miss the unintended consequences of well-intentioned acts. Dietrich Dorner is a German psychologist who studies leadership and decision making in complex environments. He has suggested that there is more harm done in today's world by well-intentioned people trying to do good, who are unaware of the unintended consequences of their actions, than by people actually trying to cause harm.[11] Remarkably, this may well be true.

Today, our standard linear, short-term, cause-and-effect paradigm for research on negotiation, mediation, and other forms of problem solving focuses on the presence or absence of predicted outcomes. It rarely attends to the unintended or unexpected outcomes that arise from interventions, which are typically dismissed as failed experiments. In other words, our approach is insufficiently mindful of how such interventions may unexpectedly affect the complex living, evolving system of a conflict over time, and how these effects may in fact be more consequential than those we set out to study. This is a serious limitation that severely constrains our understanding and capacity to address the 5 percent problem.

These limitations begin to explain why much of what we've learned to date from research on conflict and conflict resolution—ideas and strategies that do help to resolve conflict in most cases—do not seem to help with the 5 percent. These conflicts require a new way of thinking. We need to be able to see, feel, and respond to these types of problems in different ways. Our current perspectives are simply too limited to quell the tide of something as pervasive as the curse of the House of Atreus.

But that's not all. The intractability of the 5 percent goes beyond the limitations of our current models and tools. It goes to the nature and very essence of these types of problems. This is the topic for the next chapter.

chapter 2

THE 5 PERCENT PROBLEM

SCHOLARS WHO STUDY DIFFICULT CONFLICTS around the world tell us that truly "intractable" conflicts, highly destructive ones that despite people's best efforts will not go away, are relatively rare but extremely powerful. It is estimated that only about 5 percent of international conflicts since 1816 were considered intractable: they lasted more than twenty years despite multiple good-faith attempts to resolve them.[1] The same is basically true in the international arena today. That means, for those of you counting, that 95 percent of conflicts are considered resolvable through such traditional means as military victory, diplomacy, mediation, negotiation, peacekeeping, use of sanctions, the courts, and so forth. However, it also means that 5 percent are not.

These seemingly irresolvable 5 percent are so powerful because they tend to wreak disproportional havoc on everything they touch. From individual physical and mental health and well-being to marital and family satisfaction; trust in friendships and social groups to the functioning of businesses; local, state, and regional stability to the global economy, the environment, and more. These conflicts are all encompassing. They demand our attention, bleed our resources, and often leave us in despair. The longer they persist, the more widespread and destructive they become. They can mobilize individuals, families, groups, and communities against one another, sometimes for years, or even generations. Like this one.

HOUSE KEEPING

Kasha and Anthony had worked hard for years to buy a small, quiet piece of lakeside property in the country where they could build their dream house.

They sacrificed and saved year after year to put together enough money for the place, and then designed and built the house to meet their exact specifications. It was pure pleasure. They worked well together, with Anthony's drive and attention to detail complementing Kasha's aesthetics and vision. After it was built, they shared many lovely, relaxing weekends and summer vacations there with their three children. It was their paradise.

Then problems began creeping into their marriage. Over the years the couple drifted apart, and they began leading parallel lives. One day Kasha discovered that Anthony had had an affair with a work colleague. She left him immediately, and soon they began divorce proceedings. Their marriage was over. As hard as the initial separation was, they both felt it was the right thing to do and went through the process to divorce.

But then it came to the country house. Both Kasha and Anthony assumed that the other would be willing to give up the house—for surely each knew it meant so much more to the other. But they were both wrong. Neither was willing to part with the house. Not *this* house. Their lawyers negotiated over it for months and eventually brought in a mediator to try to resolve the dispute. Mediation proved equally fruitless and ended in more hostile recriminations and increased bitterness.

How could Anthony demand to keep the house? After all, it was mostly paid for by Kasha's salary and it was *he* who had cheated on her and brought on the divorce in the first place. Where was the justice in that?

Anthony could not believe Kasha's pigheadedness. Not when she knew that he had put literally years of his life into drafting the designs and building the place with his own hands. His heart and soul had gone into that home. He knew she was simply being spiteful, doing whatever she could to tear him from the thing he loved.

Both Kasha and Anthony instructed their lawyers to stop at nothing to win the house. At this point their divorce settlement, which was nearly complete with the exception of the house, fell apart. (Anthony literally tore it apart in front of her at their last face-to-face meeting.) So it went for years. The dispute eventually poisoned the family, as the children, relatives, and friends were forced to take sides. The legal fees mounted, but neither spouse would budge. In the end, they both lost the house. They were forced to sell it in order to cover their enormous legal costs, which also forced them both into bankruptcy. The dispute over the house and the ensuing legal expenses and enmity continue to this day.

SOUND FAMILIAR?

These conflicts are hard. They seem to worsen over time and seriously deteriorate when other people try to help. And they can be very painful.

Even though such extremely difficult personal conflicts are also fairly uncommon, when they do occur they can be almost as exhausting and long lasting as their more violent counterparts in the international arena. Of course, the intractable geopolitical conflicts in the Middle East and Africa are not the same as those between married couples or colleagues at the office; the differences are many and obvious. But they do share some basic similarities.

- **They are all situations where *the power of history* is considerable.** Even when past events, such as the Holocaust and WWII, were not experienced directly by the disputants, their impact can easily overwhelm current relationships and interests and lead to a destructive dynamic that feels out of their control.
- **They are all situations that tend to become increasingly difficult and *complicated* over time, but that simultaneously begin to seem incredibly *simple*.** These conflicts tend to spread beyond the initial issues and the individuals who triggered them. Over time, they gather increasing intensity and negativity with every additional person, group, and grievance they engulf. We saw this when Kasha and Anthony's hostility crept into and poisoned their extended family. At the same time, the more complex and pervasive these conflicts become, the simpler they seem to those involved. The perception is that I and my side are good people victimized by the other side, who are hateful and malicious and bent on making things worse.
- **They are all situations where the people involved tend to share an *illusion of free will*,** a belief that they are largely in control of their fate and can choose how to respond in the conflict. This was

clearly the case with the Alpha Dog R&D team early in their conflict. But the truth is that in these situations extraordinary forces are often at work shaping perceptions, thoughts, feelings, and behaviors. Disputants may even feel motivated and empowered by the conflict, but in fact lose real agency and control as they become increasingly constrained by it.

- **They are all situations where the pain and demands of the here and now focus people on responding to the current crisis, which fosters *short-term, problem-oriented thinking*.** The consequence is a neglect of the longer-term, unexpected consequences of actions. We saw this in the tragedy of Kasha and Anthony when their fixation on keeping the house (or denying their former spouse from having it) ultimately led to their loss of the home and bankruptcy. This kind of crisis orientation often leads to responses that address the immediate situation, and can help people cope, but that also have dire long-term consequences that in fact fuel the conflict.
- **They are all situations that *do not respond well* to the many conflict management strategies developed and refined over the last few decades.** Methods like mediation, group problem solving, consensus building, and town hall meetings can work approximately 95 percent of the time. But not with the 5 percent. As we saw in the stories above, they can even make things worse.
- **And, consequently, *they all last too long*.** How long is too long? Scholars differ on this. Some last years and others centuries. International conflict scholars claim that destructive conflicts that go twenty-plus years are intractable. We suggest a good rule of thumb is that too long is when most disputants and stakeholders involved in the conflict want it to end but cannot seem to make that happen.

They are also *very* expensive.

TYPICALLY, THE MONETARY *costs* associated with intractable conflicts are exceedingly high. In the personal or professional realm, they can include expensive legal fees, medical bills, counseling, property damage, harm to one's work and career, and extra time off from one's job. In communities, the expenses sky rocket and can include the costs incurred from maintaining a sufficient security or police presence, losses of investment and revenues from decreases in commerce and tourism, rebuilding those aspects of communities destroyed by violence, and providing aid and reparations to victims of the conflict.

To illustrate, in 2009 the United States provided Israel with $7 million in military aid per day (none was given to Palestine),[2] USAID provided $225 million in assistance to Colombians affected by the many conflicts there, $467 million in USAID and State Humanitarian Assistance went to Sudan, and $157 million to Somalia.[3] As of July 2010, the U.S. Congress had approved a total of $1.121 trillion in military expenditures for the three operations to fight terrorism initiated in response to the 9/11 attacks.[4] On the interpersonal level, protracted family conflict and violence in the United States alone costs from $5 to $10 billion annually in medical expenses, police and court costs, shelters and foster care, sick leave, absenteeism, and nonproductivity.[5]

In terms of human suffering, the costs of the 5 percent are incalculable. And it is important to know that civilian casualties in armed conflicts soared from around 5 percent during WWI to about 80 percent in the 1990s.[6]

But the most insidious consequence of these conflicts is the *normalization* of hostilities and violence in families, workplaces, and societies and the toll they take. This can range from psychological violence such as insults, social isolation, noncommunication, and public humiliation to physical violence such as the destruction of property, direct physical attacks, police or military engagement, or much worse.

When family, group, or societal norms legitimize hostilities or the use of force, they create an environment conducive to their continuation. In a study of ninety preindustrial societies, researchers found that intense violence was significantly more likely to occur when children were reared in cold or harsh families, especially when they were routinely physically or emotionally abused.[7] Often the hostilities associated with long-term conflicts become integrated into the socialization processes of the groups involved. Then new generations of potential disputants are propagated and fed on past resentments and negative images of the enemy, which helps ensure a long life for the conflict. For instance, findings show that Israeli and Palestinian youth accept and justify the use of violence and war more readily, and are more reluctant to consider negotiating for peace, than youth from (nonconflict) European settings.[8]

So although 5 percent problems differ from one another in myriad ways, each possessing its own unique set of issues, people, and circumstances, they do share some common features. In fact, they seem to have their own particular set of *rules* which distinguish them from more solvable problems.

It is clear that *many* of life's conflicts are complex and difficult, yet eventually get resolved anyway. People face hard conflicts over moral or value differences, power struggles, and scarce critical resources all the time. Somehow they manage to find a way to work them out. The 5 percent are different. How?

There are a few other reasons the intractability of the 5 percent is beyond the limits of the current tools of the trade: the *essence* of these particular types of conflicts, how we tend to *view* them, and, subsequently, how we tend to *respond* to them. Let's walk through them.

THE ESSENCE OF THE 5 PERCENT

About ten years ago I set out to try to isolate the main source of intractable conflicts. I hoped, in the process, to identify what social psychologist Kurt Lewin called "the *essence* of the phenomenon" of intractability. Lewin argued that whenever you study something new of which little is known, you should try to get a sense of its essence, its core.

I spent a couple of years of combing through the considerable amount of scholarly and applied literature in international affairs, psychology, and conflict resolution. After comparing various accounts, the good news is that I was able to identify the essence of the problem of impossible conflicts. The bad news is that there are roughly fifty-seven of them. Fifty-seven essences!

THE FIFTY-SEVEN ESSENCES OF INTRACTABLE CONFLICT

1. Domination: a deep desire for power and control of others.
2. Inequity: history of colonialism, racism, sexism, ethnocentrism, or human rights abuses.
3. Gender: situations where men, who are responsible for the vast majority of violence, are in charge.
4. Divide and conquer: high-power groups (HPGs) manipulating low-power groups' (LPGs') ethnic differences.
5. Cracks in the facade: conditions where HPGs' control of historical and cultural meaning through history textbooks, media, official accounts, etc. becomes compromised.
6. Delegitimization of hierarchy-legitimating myths: challenges to ideologies, narratives, and policies that validate hierarchical power arrangements.
7. Structural victimization of LPGs: denial of identity, security, and voice.
8. Structural violence toward LPGs: unequal access to housing, health care, nutrition, education, etc.
9. Lack of awareness: an insulated and inattentive HPG.
10. Accumulation of indignities: pervasive patterns of "civilized oppression" by HPGs against LPGs.
11. Seismic shifts: periods of rapid social change and instability.
12. Tainted infrastructure: compromised institutions, laws, and social norms for conflict regulation.
13. Looking up: changes in LPGs' aspirations.
14. Power shifts: changes in the balance of power between HPGs and LPGs.
15. Ambiguity of power: unclear relative status of groups in conflict, leading to more volatility.
16. Anarchy: the complete collapse of social order.
17. Dialogic poles: underlying issues rife with consequential trade-offs.
18. Paradoxical dilemmas: issues that, when resolved, create new problems.
19. Intricate interconnections of issues: complex connections among distinct issues.
20. High centrality: issues that have high personal or group-based importance.
21. Truth: issues that revolve around important, basic beliefs.
22. Hub issues: grievances embedded within broad beliefs, ideologies, and basic assumptions.
23. Exclusive structures that keep groups isolated and out of contact from each other.
24. Inescapable relationships: relationships from which it is virtually impossible to exit.
25. Collapsed relationships: relationships damaged beyond repair by conflict.
26. Intense mixed motives: high-stakes conflicts with a mix of cooperative and competitive goals.
27. Intractable core: fundamentally unsolvable issues.
28. Polarized collective identities: group identities based on the negation and destruction of the "other."
29. Conflict identities: group identities organized around an ongoing conflict.

30. Monolithic and exclusive identities: all different aspects of in-groups and out-groups collapse into single entities.
31. Frozen identities: personal and group identities become rigid and unresponsive to change.
32. Unconscious needs and defenses: motives that are operative but difficult to identify and address.
33. Intragroup divisions and factions: internal group divisions drive intergroup conflict.
34. Hidden agendas: covert or criminal objectives that drive the overt conflict.
35. Emotional contagion: the pervasive spread of toxic emotions such as humiliation, deprivation, loss, and rage.
36. Memorialized conflict: conflict driven by a sense of duty and loyalty to those harmed in the past.
37. Socially constructed volatility: in-group processes that create rules and norms that sanction destructive emotions.
38. Impaired cognitive functioning: resulting from protracted, high-intensity situations.
39. Malignant social processes: self-perpetuating, inescapable emotional dynamics.
40. Escalatory spirals: basic tit-for-tat escalatory dynamics that run amok.
41. Structuralization: changes in social and institutional structures due to escalation that perpetuates conflict.
42. Moral exclusion: conditions where groups see out-groups as deserving of immoral treatment.
43. Violent exchanges and atrocities: a tipping point when violence justifies and begets more violence.
44. Pervasiveness: conflict spreads into functional aspects of life (education, cultural systems, etc.) and transforms them into tools of conflict.
45. High complexity: conflicts become too complex to comprehend.
46. Multilevel: negative aspects of conflicts link from people to groups to institutions to cultures.
47. Multiparty: increasing numbers of stakeholders contribute to the perpetuation.
48. Chaotic and mercurial: constantly changing dynamics that perpetuate conflict.
49. Individual and community trauma: families and communities lose the capacity to trust one another and therefore lose their ability to function and repair.
50. Betrayal of trust: a rupture of the basic understanding of a predictable world.
51. Beyond posttraumatic stress disorder: when atrocities lead to extraordinary levels of trauma that impair basic functioning.
52. Trauma unaddressed: when past trauma is left untreated to fester.
53. Historical rivalries: robust, long-term animosities among people and groups.
54. Enduring cycles of low to high intensity: cycles of conflict that alternate between high and low intensity that can lead to temporary states of complacency.
55. Destructive norms: hostility and violence become the accepted norm.
56. Intergenerational perpetuation: children and newcomers are socialized into the conflict.
57. Entrapment: a conflict's long duration justifies its perpetuation.

That's right. The literature on difficult conflicts (alternatively called moral conflicts, deeply rooted conflicts, divided societies, enduring rivalries, protracted social conflicts, and intractable conflicts) was filled with proclamations claiming the various essences of the problem. The back and forth went something like this:

> "Intractable conflicts are all simply about getting and keeping power and control."

> "Actually, they're basically all about hidden agendas and covert investments in maintaining the conflict."

> "Okay, but underneath it all, they're really about how instability and change fosters more instability and conflict."

> "No, they are rooted deeply in past instances of personal and communal trauma, in powerful emotions and unconscious, irrational processes."

> "No, no, they are in fact about scarce critical resources and other nonnegotiable issues. That's why they can't be solved."

> "No, please, can't you see—they are of course all about the basic need of people and groups to protect their sacred rights and identities."

> "No, no, no. They're simply conflicts that are too complicated to figure out!"

And the problem is that they are right. They are *all* right. Impossible conflicts are often about nonnegotiable issues and important identities and intense emotions and past trauma and hidden agendas and power and instability. And they do tend to be very complicated and pervasive and mercurial. *And* they are all unique. So each claim is right, to a degree.

Look, for example, at the story of the resurgence of World War II over a friendly dinner in Greenwich Village. What happened there? Why did this tightly knit group of friends and coworkers implode like it did? Was it because of latent feelings of guilt and shame that the German and the Pole felt for things they suspected their ancestors did or did not do during WWII? Was it about past or even current relations and the balance or imbalance of power between Germany and Poland? Did the fact that the colleagues were all guests in an Israeli's home, eating her food and drinking her wine, simply intensify everything? Was trauma involved? Was it the historical transmission of trauma from their parents and grandparents that gripped several of them that night and refused to let go? Or was this some perverse form of sibling dynamic? Did the colleagues suffer from the absence of authority in the room and thus feel free to let loose on their peers?

We suspect the answer is yes, to all of the above.

As soon as one looks more deeply into the collection of fifty-seven factors, which are each *the* source of intractability, it becomes clear that there is something even *more basic* that intractable conflicts seem to share. These essences, all fifty-seven of them, are often connected to one another in a very particular way. They tend to be linked in such a way that they *support and reinforce* one another. In other words, they function like a system: one complicated, well-oiled system. That is their essence.

Five percent problems are the result of complex systems dynamics created by many different elements interrelated in a weblike fashion that come together into one strong, coherent conflict. One destructive, complicated, evolving unit, as illustrated on the following page.

At our dinner party in the Village, the fact that half the members of the group had been raised in cultures where the Holocaust and other atrocities committed during WWII are still very much alive—salient, discussed, and debated—played a key role.* The three colleagues from Germany, Poland, and Israel came to the party holding latent but strong, internalized feelings and beliefs on the issues, interlinked like the image below, that had never been triggered in the group. With this background, the Israeli's description of the Silent March, coupled with the wine, the late hour, their youth, and the comfort they felt with each other because of their peer relations, provided a strong cocktail for the eruption. A conflict cocktail.

---

*Even today, investigators in Europe are discovering previously unidentified "camps" used by the Nazis in WWII, and large tracts of land taken by the Nazis during the war are still fenced off pending court action.

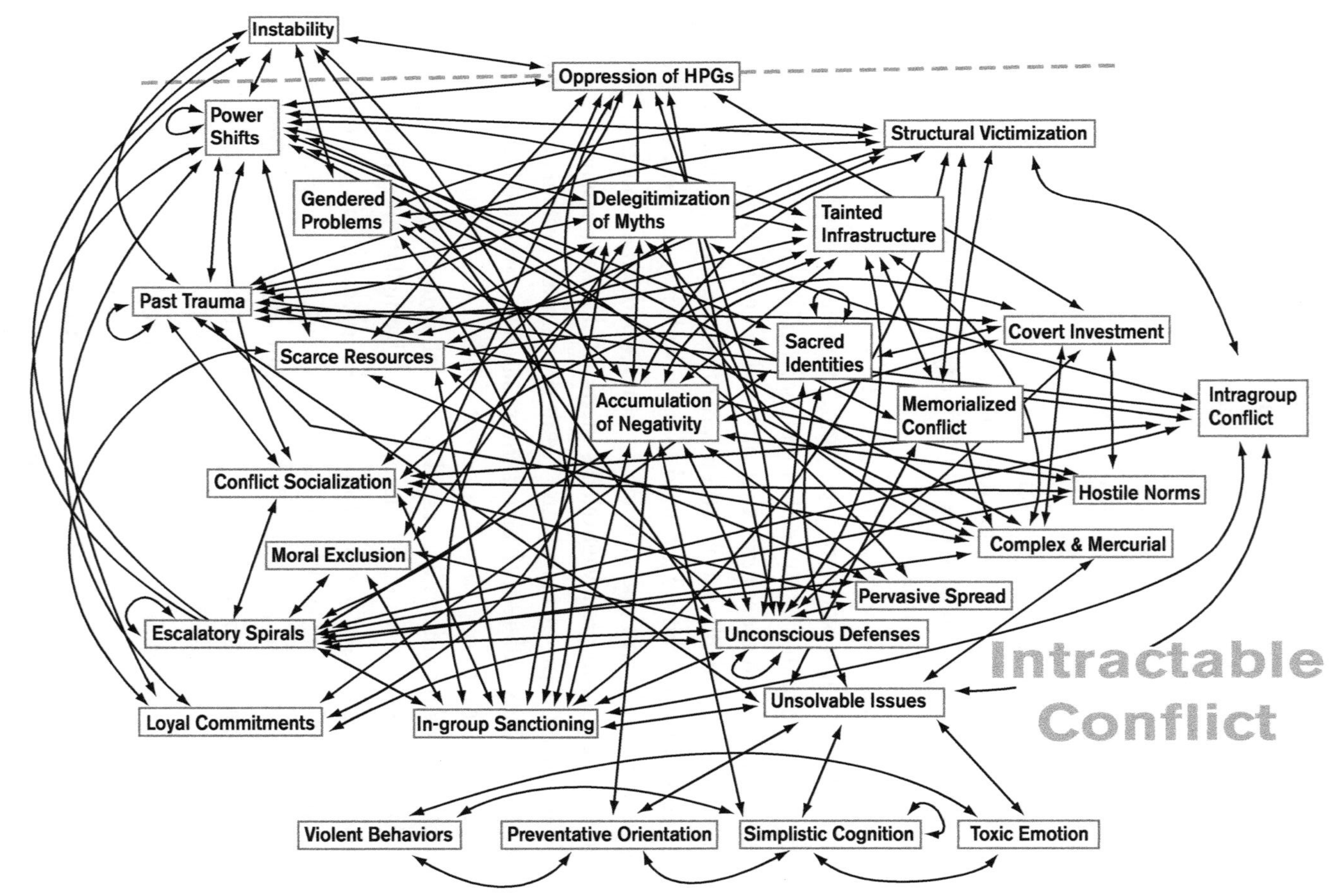
Instability
Oppression of HPGs
Power Shifts
Structural Victimization
Gendered Problems
Delegitimization of Myths
Tainted Infrastructure
Past Trauma
Covert Investment
Sacred Identities
Scarce Resources
Accumulation of Negativity
Memorialized Conflict
Intragroup Conflict
Conflict Socialization
Hostile Norms
Complex & Mercurial
Moral Exclusion
Pervasive Spread
Escalatory Spirals
Unconscious Defenses
Intractable Conflict
Unsolvable Issues
Loyal Commitments
In-group Sanctioning
Violent Behaviors
Preventative Orientation
Simplistic Cognition
Toxic Emotion

Afterward, it was simply too hard to overcome the shame and humiliation unleashed that night, the breach of trust. And too easy to disband the group. And so they did. It felt impossible to consider anything else.

This collapse of the different components of conflicts into one unit—one malignant system—is the core of intractability. It is not only that when this happens people are forced to face multiple problems at once. When problems converge like this they begin to feed off each other, triggering and exacerbating one another. Over time they come to severely limit our sense of what is possible in the conflict. That's when they become intractable.

THE 5 PERCENT ARE ALSO HARD TO SEE

There is another important reason why the 5 percent are so impossible to solve: we often tend to misread them. Long-standing conflicts that are complicated, threatening, and constantly changing are often extraordinarily difficult to make sense of. Take this case.

Big Oil in Nigeria

They were on their way to nursery school. In September 2010, fifteen children in the oil-rich Niger Delta region of Nigeria were abducted from their school bus by armed men. This was the latest in a pattern of kidnappings of foreign oil workers and prominent Nigerians and their families that began in the early 1990s. It happened in the state of Abia, where middle-class Nigerians, who are frequently attacked in their cars, travel with armed escorts.

In October 2010, two bombs killed eight people during an independence day ceremony in the capital of Abuja. A militant group, the Movement for the Emancipation of the Niger Delta, which has waged an insurgency campaign against the oil industry in Nigeria for five years, took responsibility. In a warning issued before the bombings, it wrote, "There is nothing worth celebrating after 50 years of failure. For 50 years the people of the Niger Delta have had their land and resources stolen from them."[9]

It has been said that Nigeria's oil boom has been more of a curse than a blessing. Africa's most populous country and second-largest economy, it has three major international oil companies operating there: Royal Dutch/Shell,

ExxonMobil, and ChevronTexaco. Petroleum extraction is 60 percent of its GDP. Although a leading exporter of oil, it is chronically short of gasoline and electricity. Although the nation takes in billions of dollars in oil revenue annually, the majority of its people live on less than a dollar a day. Poverty is on the rise and corruption is rampant. By some estimates, Nigeria has endured the equivalent of the *Exxon Valdez* spill every year for fifty years.[10] The oil pours out nearly every week, yet these spills receive little to no media coverage. The country's oil industry, operating within a complex context challenged by poor governance, unbridled corruption, and multiple layers of conflict, has hardly proven a boon to the majority of Nigerians.

The complexity of socioeconomic dynamics in Nigeria's oil-producing Delta states—continually impacted by extreme poverty, ethnic tensions, and the presence of oil companies—creates a context that is a virtual tinderbox for conflict. Competition for oil wealth has fueled ethnic violence and militarization in a country with about 250 ethnic tribes, approximately half of which are Christian and half Muslim. Ironically, the country's conversion to democracy has not seemed to help. Much of the violence was kept in check by a succession of military regimes until 1999, when Nigeria returned to civilian rule. Since then, rioting in 2001 killed over a thousand people, and violence in 2004 and 2008 claimed another thousand.

With casualties from violence in these numbers, the Niger Delta region reached a category of high-intensity conflict comparable to places like Chechnya and Colombia. In response, in 2009 the government established an amnesty program for thousands of Niger Delta gunmen. In 2010, Human Rights Watch reported:

> Since the latest escalation of violence began in early 2006, hundreds of people have been killed in clashes between rival armed groups vying for illicit patronage doled out by corrupt politicians, or between militants and government security forces. Armed gangs have carried out numerous attacks on oil facilities and kidnapped more than 500 oil workers and ordinary Nigerians for ransom during this period. The amnesty offer, announced in June 2009, followed a major military offensive in May against militants in the creeks of Delta State, which left scores dead and thousands of residents displaced.[11]

The situation in Nigeria has grown increasingly intractable.

WHEN FACED WITH ANY COMPLEX PROBLEM in living systems, humans encounter several basic challenges to understanding them and taking effective action. As a thought experiment, consider for a moment the problems in Nigeria. Begin by asking yourself, "What is germane to addressing the conflicts in the Niger Delta?" In other words, given the vast array of potentially relevant factors, which do you consider most central to the problem? Notice where your mind goes. Does it identify government corruption, corporate greed, America's thirst for oil, or the international community's general neglect of the plight of African countries? Does it go to scarce resources, class warfare, structural oppression, and the eternal struggles between the haves and have-nots around the world? Or does it focus on basic tribalism, ethnocentrism, stereotyping, and other classic intergroup dynamics? Does it orient you to the extraordinary constellation of problems facing this beleaguered country, or to the exceptional opportunities and resources available for enhancing the well-being of all Nigerians? And why do you suppose your mind went where it did? Was it because of previous personal or professional experiences? Or an influential editorial, article, or book you once read?

The problems in present-day Nigeria are highly complex and dynamic. They combine very traumatic personal tragedies with other important historical, environmental, social, cultural, political, economic, and international dimensions. As your own ruminations may have indicated, they are problems that manifest on a variety of levels, which are different today than they were yesterday. This small experiment illustrates some of the many challenges we encounter when we attempt to comprehend and respond effectively to complex, evolving problems.

THE FRAME PROBLEM

Researchers studying artificial intelligence (AI) have labeled our difficulty in comprehending dynamic complexity *the frame problem.*[12] The question we face is, Given a specific problem, what is or is not germane to solving that problem?

This is essentially a problem of determining relevance and irrelevance. For example, when AI researchers attempt to train a robot to accomplish a simple task such as retrieving a ball, they face the extraordinarily difficult problem of predetermining which stimuli (from an infinite field of stimuli) are or are not relevant to the task at hand. In fact, the ability to discern what is and is not germane to a problem is what researchers working in AI define as *the essence of intelligence.*[13] The frame problem, even for simple tasks, is enormously demanding; it becomes increasingly more unworkable as tasks or situations become more complex. So given the multitude of fifty-seven things that may be driving any 5 percent conflict, the issue becomes what is relevant—and, more important, what is *not* relevant—to addressing it?

Under normal circumstances the frame problem has four primary dimensions:

- **The *object problem,*** which concerns how a given object (such as an oil company operating in Nigeria) can be segregated meaningfully from the parts that compose it (employees, corporate leadership, policies, business practices), its situation or context (government regulations, local economy, the developing world, Nigeria's history with big business, continental and global business trends), related entities (other industries operating in Nigeria, the neighborhood in West Africa, Muslim-Christian religious divisions within the country, relations with the World Bank and other international agencies and NGOs), and the observer (the nature of the relationship of the observer to the company). In other words, when faced with a problem, at what level and within what scope do we usefully define and distinguish the main aspects of interest?
- **The *subjectivity problem.*** This is based on the premise that there are an infinite number of ways to perceive or construe a situation and its consequences. However, each perspective is aspectual: it focuses attention on certain aspects of a problem and away from others.

  Because we all deal with conflicts every day throughout our lives, each of us has developed our own preferred perspectives: what we call *implicit theories* or *frames.*[14] We may not be aware of them, but we have them. I once interviewed an eminent international peacemaker who said to me, "I don't have any use for models or theories in my work." He then went on to describe his model, in detail, which involved dealing with every situation anew on its own terms. It was a *nonmodel* model (a situational-contingency model), but a model nevertheless.

These models usually have a combination of origins. They may come from our formative personal or professional experiences with conflict (including how we saw our parents, teachers, coaches, politicians, etc. model how to deal with conflict) or else from our formal education: how we were trained to see problems and solve them. Experience shows that engineers, physicians, military officers, social workers, teachers, therapists, political scientists, diplomats, economists, union organizers, and so on all see and approach conflicts in distinctly different ways. They all bring to conflict their own *frames:* ways of seeing and thinking.

We are inclined to prefer certain perspectives over others for a variety of reasons. These could include our past history with a situation, values, political attitudes, disciplinary and professional training, level of optimism, current mood, and other relevant factors. Different frames highlight certain aspects of conflict situations and ignore others, as they shape our sense of reality and of what is and is not relevant to a solution. In fact, cognitive scientists tell us that our frames are often stronger determinants of our perceptions and actions in social situations than are the facts on the ground. As the linguist George Lakoff has put it, "frames trump facts."

- **A set of two *data-processing problems*** especially relevant to processing complexity. One involves our limited capacity to attend to multiple objects. Research demonstrates that humans can only process a small number of objects at any given time.[15] Typically, a set of seven, plus or minus two, is what we can manage. Under conditions of threat, this number drops precipitously. Additionally, when attempting to solve problems, humans tend not to *maximize* but rather to *satisfice.* Instead of systematically assessing each response option, weighing the costs and benefits of each, comparing them, and choosing the best, they will simply choose the first decent option that emerges.[16] This usually occurs through an automatic application of mental guidelines or rules of thumb, called *heuristics,* that aid us in processing information more efficiently, particularly under conditions where other demands are competing for our attention. It thus proves extremely difficult for us to both attend to the many aspects of complex scenarios and to effectively process the many potential solutions to these problems.

- **The problem of *dynamism*.** Simply stated, people, groups, and social situations are in a constant state of flux and transformation. Some aspects of situations remain relatively stable, while others change in either important or unimportant ways. Thus, our earlier framing of a conflict may become obsolete due to important changes that have occurred. For example, in Nigeria kidnapping has been used by insurgent groups for some time now not only to bring attention to their cause, but also to terrorize oil company executives and bring in revenue for their movements. However, experts believe that the recent spike in kidnappings is due to criminal gangs who have taken advantage of the instability in the region. Understanding this shift is critical to comprehending the current dynamics of the political conflict and identifying new opportunities for peace.

Making matters worse are conditions of prolonged conflict, high tension, threat, or polarization, which serve to exacerbate the frame problem. In high-stress situations, our capacity for thorough, effective decision making becomes increasingly impaired by perceptual distortions, anxiety, and inflexible thinking.[17] Research identifies several basic psychological shifts that occur over time under these conditions. They include the following:

- **Promotion to destruction.** Shifts from a *promotion* orientation (people are motivated to seek their best possible outcomes in a conflict) to a *prevention* orientation (peoples' motivation shifts to avoiding negative outcomes and loss) to a *destructive* orientation (people become motivated to inflict as much harm as possible on the "other") as the conflict intensifies.

- **Concrete to abstract.** Shifts from *low action-identification* (people can identify and process concrete and nuanced aspects of situations) to *high action-identification* (people are more focused on abstract principles such as right and wrong and good and evil).
- **Objectivity to subjectivity.** Shifts from *objective* concerns (people want to obtain accurate information regarding substantive issues in dispute) to *subjective* concerns (people are more focused on their sense of respect and dignity, and the need to defend their identity and core values).
- **Long term to short term.** Shifts from longer-term, even generational, thinking ("How will what we do today affect us and our children in the long run?") to an immediate focus on the here and now.

Once these perceptual and motivational shifts occur, the logic of immediate coercion and violence prevails. Threats, contentiousness, and other escalatory actions emerge as the most reasonable response to conflict. Anything else feels impossible to consider.

RESPONDING TO COMPLEX PROBLEMS

When faced with complex problems, we typically respond in one of three ways.[18] Often, our initial reaction is to feel overwhelmed. We may feel anxious and despair of our ability to respond effectively. This motivates our attempts to *deny or avoid* a problem. We might fail to recognize it altogether, or acknowledge the issues while simultaneously refusing to engage them. This characterized Anthony and Kasha's initial approach to their divorce proceedings, when they chose to leave discussion about their vacation house until the end of the process. This strategy can have short-term benefits, such as the temporary management of anxiety, and long-term negative consequences, such as a missed opportunity to deescalate the conflict. It could even intensify the problem.

A second common response to complex problems is to *prematurely simplify* the problem. The demanding nature of these situations understandably attracts us to simplification: to thinking that circumscribes their intricacies by focusing on very few aspects. When situations offer contradictory information, simplification often involves a cursory comparison of different sides of the information, resulting in a polarized decision that one side is right and the others wrong. Such responses help alleviate our anxiety, cope, identify what to do, and begin to feel a sense of efficacy and control over the problem. But they can also lead to a misreading of the problem, resulting in what cognitive scientists label *the revenge of the unjustly ignored.*[19]

In other words, premature oversimplification can lead us to actions that result in unintended negative consequences—consequences regarding important but neglected aspects of the problem. For example, some have argued that the Oslo Accords between the Israelis and Palestinians, despite their merits, failed because they neglected to address many of the key concerns of marginalized factions in the conflict and other serious issues voiced in the streets.

The third type of response to complex conflicts, much less common than the others, is to *actively engage with complexity.* This can take different forms but typically entails an iterative process of *differentiation* of the relevant aspects of and perspectives on the problem. *And then* an *integration* of this information within some coherent framework that makes it comprehensible and useful.[20] This does not mean getting lost in the nuances and complexities of problems or prematurely simplifying them. It means doing both in an iterative, ongoing fashion. In other words, we break it down and then put it together *before* and *after* we decide.

Research on this type of information processing, called *integrative complexity,* has been conducted on the writings of a variety of effective decision makers, including diplomats, presidents, revolutionary leaders, and Supreme Court justices.[21] Generally, higher complexity is associated with reaching mutually beneficial compromise agreements, successful diplomatic communications, employing cooperative tactics during negotiations, and increased managerial effectiveness. Additionally, leaders with high levels of complexity are more likely to be open minded, more effective in highly turbulent environments, and less likely to jump to conclusions too quickly when facing ambiguous situations. Although this manner of problem engagement can be demanding and requires certain skills, and is unnecessary with more mundane problems, the benefits of employing it with the 5 percent will greatly outweigh the consequences of denial, avoidance, or oversimplification.

Clearly, complex problems like the 5 percent present daunting challenges to our human capacity for comprehension and effective action. Determining the relevance or irrelevance of the countless aspects of such problems can overwhelm even the most careful, rational thinker. Under normal circumstances, we must locate the problem at an appropriate level and scope, mindful of how our point of view affects what we come to see as fact. We must struggle with limitations to our cognitive processing of information and remain open to how important unfolding changes may impact the situation. And if we face conditions of protracted threat, the demands on us are further exacerbated by anxiety, impaired cognitive functioning, a chronic concern for safety, and a context that provides contradictory and politically consequential forms of information. Like athletes who play extreme sports, we must be aware of the challenges the 5 percent present to our perception and judgment, and respond accordingly.

COMPLEX PROBLEMS AND OVERLY SIMPLISTIC PERCEPTIONS AND RESPONSES: A PERFECT STORM

Of course, various aspects of the 5 percent problem—their complex, intertwined spaghetti-like nature and how they are often misperceived and mishandled—work perfectly together. And when very complicated situations collapse into simple "us versus them" problems, then certainty, hate, and escalatory spirals proliferate and become a driving force for perpetual conflict. They become Orestes avenging Agamemnon, who was slaughtered by Clytemnestra, who was avenging Iphigenia, who was slaughtered by Agamemnon, who was avenging his brother Menelaus, whose wife was abducted by Paris, and so on. They become impossible.

That was the state of relations between the pro-choice and pro-life communities in Boston prior to the clinic shootings in 1994. The villains and the heroines of the conflict were crystal clear to both sides.

Every word uttered by the other side, every comment, every gesture, every move was seen as heinous and further fuel for conflict. Every march, every rally, every speech was predictable and provided more justification for the status quo. It was all very complicated and fundamentally simple. It all fit together perfectly and demanded a unified front. It was an impossible conflict.

But beneath this impossibility in Brookline, Massachusetts, lay the seeds of something else. Beyond the history, the predictable moves, the inflammatory gestures, the very denial of the other side's humanity was a faint but very real possibility. An alternative. Another way. And it was this dormant possibility that was awakened in 1994 by the extraordinary combination of crisis and human contact, triggered ironically by the clinic shootings. Just how this all comes to pass—how some conflicts grow and spread and fit together in such a way that they seem impossible to solve, and how, sometimes, people are able to find a way out—is the essential story of this book.

How Do I Know If I'm in a 5 Percent Conflict?

When something triggers a conflict and you find yourself immediately, deeply in it, and it all feels very familiar and simple and yet you also feel weary–tired and wanting desperately for it to end and yet, somehow, again and again you find yourself back at square one–chances are it's a 5 percent. Its two telltale signs are (1) you find yourself denying or discounting any and all positive information about your opponent and (2) you feel overwhelming resistance (from yourself and others) to act differently toward your opponent.

part two

THE APPROACH

THE ATTRACTION OF IMPOSSIBLE CONFLICTS

chapter 3

THE BIG IDEA: COMPLEXITY, COHERENCE, AND CONFLICT

THE INTRACTABLE CONFLICT LAB

In the Intractable Conflict Lab at Columbia University sit two participants from one of our studies on polarizing moral conflicts. They are seething. They are both black women, brought together by us to discuss their views on affirmative action. One identifies herself as African American, the other as Jamaican American. They have been working hard trying to reach consensus on a position statement on affirmative action in U.S. higher education. But they discovered right away that they hold opposing views on the issue.

Session 1

A: "I disagree with the [pro-affirmative action] statement, because when two equally qualified persons apply for a job, you can't choose one because of race."

B: "Umm . . . I would agree with the [pro-affirmative action] statement because sometimes when we think about equal opportunity . . . If you have two qualified people and one is black and one is white . . . I don't know how to put it . . . just because people have equal credentials doesn't mean it isn't discriminatory in nature. Because, like, from the day you are born white or black you automatically have privileges afforded to you as a white person that you don't have as a black person. So let's say they are equally qualified, I just feel like . . . there are more white people in every other position in life so why not hand it to the person of color, whether that person is black or another person of color?"

A: "But what would happen if the workforce right now had ninety percent black and ten percent white?"

B: "Well . . . when you say the workforce? . . ."

A: "For that job. In that department, it's ninety percent black, ten percent white."

B: "I would say that's *one* job, as opposed to every other job in America. America where there are only thirty-three percent of Americans who are white, male, middle-class men with money. Yet, they occupy eighty percent of CEOs, ninety-nine percent of athletic team ownerships, a hundred percent of the presidents, except for, you know, besides yesterday. So it's like, even though there is this one job, there's like a million other instances where there is always a hundred percent white people."

A: "Yeah, but you are *generalizing* based . . . and we're talking about one specific situation. So, that would be reverse discrimination. Because, here you have a workforce that is predominantly black. And you are saying that with two equally qualified persons . . . and the black person should get the job. Then that white person could say, hey, this is reverse racism, because right now that workforce is not diverse. So how do you create a diverse workforce? So there's pros and cons. You can't just look at the situation just like that and give a blanket answer."

B: "Okay, so, one word you said was *reverse racism.* That wouldn't be reverse racism, 'cause the definition of racism . . . people have to have the power to be racist. Black people don't have the power in this country so they cannot be racist . . . so if I were to afford a job to a black or a white person that would not be . . . first of all, that would not be racism there. I could give it to you if you said prejudice, because anyone could be prejudiced, but in America, only white people can be racist because they are the people who have power."

A: "I would *totally* disagree with that statement!"

The conversation escalates and becomes increasingly polarized. For one participant, it is clear that the legacy of black slavery in the United States combines with white privilege, structural oppression, and institutionalized, covert racism to keep U.S. blacks at a disadvantage, providing ample evidence of the need for reparations like affirmative action. She cries out:

B: "Name me anything in American that is predominantly black, and I'll always tell you that a white man is signing the check. That's what I'm saying about power. Athletics, black people, all in that, but there will always be someone signing the checks, someone owning it. Black people don't *own* anything in this country."

B: "The SAT test is racist and discriminatory. It's for white men. I didn't understand it, it was not my reality. . . . If they had relied on that, I would have never graduated from college with a 3.5 GPA and made it into an Ivy League graduate school."

B: "I'm the first one in my family to go to college, even though my great-grandmother lived here for over seventy years. Do you know in Harlem, fifty percent of black men will not graduate high school, as opposed to eighty-nine percent of white people?"

B: "So you think that black people in this country are just lazy and need to get over it, right?"

The other participant sees things differently. She argues that despite the discrimination and humiliation she and her daughter have faced time and again, she will not give up her power. She locates the *real* problem for U.S. blacks within black families:

> A: "I have a very difficult time with this because you're automatically giving someone else power over you. I'm a black person. I feel that no white person has any power over me. We equally have the same right. I might be living in a dream world, but I use that to my advantage. I'm never going anywhere, under any circumstances, and think that somebody because of the color of their skin, they're allowed any preferences over me, they have any kind of power. So I think this power is in the mind. And if you have in your mind-set . . . oh, this white person has power over me, they will always have power over you."

> A: "You keep generalizing everything, that's where I have the problem. Everything is *always,* everything is like that's the way it is . . . it's not always like that . . . I believe that each situation has to be looked at in that context."

> A: "As black parents, what do they do? They pass on the debt, they pass on everything else, but they don't teach their children how to survive, how to succeed, how to be the one to write the check . . . If you think you can never write the check, you'll never write the check."

> A: "You know who needs to show you? You know who needs to show you? Nobody outside the door needs to show you. Your mother and your father need to show you. That's their responsibility."

> A: "As an immigrant, I've been here twenty-something years, I've never collected welfare, I've never been on any social service. Not that I haven't had hard times. And I'm a citizen and I've paid my taxes since the day I walked into this country. Every time where I find myself that I might have been knocked down, I did everything in my power and worked twice as hard or three times as hard to get myself up . . . I never went into a line and said I need to get a Social Security

check because now I'm not working and a white man is holding me down."

A: "My daughter was called every single name in the book by black kids, 'Oh, she's not black enough, she's not this enough, she's too smart.' Because she never talked the slangs that they did."

The pain and frustration and indignities suffered by both women and by generations of their family members fill the room. As they speak, they become more and more angry, moving further and further apart in their views, until the facilitator ends the session.

In our research on difficult moral conflicts, my colleagues and I have brought together hundreds of people like these in our labs at Columbia University in New York and at Ludwig-Maximilians University in Munich, Germany. Most contemporary research on social conflict involves case studies of past events, large surveys of people's attitudes and perceptions of current events, or small lab studies that use games or role plays to simulate conflict. We take a very different approach in our research because we are interested in studying the *real* and *real-time* experiences and actions of people locked in difficult conflicts.

It's fairly straightforward. First, we premeasure people's attitudes on sociopolitical issues important to them. Then, after matching people who hold opposing views on the same issue, we invite them into our lab and ask them to try to reach consensus for a position statement. They are told they will be asked to share their written statement with an on-campus student group looking for information on that issue. Typically, the participants discuss the topic for twenty minutes or so, and their conversation is recorded. We then ask them to listen to the recording and tell us how they felt from moment to moment during the discussion. (John Gottman uses a similar method in studying marital conflict and divorce in his Love Lab in Seattle.[1])

As you can imagine, the conversations that take place in the lab are difficult. Picture yourself sitting down with someone who has a strong opinion on abortion, one that is opposed to yours, and then trying to discuss the issue and reach *consensus* on a statement that will be publically shared with others.

It might not surprise you to learn that many of these conversations get hostile and need to be ended early, before the study is complete. Like the session described above, they become deeply personal and historical. But what might surprise you is that they do not all go terribly bad. They do not all escalate, get locked in, and remain stuck. For example, here's another brief excerpt from a different session, this time from a European American man and an Asian American woman who are also discussing affirmative action.

Session 2

M: "So, what's your take on affirmative action?

W: "My take on affirmative action? Um, overall, or specifically on these questions?"

M: "Overall."

W: "Overall? The first thing that comes to mind when you ask the question is . . . an idea to fix a wrong that may not be the right fix . . . that's my take, generally."

M: "And when you say *may be wrong* do you mean that you may be more for or against it?"

W: "The reason that I say I think it's wrong . . . I think it may be ineffective as a solution to the issue we are talking about . . . because I think it might be a setup for students who are involved in these programs. It might be setups for failure. So it actually makes things worse for them. That's how I feel about it."

M: "Do you think it's ineffective or something you disagree with? I'm just trying to understand."

W: "I think it's ineffective . . ."

W: "If I was to see someone else of color that scored much lower than I did and got into the program choice that I wanted to get into, and I was denied that, I would be very upset about it, I would think it was unjust."

As in the first session, the man and woman in this discussion were paired because of their contrasting views on affirmative action. And as before, the participants quickly discovered they held opposing views on the subject and that their stances on the issue came from their personal history—how they had been raised and taught and where they had been brought up, in this case, Minnesota and New York City.

But something different took place in this second session. Although emotional, even sometimes caustic, the dialogue was less constrained and more emotionally *expansive.* Both conversations involved negative emotions, attributions, and even some verbal attacks, but they diverged dramatically in the degree to which session 1 had become stuck in a narrow well of negativity and polarization. The participants in session 1 had become engulfed by the conflict.

Session 2 participants did not suffer the same fate. When we asked the participants from both sessions how it went for them, it was clear that those from session 2 felt significantly better about the discussion, their relations with the other person, whether they would want to work with them again on something, and even with the statement they generated. Even though both dyads in the study were discussing the same difficult, politically polarizing issues on which they held strong, morally opposing views, one dyad had discussions that got mired in negativity and the other, although not absent of negativity, was able to speak to the issues in ways that, even though hard, remained constructive.

These same differences in the patterns of more constructive versus more destructive moral conversations—differences in the *expansiveness* of how the participants thought, felt, and behaved—were found again and again in the various sessions in our research. It was as if the more destructive dyads got mired in a place that became more and more constraining.

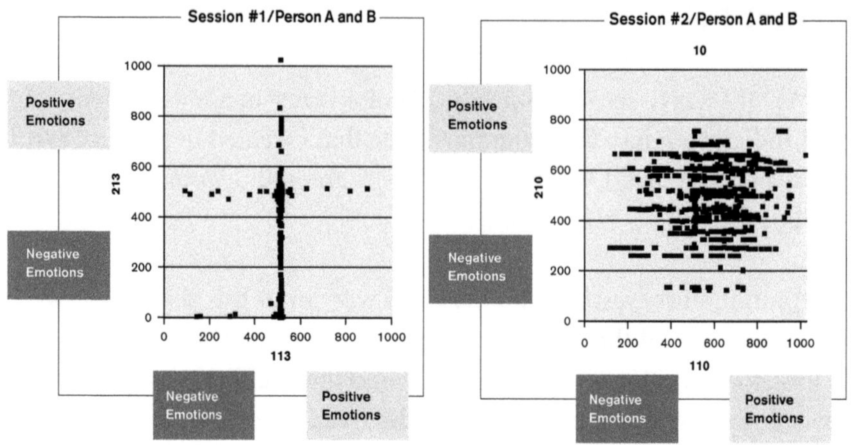

Like being caught in quicksand, the more they struggled the more stuck and exhausted they became. The constructive dyads were somehow able to avoid this trap.

What was particularly interesting to us was that, underneath it all, the main thing that distinguished the session 1–type discussions (destructive) from the session 2–type discussions (constructive) was the difference in their degrees of *complexity*. That difference could be seen in the dramatic contrast between the *lower-complexity patterns* of the thoughts, feelings, and behaviors of dyads in the destructive encounters and the *higher-complexity patterns* of the dyads in the constructive conversations. Above, for instance, is what the emotions of the two different dyads looked like during their twenty-minute sessions.

Without paying too much attention to the specifics of the graphs above, just notice the differences in the gray dots and lines from sessions 1 and 2. In session 1, the dots are all tightly organized along two lines, meaning that the people in this discussion felt mostly neutral to negative emotions as they discussed affirmative action.

In session 2, the dots and lines are all over the place. This shows that the emotions of the participants moved back and forth, from positive to negative, as the discussion unfolded. And as we looked further, we found similar differences in *simple versus complex patterns* in the data between the two sessions, for thought and behavior as well. In other words, the more constructive dyads thought about the issues in more complex, nuanced, and flexible ways. They felt many different types of emotions, both positive and negative, over the course of the discussions. And they behaved in more varied ways that demonstrated a greater degree of openness, flexibility, and curiosity in addition to a strong advocacy for their positions than did the session-1 types.

The findings from this study were particularly striking to us because they flew in the face of conventional wisdom, which argues that the simplest approaches to complicated problems are always the best. In our research, more complex approaches, in terms of how the participants thought about the issues, felt, and behaved, were in fact better. To explain why, it's necessary to back up and address the psychology of complexity.

THE PSYCHOLOGY OF COMPLEXITY, COHERENCE, AND CONFLICT

In 1910, the philosopher Max Wertheimer bought a small toy while away on vacation. This toy ended up turning the field of psychology on its head. On his journey, Wertheimer had been staring out the window of a train, puzzling over the blur of perceptions before him. He got off the train during a station stop and purchased a stroboscope, a spinning drum with viewing slots and pictures on the inside, like a primitive movie machine.

While playing with the toy, Wertheimer was struck by something. He noticed that the pictures in the toy looked like they were moving, but were not. It occurred to him that at times we perceive motion when it is really not there, when there is nothing more than an effect called *apparent motion,* a rapid sequence of individual sensory events. He realized that we often experience things not part of our simple sensations, that what we see is an effect of the *whole* event we are perceiving, not just the sum of its parts. He later wrote: "What is given me by the melody does not arise . . . as a *secondary* process from the sum of the pieces as such. Instead, what takes place in each single part already depends upon what the whole is."[2] In other words, while listening to music, only after first hearing the melody do we perceptually divide it up into notes. Similarly with perception, we see the form of the circle first and only later notice that it is made up of lines or dots or stars.

At the time, psychology was interested in the small things. Psychologists studied learning, perception, and cognition by breaking things down into their smaller parts, like sensations, images, and feelings, and then investigating them in their own right. Wertheimer rebelled against this approach, arguing that psychology should take a *unified* approach to the study of human perception and behavior, and view it as a meaningful whole. That is how we make sense of things. How we feel and behave depends on our broader context of experience and cannot be understood by merely studying the pieces. This idea resembles the Taoist and Aristotelian principles of *holism.* It was the basis for Gestalt psychology, a radical paradigm shift in the field away from atomistic, micro, and mechanical perspectives toward a more holistic and dynamic view of psychological phenomena.

Enter Kurt Lewin, a bright, gregarious German Jew who studied psychology in Berlin under Wertheimer's former teacher, Carl Stumpf.* Lewin was forced to flee Nazi Germany in the 1930s and traveled to the United States. There his work had a major impact on social psychology, in particular the theoretical study of group dynamics, prejudice, authoritarianism, and, most important for us, social conflict.†

While in the United States, Lewin developed his *field-theoretical* approach to the study of social conflict, which incorporated much of what he had learned from his Gestalt colleagues, as well as some new ideas coming out of physics (which was undergoing a similar paradigm shift at the time from Newtonian mechanics to field theory). In particular, there were two main principles from Gestalt that influenced his work.

1. All social phenomena should be conceived as occurring in a "field." This means that in order to best comprehend any social phe-

*Lewin later worked with Wertheimer and two of his assistants, Wolfgang Kohler and Kurt Kafka, the three of whom are known as the founders of Gestalt psychology.

†It is interesting to note that some scholars go so far as to credit Adolph Hitler with inspiring the ascendance of social psychology, because his rise focused so much attention on the systematic study of dire social problems.

nomenon such as conflict, we must not prematurely oversimplify it, but be able to see the broad field of forces operating to move it in a positive or negative direction. For example, take a look at the electromagnetic field below.

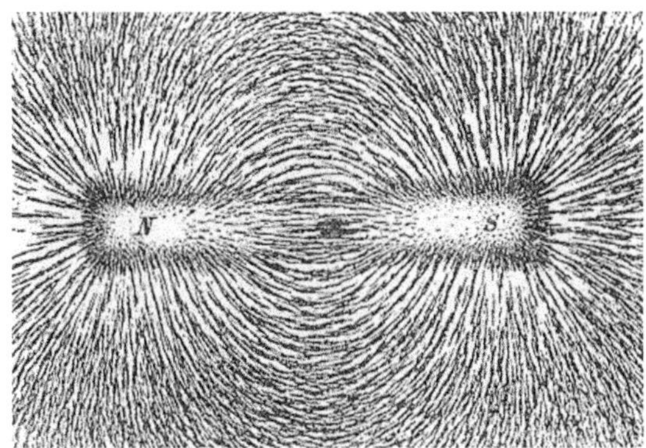

Before the discovery of such fields in the latter part of the nineteenth century, physicists understood most natural phenomena as the result of forces acting between one body and another in an empty space. But a series of brilliant experiments on electromagnetic phenomena, conducted by Hans Christian Oersted and Michael Faraday, challenged this basic view and profoundly altered scientific conceptions of physical reality. They demonstrated that between two magnetic poles, instead of empty space, there lies *a complex field of forces acting to attract or repel* the poles.

The impact of these ideas crumbled the foundations of popular philosophical viewpoints at the time and served as a model for new conceptions in the biological and social sciences. The Gestalt conceptualization of psychological perception occurring in a field and Kurt Lewin's development of a field theory of human motivation and social conflict were two of the more influential models emerging from this view.

The second Gestalt principle was derived originally from psychological research on perception.

2. Psychological processes act to move us toward states of the field that are as simple and orderly as conditions allow. Allow me to illustrate. Turn the page and look at the image. What do you see? Anything?

Source: The Intelligent Eye. R. L. Gregory, Weidenfeld and Nicholson, 1970.

People see all kinds of things in this image. Alligators, fish, trees, ant hills, boats, faces, dogs, even a lady dancing in the upper left-hand corner. So what do you see?

Eventually, most people see a dog, a Dalmatian, in the center of the image, leaning away from the viewer and eating something on the ground. Can you see it?

Now notice what just happened. What did your mind do? Your eyes saw some black blotches on a white background, and then what? Did you see an object right away or did it take a while? Did you see the Dalmatian or something else? If something else, was it hard to then change your perspective to see the Dalmatian? Were you ever able to see the dog?

Research shows that when we are faced with abstract or ill-defined images, we are *driven* to make sense of them. We feel we have to. It is as though we are hardwired to impose meaning on the world.

The Impressionist painters knew this and used it to engage the public with their art. Of course, we do this all the time as we walk down the street, processing trillions of bits of data coming in through our senses. It is mostly automatic. But it becomes noticeable and most interesting when we *cannot* make sense of things. When we cannot see anything in the image or, worse yet, when most other people see a Dalmatian but no matter how hard we try, we simply cannot. How does that feel?

It usually feels bad. Most of us do not like *not* being able to see what others see or make sense of something new. We do not like it when things do not come together and fit together nicely for us. That is why most popular movies have Hollywood endings. The public prefers a tidy finale. And we especially do not like it when things are contradictory, because then it is much harder to reconcile them (this is particularly true for Westerners).[3] This sense of confusion triggers in us a feeling of noxious anxiety. It generates *tension.* So we feel compelled to reduce it, solve it, complete it, reconcile it, make it make sense. And when we do solve these puzzles, there's relief. It feels good. We *really* like it when things come together.

What I am describing is a very basic human psychological process, captured by the second Gestalt principle. It is what we call the *press for coherence.* It has been called many different things in psychology: consonance, need for closure, congruity, harmony, need for meaning, the consistency principle. At its core it is the drive to reduce the tension, disorientation, and dissonance that come from complexity, incoherence, and contradiction.

In the 1930s, Bluma Zeigarnik, a student of Lewin's in Berlin, designed a famous study to test the impact of this idea of tension and coherence. Lewin had noticed that waiters in his local café seemed to have better recollections of unpaid orders than of those already settled. A lab study was run to examine this phenomenon, and it showed that people tend to remember uncompleted tasks, like half-finished math or word problems, better than completed tasks. This is because the unfinished task triggers a feeling of tension, which gets associated with the task and keeps it lingering in our minds. The completed problems are, well, complete, so we forget them and move on. They later called this the *Zeigarnik effect,* and it has influenced the study of many things, from advertising campaigns to coping with the suicide of loved ones to dysphoric rumination over past conflicts.

In the United States, Lewin went on to integrate these two basic Gestalt principles of complex force fields and the press for coherence into his field-theoretical approach to the study of human motivation and social conflict. He also borrowed a lot from physics, but was clear that he saw physical systems and psychological or social systems as very different, although he believed that the underlying *logic of dynamics* might be very similar across different areas of science.

Lewin's approach to understanding social conflict had five main components.

1. Start with the *total* situation, then essentialize. Although Lewin found it critical to identify the essence of things, he believed we needed to start with an understanding of the whole, of the many forces operating in a situation, before we focused in on the core. He defined *conflict* in holistic field theoretical terms as "a situation in which oppositely directed forces of about equal strength play upon a person simultaneously."[4]

2. Understand the constellation of forces operating *now*. Lewin believed that the current situation was what mattered most; the past was only important in how it affected people in the present.

3. Do not emphasize things; focus on the *relations* between things. Psychology in Lewin's time was focused on things like sensations, instincts, and habits (the classificatory approach) and tended to discount the relations *between* things (the constructive approach). Lewin flipped this and said it was the relations between things—the social bonds between people, competing goals in groups, communication links—that really mattered. In fact, he came to define the *essence of groups* as how the members see their goals linked together: are they with, against, or unconnected from one another? This inspired his student Morton Deutsch to define the essence of constructive versus destructive conflict as cooperative versus competitive goal linkages between people and between groups.

4. Remember that people and groups are *alive*. Unlike the more static views of psychology at the time, Lewin saw humans and groups as living, evolving systems that seek some type of balance with their environment. This view of humans as living systems was a hard sell in psychology, but it has risen in prominence over the last two decades.

5. Do your *math* homework. Finally, Lewin believed that for psychology to ever really grow up and mature into a rigorous scientific discipline, it would have to come to understand human behavior through the use of formal mathematical models. Note that this requires careful specification of the essence of phenomena, but only after they are understood in their broader context. Unfortunately, mathematics and computers were not sufficiently advanced during Lewin's time. But that, too, has changed.

Tragically, Lewin died quite young, at age fifty-seven. And although he inspired many and blazed a trail for the study of conflict, he left much unfinished business.

THE BIG IDEA

Nevertheless, Lewin and his Gestalt colleagues brought to light a major idea central to our work on impossible conflicts; namely *the relationship among complexity, contradiction, and coherence.*

It is critical to recognize that we live in an increasingly complex world—biologically, socially, politically, technologically, you name it—that holds many inherent contradictions. In the middle of this complex world are we humans, who have a natural tendency to seek coherence in what we see, feel, think, and do.

When we experience conflict, this tendency intensifies. Conflict is essentially a contradiction, an incompatibility, oppositely directed forces, and a difference that triggers tension. When we encounter conflict, within the field of forces that constitute it, the natural human tendency is to reduce that tension by seeking coherence through simplification. Research shows that this tendency toward simplification becomes even more intensified when we are under stress, threat, time constraints, fatigue, and various other conditions all absolutely typical of conflict.

So what is the big idea? It is *not* that coherence is bad and complexity is good. Coherence seeking is simply a necessary and functional process that helps us interpret and respond to our world efficiently and (hopefully) effectively. And complexity in extremes is a nightmare—think of Mogadishu, Somalia, in the 1990s or the financial crisis of 2009 or Times Square during rush hour on a Friday afternoon.

On the other hand, too much coherence can be just as pathological: for example, the collapse of the nuances and contradictions inherent in any conflict situation into simple "us versus them" terms, or a deep commitment to a rigid understanding of conflicts based on past sentiments and obsolete information. Either extreme—overwhelming complexity or oversimplified coherence—is problematic. But in difficult, long-term conflicts, the tide pulls fiercely toward simplification of complex realities. This is what we must contend with.

And if you look around, you see that this basic idea of complexity and coherence is all over the research on well-being: in brain science, physical and mental health, innovation, learning, psychology, and conflict. Here are some examples.

Physical health. In an article published in *Science* in 1989, researchers summarized a series of research results, stating that "chaos [a highly complex pattern] may provide a healthy flexibility to the heart, brain, and other parts of the body. Conversely, many ailments may be associated with a loss of chaotic flexibility."[5] For instance, a healthy heart rate tends to show a highly complex, variable pattern but collapses into a much simpler pattern days and hours before a cardiac arrest.[6] Similar patterns have been found for healthy versus pathological EEGs of brain behavior associated with seizures.[7] Health scientists conclude that "individuals with a wide-range of different illnesses are often characterized by periodic and predictable (ordered) dynamics, even though these disease processes themselves are referred to as disorders."[8]

Psychological well-being. A review of the *Diagnostic and Statistical Manual of Mental Disorders* shows that most psychopathologies are associated with either too much rigidity in psychosocial functioning or too much complexity, or wide swings between both. Psychologists suggest that psychosocial movement toward complexity that accomplishes some balance of both structure and chaos in mental health is the most stable and adaptive.[9]

Integrative complexity. This refers to the level of complexity of the cognitive rules people use to process and analyze incoming information. Research spanning decades shows that people who have higher levels of integrative complexity tend to be more conciliatory in conflict and also that as conflicts escalate, peoples' level of cognitive complexity diminishes.[10]

Political thinking. Differences in the cognitive structures associated with how people think about political issues have been labeled *political thinking*. Higher-level, more systematic political thinking is associated with a tendency for cooperation and compromise in political conflict. Lower-level, linear political thinking is associated with a simple, dualistic view of conflict situations and with a more competitive and destructive orientation.[11]

Need for closure. This is defined as the degree to which people feel a need for closure in life, for order and structure. Research demonstrates that those with a high need for closure tend to escalate conflict more rapidly and dramatically, after reaching a threshold.[12] The need for closure is also tied to black-and-white thinking (you're either with me or against me, for instance) and can be found in those uncomfortable with enduring ambiguity.[13]

Emotional complexity. People whose emotional experiences have been broad and well differentiated can be distinguished from those whose emotional experiences have been more narrow and homogeneous. This quality is called *emotional complexity*. People with greater emotional complexity tend to be more open to experience, empathetic, cognitively complex, and have a better ability to adapt to different interpersonal situations.[14] Research on moral conflicts has also found a strong association between high emotional complexity and constructive conflict processes.[15]

Behavioral complexity and flexibility. This refers to the ability to engage in a wide array of roles and behaviors to effectively meet multiple and competing needs of groups and organizations. Leaders who display higher levels of behavioral complexity tend to be more effective and successful in achieving their goals.[16] Research on social conflict has also found behavioral complexity to be associated with more constructive and innovated processes.[17]

Social identity complexity. This describes the degree to which people see themselves as members of different groups that are aligned and coherent versus groups that are contradictory and do not overlap. A liberal, pro-choice, pro–gay rights, antiwar individual would therefore have much lower social identity complexity (more coherence) than a gay,

Republican, antiwar NRA supporter (higher internal contradiction). Research shows that people with higher social identity complexity are more tolerant of out-groups and more open in general.[18]

Out-group perception. This concerns differences in the tendency to view members of out-groups in individualized, complex, and multifaceted ways, as opposed to essentializing out-group members in corresponding stereotypical terms. Research shows that perceptions of out-groups in single-categorical versus multiple-categorical terms have significant implications for understanding and attenuating intergroup discrimination and conflict.[19]

Person-situation fit. There is considerable evidence to support the idea that people prefer situations that *fit* with their dominant personality characteristics. Extraverts tend to like busy environments, whereas introverts prefer less stimulating places. When a person gets stuck in an antithetical environment for a long period of time (like a prison or university), his or her personality will tend to change over time to better fit the situation.[20]

Relational balance. Research also shows that people prefer their relationships with others to be aligned and balanced. In other words, we prefer that all our friends be friendly with each other and that they dislike our enemies. Any imbalances between our friends and enemies results in the motivation to change friends to enemies or enemies to friends.[21]

Creativity and innovation. Classic research in social psychology demonstrates the strong press for uniformity operating in most groups, particularly those that are cohesive, public, or under threat from other groups.[22] However, recent research on strategy groups in business shows those who are less constrained and have more emotionally, cognitively, and behaviorally complex processes among their members are more effective and innovative at work.[23]

Social network complexity. People with more diversified, complex social networks have been found to be more tolerant of out-groups and more supportive of policies helpful to them. They tend to have more positive out-group experiences, share more interests with people outside their own groups, and learn more about the contributions of out-group members and the problems they face.[24]

Cultural rule complexity. Research also shows that when cultural groups either have or are given very simple rules for negotiating with others ("When others deceive you, never trust them again"), they tend to have more contentious negotiations and come away less satisfied. But when groups have or are given more complex, nuanced rules for conflict negotiations ("When others deceive you, never trust them unless they were forced to deceive you or were unaware of their actions or generally meant well"), their negotiations tend to go far more successfully.[25]

Culture and contradiction. Cross-cultural research shows that cultural groups differ in the degree to which they avoid or prefer contradiction. Cultures based on Confucianist philosophy prefer contradiction. This results in a dialogic or compromise approach to conflict resolution that retains basic elements of the opposing interests and perspectives in a conflict. Cultural groups derived from a lay version of Aristotelian logic are less comfortable with contradiction. They tend toward a differentiation model of conflict resolution that polarizes contradictory perspectives in an effort to determine which position is correct.[26]

Cultural tightness or looseness. Other cross-cultural research finds that cultural groups differ in the relative tightness or looseness of their culture. This is the degree to which groups have constraining social norms actively enforced by their members versus more open, flexible norms that are not readily enforced.[27] Tighter cultures have been found to have more consensus and agreement on the meaning of common concepts than looser cultures. For example, cultures that display a tight *culture of honor*—a concern for the public image of status and toughness—encourage much harsher reactions to provocations than those with looser cultures of honor.[28] The specific implications of this for conflict and peace are currently being explored.

Structural and institutional complexity. Anthropological research demonstrates that societies differ in the degree to which they are structured in isolated versus integrated ways. Some societies are organized in nested groups (low complexity), where members of distinct ethnic groups tend to work, play, study, and socialize with members of their own group; they have little collaborative contact with members of other groups. Other societies are organized through crosscutting structures (high complexity), including ethnically integrated business associations, trade unions, professional groups, political parties, and sports clubs. This has been identified as one of the most effective ways of making intergroup conflict manageable and nonviolent.[29]

Linked conflicts. At the broadest level, research on international conflict shows that when conflicts between state rivals become linked with other conflicts between other nations or groups, the potential for serious conflict and escalation increases significantly. In other words, when multiple bilateral conflicts link together into one interrelated problem, they become exponentially more intractable. In fact, the vast majority of intractable conflicts between nations involved connections with at least one other enduring rivalry.[30]

THIS IS A BIG IDEA. And it seems that all of this is essentially the same idea. Whether it is how people tend to think, feel, or behave; how they view their own group identities or members of out-groups; how they approach their relationships and group processes; or how their cultural groups and societies are structured and organized, the degree of complexity and coherence matters. Of course, there are meaningful differences in the various models outlined above, but basically they are all about complexity, contradiction, and coherence.

So although psychology, unlike physics, doesn't yet offer us any *laws* of human behavior, it does offer us a few big ideas, and this is one. Which leads us to a rule of thumb for 5 percent conflicts:

> **THE CRUDE LAW OF COMPLEXITY, COHERENCE, AND CONFLICT (C^3)** Human beings are driven toward consistency and coherence in their perception, thinking, feeling, behavior, and social relationships. This is natural and functional. Conflict intensifies this drive, which can become dysfunctional during prolonged conflicts. However, developing more complex patterns of thinking, feeling, acting, and social organizing can mitigate this, resulting in more constructive responses to conflict.

Family Ties

Dominic, age fifteen, and his stepfather, Charlie, age forty-eight, lived together in a small duplex apartment in the Midwest with the boy's mother and two siblings. Dominic had been raised by his biological parents in a middle-class area of a major city, but after their divorce he was moved by his mother to a small, working-class town where she met the boy's stepfather. Charlie had been raised on a farm in a small rural town and now worked in a factory.

When this new family first came together, they were very happy. New to the town, Dominic and his younger siblings were thrilled to have a man around to show them the area, fix things up around the home, and in particular help Dominic navigate the perils of being the new kid in a tough working-class neighborhood. Charlie really enjoyed having these young children around because he had become estranged from his now grown-up children from his first marriage.

Shortly after Charlie's marriage to the boy's mother, however, the relationship between him and Dominic began to sour. Initially, the arguments were over chores around the house, habits, and household rules. Gradually, they escalated into more serious territorial and power conflicts, with screaming, name-calling, threats, destruction of property, and physical violence. In time, the relations between the two escalated to the point where virtually every interaction they had resulted in hostilities. They began avoiding each other and went for weeks without speaking. The entire family was affected by these relations. Dominic's siblings, other relatives, friends, and neighbors attempted to intervene. They took sides and then eventually lessened contact with the family. The boy's mother was consistently put in the middle and told to decide between them. This continued for approximately two years.

Eventually, the family was referred to community mediation by the police. Events had escalated to the degree where severe violence was imminent. The police had been called in on several occasions, and both the boy and stepfather were demanding that the mother decide "who should stay and who should go." The mother, having suffered a painful divorce from her first husband, was determined to keep her family together.

Living in a new town with a new family, Dominic and his siblings were very happy to meet someone who could bring some stability to their lives. Charlie's guidance and support, even his strict sense of discipline, were a welcome shelter during this disorienting transition. But in time, and particularly when in conflict, Charlie's rigidity and Dominic's adolescent rebellion were an explosive cocktail. The dynamics that ensued from their increasingly hostile encounters became more and more widespread in terms of the problems and people they involved. They also became more and more simple. "He" was the problem.

To sum up, coherence is natural and necessary. It can provide people and groups with a sense of stability, predictability, and a platform for decisive action. It simply makes life easier for us to navigate. But when taken to extremes, this natural tendency has its associated pathologies. This is especially true in conflict, where the press for coherence intensifies, and much more so in intractable conflicts, where we see the virtual collapse of contradiction and complexity. Left unchecked, this super coherence can lead to the escalation and spread of conflict, as well as to the development of strong, destructive, ingrained patterns of thinking, feeling, and behaving—in other words, to impossible conflicts.

THE MATHEMATICS OF COMPLEXITY, COHERENCE, AND CONFLICT

Understanding how the psychological dynamics of complexity and coherence lie at the core of intractability in conflicts was a critical step toward grasping how they operate and, ultimately, how they might be resolved. Following Lewin's guidance, the next step was to move toward a more careful specification of the essence of this phenomenon by working with more formal mathematical concepts and models. Constructing such models requires that you carefully examine your basic assumptions about how complexity and coherence operate in social relations experiencing conflict, which is not a trivial matter. However, if you can identify the critical variables and the nature of how they affect one another over time, these models can provide deep insights into difficult conflict dynamics.

A branch of applied mathematics called *complexity science* provides us with the basic platform and tools to understand how complex systems can evolve into more simple, coherent structures. Although rooted in mathematics, complexity science is a highly interdisciplinary field that seeks the answers to some fundamental questions about living, adaptation, and change. It teaches us that complex systems have three important characteristics: emergence, unintended consequences, and self-organization.

- **Emergence.** Emergence is the way complex patterns and coherent structures arise from a series of very simple interactions. The spatial patterns of beehives are not at all predictable from knowledge of each individual bee. The dynamical patterns of market bubbles and crashes are not at all predictable from knowledge of each individual investor. As Wertheimer noticed, the whole is quite different from the sum of its parts.
- **Unintended consequences.** These are simply surprises, good and bad, that result from how our actions operate in complex systems. We try to reduce the cost of gasoline, and thereby the cost of living, by substituting corn ethanol for gasoline. But all this does is raise the price of food, which depends so heavily on corn products. As Wallace White said, "When you pick up one piece of this planet, you find that, one way or another, it's attached to everything else—if you jiggle over here, something is going to wiggle over there."
- **Self-organization.** The self-directed actions of individuals alone can lead to organization of a whole group of people. According to Richard Feynman, the actions of a single despotic leader are not needed to organize a curved line of humans, all brushing their teeth once a day just after sunrise, that circles the globe.

Mathematics has helped us understand how emergence, unintended consequences, and self-organization arise from the interaction of individual elements. Mathematics gives us a way to compute how low-level individual actions, like simple rules for behavior, lead to higher-level global properties, like the V-formation of flocks of birds, synchronized patterns in schools of fish, or common adolescent dating rituals.

It's a great game. You make up any rules you want for the players, and the mathematics then describes for you the plays, strategies, and who wins. There are lots of different possible rules and lots of different mathematical methods that can be used to compute their consequences. Thus, there are many different mathematical flowers in the garden of complexity—self-organized critical systems, small-world networks, artificial neural networks, differential equations—each with its own shape, color, and fragrance. Used as a metaphor, each of these mathematical approaches gives us its own unique insight into conflicts. In work on enduring conflicts, conflict specialists rely mostly on insights provided by the mathematical method called *ordinary differential equations,* or ODEs.

Ordinary differential equations predict how the values of variables in a model change over time. Usually, there are only a few different things being measured in any one model; for instance, conflict intensity, relative power, cooperation, or emotion. Yet ODEs can have fascinating properties. Sometimes, the deterministic rules you put into the equations produce values that vary as if they were random. This is called *chaos.* Even stranger, although you know all the rules, you typically cannot predict all the future values. Sometimes, you change one thing just a little, and then all the current and future values change quite a lot. This is called a *bifurcation.* This type of equation has been useful in understanding turbulence and the motion of air in the atmosphere, the rattling of mechanical gears, dripping faucets, and teams of people working together in an organization.

One way to think about ODEs is of them representing the journey of variables across an artificial landscape. The variables are simply the things we can measure about a conflict; for example, the different types of emotions of the people involved or their intensity. We can watch the trail of these variables as they move through the valleys, hills, and mountain passes of the landscape.

Just like a real landscape, it is a lot easier to walk downhill than uphill. So we watch the trail most often settle into the depths of the nearest valley. These valleys are called *attractors* because they are what the conflict settles into. The peaks are called *repellers* because the conflict never stays there; it rapidly falls downhill into someplace else. The mountain passes are called *saddles.* Like the saddle on a horse, it's easy to go downhill along the direction that curves off the side of the horse and hard to go uphill along the direction toward the horse's head or tail. In a conflict, emotions can drive a situation into a positive or negative attraction.

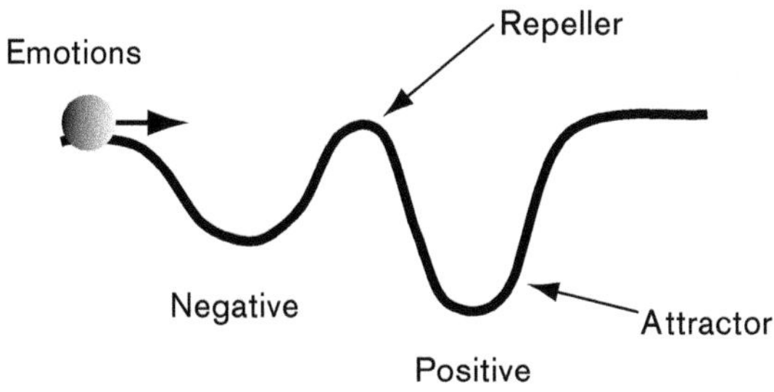

A Conflict Landscape

ATTRACTORS

The ideas from mathematics are being used here as a metaphor, as an illustration of the way social science uses concepts as ways of thinking, categorizing, and recognizing phenomena. The deep valleys in the landscape are the attractors, the somewhat stable patterns or tendencies in systems that draw us in and that resist change. For instance, when we go to a funeral in the Western world there is a strong tendency to wear dark colors, sit quietly and respectfully, and look sad. Even if we did not know the deceased, we tend to do this. We are pulled into it. Alternatively, when we are at a football game, even if we are not big fans of the team, we are likely to begin to jump around a little and cheer and talk trash with the opponent's fans. It is hard not to.

The behavior patterns that attractors pull us toward are influenced by many, many different things, from the smell of a funereal bouquet to the sound of a marching band. *But it is not any one thing that creates an attractor. It is how the many pieces come together that matters.* It is how they fit together or not. *It is their degree of coherence.*

Weaker attractors will have many pieces moving against or away from each other; many mixed signals and low coherence. This results in less clarity about what the situation requires of us and less of a pull toward conformity. In other words, this looks more like a flat landscape where movement in any direction is equally possible. With stronger attractors the pieces all come together. They fit into a coherent picture that draws us all into fairly uniform patterns of thinking, feeling, and behaving. These create deep valleys (attractors) and high peaks (repellers) in the landscape, which make it much more likely that we will journey into the valley of the attractor and be forced to act in ways consistent with it.

Research reveals that conflict can take place within a variety of attractor landscapes. They tend to have *current* attractors (how people are responding to a conflict right now) and *latent* attractors (hidden tendencies to think, feel, and act in very different ways in the conflict). They can have *positive* attractors, drawing people into more constructive and satisfying conflict interactions, and *negative* attractors, encouraging the opposite. These may be *weak* attractors (faint impulses to respond in a certain way) or *strong* attractors (extraordinary determinants of our experiences of and reactions to conflicts). Together, the current and latent, the positive and negative, the weak and strong attractors make up what we call *landscapes for conflict.*

The Kashmiri Landscape

A largely frozen and uninhabitable mountainous region that lies at the border between India and Pakistan, Kashmir has sparked three wars between those two countries since 1947. An average of twenty-five hundred violent incidents occur there every year. Official Indian estimates have seventy thousand people killed in fighting in Kashmir since 1989. Some claim the number is twice that. Two hundred thousand people have fled the valley. Half a million Indian security forces occupy the area, which today is the most highly militarized zone in the world. This is Kashmir.

Largely Hindu India and predominantly Muslim Pakistan became independent of the British Empire in 1947 and quickly went to war over Kashmir, a Himalayan territory that had been a princely state with a Hindu maharajah and mostly Muslim populace. The war ended with India controlling two-thirds and Pakistan one-third of the state. In 1989, Kashmiri independence rebels began a separatist struggle against India and were soon joined by Pakistani militants. India reacted by flooding Kashmir with soldiers and paramilitary troops. Conventional and guerrilla war ensued. In recent years, the conflict has attracted a growing number of Islamic fundamentalists who define the conflict as a jihad, or holy war.

In 2001, Atal Bihari Vajpayee, the prime minister of India, ended India's six-month cease-fire in Kashmir, calling it a sham. The next day, Mr. Vajpayee officially invited Pakistan's military ruler, General Pervez Musharraf, to India for peace talks. On a violent day in Kashmir, when fourteen people were killed, Mr. Vajpayee's letter read: "Our common enemy is poverty. For the welfare of our peoples, there is no other recourse but a pursuit of the path of reconciliation."[31] In response, Pakistan's foreign minister accused India of "state terrorism," "repression," and the massacre of seventy-five thousand Kashmiris, while announcing that his nation would accept India's invitation for talks "in a positive spirit."[32]

Today, there is an ongoing ethnopolitical struggle between India, Pakistan, and Kashmiri independence rebels over Kashmir. It is a story that combines the increasingly common elements of terrorism, religious militancy, human rights abuses, movements for local independence, and nuclear threat.

Politicians on both sides have used Kashmir as a rallying point for so long that compromise is viewed as political suicide. Even the most liberal, optimistic Indians and Pakistanis tend to turn conservative and belligerent when discussing Kashmir. It is as if it is impossible not to. The potential use of nuclear weapons by both sides is a persistent reality.

And still, every evening at sunset, an extraordinary spectacle occurs. Pakistani and Indian troops, stationed a stone's throw across from one another at a checkpoint, meet. Dressed in full military regalia, these armed units march ceremoniously in formation directly toward one another to within a few feet, swing and slam closed their respective border gates in unison, then turn their backs abruptly to one another and march away. This too is Kashmir.

In Kashmir, the landscape is both treacherous and hopeful. The misery, volatility, and danger of the situation there are painfully obvious. The destructive attractor reigns. But there are also hints of other possibilities. Slight glimpses of what might one day be. The mixed messages of the leaders. The peculiar, almost intimate rituals of the soldiers. The desire for peace of the people. They point to another way of being that is perhaps latent in Kashmir, and in India and Pakistan, waiting for its moment.

THE ATTRACTION OF THE 5 PERCENT PROBLEM

What is important to understand now is that the 5 percent problem represents a special kind of attractor landscape for conflict. Picture being trapped on the icy face of K2, the second-highest mountain on earth.* In addition to the treacherous terrain of the mountain slope, you find yourself plagued by mounting physical ailments and exhaustion, as well as impaired decision making, hallucinations, and a rising sense of hopelessness. These are perilous conflict landscapes, with very strong, coherent current attractors for destructive interactions pulling you down, and relatively weaker latent attractors for other, more constructive types of interactions just over the next ridge. This means that even a random thought we may have about the "other," not to mention an actual encounter with them, will tend to pull us down into the negative responses of the destructive attractor valley—no matter what the other person does and whether or not we really want to act that way. It is so much easier and makes much more sense to go down the slope!

The power of this negative attraction is bolstered by many different things—memories, social norms, beliefs about the "other," strong feelings, the other's current behaviors—but our experience of it is simple. They are bad and we are good. At this point, our sense of our options in this situation is extremely limited. And the ways we do respond will tend to build an even stronger attractor for destructive conflict between us and them. It all works very well together.

---

*Known as "Savage Mountain" due to the difficulty of the ascent and the high fatality rate among climbers; one in four climbers has perished trying to reach the summit.

chapter 4

THE MODEL: INTRACTABLE ATTRACTORS

IN THE INTRACTABLE CONFLICT LAB in Munich, Germany, we manipulate complexity. We are again running studies of polarizing moral conflicts, but this time instead of letting the participants wander off into constructive or destructive conflicts on their own, we are actually altering their levels of complexity beforehand. We do this with information. We again pretest all the participants on their attitudes about abortion (an issue particularly polarizing in Germany today) and match people with opposing views, but then we do something different.

First, each dyad is randomly assigned to either a low-complexity or a high-complexity condition. In the low-complexity condition, participants read information about abortion presented in pro and con categories (one side is always consistent with the opinion of the person and the other contradicts it). In the high-complexity condition, participants read a text that presents various positions and arguments on abortion from different angles, describing them in relation to each other. We do not only give the high-complexity dyads information that supports and contradicts their attitudes. What we do instead, which is consistent with what some dialogue groups do in conflict settings, is provide several different perspectives on the issue of abortion. Positions such as the moral responsibility of having a child; the moral status of the embryo; the rights, obligations, and autonomy of the woman and the embryo; the need to protect the mother and the embryo; alternatives to abortion; and the need to consider extreme cases of rape and disability. We conclude by writing: "In summary it can be said that the debate about the topic 'abortion' is very multifaceted and includes many aspects. All aspects have their relevance and their importance and should be considered and seen in relation to each other."

Notice that while the *amount* of information and the basic *content* of the information are the same in both high- and low-complexity conditions, it is presented in fundamentally different ways: either *pro and con* or from *multiple perspectives.* The different types of information matter. In fact, the effects of presenting the dyads with pro-con information versus more complex forms of information are striking. This simple intervention leads to radically different conflict dynamics.

Compared to the dyads in the low-complexity condition, those in the high-complexity condition (who held important, opposing views from one another on abortion) were able to reach consensus on position statements more often and generate better-quality agreements; were more satisfied and cooperative; had higher ratios of positive-to-negative emotions over the course of their discussions; and their levels of cognitive complexity actually increased after the sessions. Complexity rules!

OUR MODEL

Our approach is a hybrid, a combination of social psychology and complexity science. It is also informed by important research on conflict from areas like anthropology, physics, political science, and international affairs, as well as other types of psychology. Our project team includes conflict specialists, social psychologists, an anthropologist, complexity scientists, a physicist, and experienced peacemakers. It is important to emphasize that we have not been hiding away in an ivory tower to develop our model; we have also been carefully studying real people in real conflicts. Mediators, negotiators, diplomats, peacemakers: conflict resolvers of all stripes.

From this fairly unique interdisciplinary scholar-practitioner primordial sea, a new model has emerged. It is based on the idea of attractors, the somewhat stable patterns or tendencies in systems that draw us in and that resist change. Like the forceful gravitational pull of a valley at the base of K2, they propel us down, down, down.

Here's the basic story. Imagine a climber on a mountainside, as shown in the figure on the next page. The climber represents *the conflict*

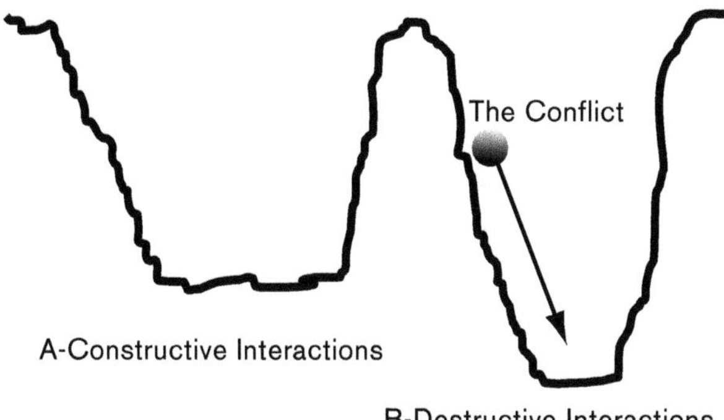

Intractable Attractor Landscapes

right now. While clambering around on the steep slope, the climber is constantly compelled to slide down the mountain and come to rest at the bottom of the valley. The valley (along with gravity) serves as an attractor for the system. Any attempt to move up and out of the valley and over the peak takes considerable effort and may even be fruitless.

The picture also illustrates that a conflict system may have more than one attractor, in this case, two. Each attractor has its own *width,* that is, a set of states "attracted" by the attractor. Here, attractor A is somewhat wider than attractor B. On a mountain range, that simply translates to more real estate sloping down in the vicinity of valley A, which would compel you down that incline. Psychologically, the wider the attractor, the greater the range of thoughts and actions that eventually evolve toward its basin—the mental and behavioral patterns associated with that attractor. This means that even contradictory information entering into the range of an attractor, say, positive information about an enemy that contradicts the current negative view of them, is likely to be transformed until it fits the dominant perspective of that attractor and is perceived as negative. So I may hear about a kind or generous act that my enemy did for someone, but I will construe it as manipulative or cunning, and it will then further support my negative sense of them.

Attractors can also vary in their relative strength, shown here as the *depth* of the two valleys in the figure. Attractor B is a stronger attractor than attractor A. This means that once a climber is caught in the pull of this deeper attractor, it is more difficult for them to be dislodged, even when strong external influences make escape more likely (for instance, when a rescue team is on the scene). It is as though the climber becomes wedged into a deep crevice in the valley.

The psychological equivalent occurs when a disputant holds a strong, immutable conviction that makes it nearly impossible to change their mind-set. So it would take a much stronger force to dislodge the climber (disputant) from attractor B than from attractor A. That is the basic idea: attractor valleys and craggy, mountainous landscapes for 5 percent problems and the journeys people take across them over time. But here are a few other things, presented in the form of FAQs, that are important to know about this story.

1. Where do conflict attractors come from? They come from both our past and our current experiences. They are made up of many different factors that come together to help establish the patterns we tend to fall into when we get into a conflict. Recall Lewin's constellation of forces: past encounters with people and groups, beliefs, expectations, social norms; how we have been taught and socialized; cultural influences. Of course, some things will matter more than others (a past act of violence committed by someone will be a stronger determinant of your future reactions to him than a less consequential encounter), but their effects on an attractor will always be in combination with many other factors. Here is an example of how attractors develop on the global scene.

Conflict Rules

They believed it would end quickly. At the onset of World War I, "the war to end all wars," none of the major powers that entered into war that summer of 1914—Russia, Germany, Austria-Hungary, Turkey, France, Britain—wanted or expected a prolonged conflict. But they got it. Four years later, seventy million troops had been mobilized and nine million combatants lay dead in what was the second-deadliest war in human history. Why? Because the conflict took control. Sure, the leaders made mistakes in judgment. They believed in the possibility of quick victory, held outmoded assumptions about warfare and war etiquette, thought free trade among the countries would prevent the war's escalation, and failed to consider the political backlash of their actions at home. But it was more than that.[1]

Essentially, the system was ready for conflict. An arms race between Britain and Germany at the turn of the century had spread to the other major European powers, which then devoted much of their industrial base to manufacturing weapons and logistical equipment for combat. From 1908 to 1913, military spending increased in this region by 50 percent. Then various conflicts sprang up, over competing territorial claims and growing nationalism in the Balkans, while the Ottoman Empire crumbled and Germany thrived and expanded. This combination began to tip the balance of power in the area, a balance that Europeans had relied on for stability for a century. All this began to unfold within a complex network of political and military alliances among the countries—formal and informal, public and secret—and within a context of imperialist foreign policies, animosity between states over past grievances, and a series of aggressive interstate maneuvers that caused further destabilization.

So when a young Bosnian-Serb named Gavrilo Princip lit a fuse by assassinating the archduke Franz Ferdinand of Austria in June of 1914, the conflict detonated almost overnight, and most of the major powers got sucked into the war within weeks. It soon polarized into two opposing alliances. As all these European powers had colonies abroad, the conflict quickly spread around the world. At that point, it was in charge. The options of each of the major powers diminished before their eyes as their constraints grew. The conflict ruled.

Of course, this war only lasted four years, so was it really intractable? It apparently seemed so at the time, because it was extremely destructive and lasted much longer than the major powers desired. It has also been argued that the conclusion of WWI, resulting in a rise in nationalism in Europe and the humiliation of Germany at Versailles, established the conditions for World War II.[2] But that is another story.

2. Why do conflicts fall into attractors? Mostly because it is easier. We fall into these ingrained patterns of thinking-feeling-behaving because we are used to them, or because everyone else is doing the same thing, like in Europe in the early 1900s. And because it takes less energy to fall into them than to try to climb out of them or fight against them: to do something different. But we also fall into attractors because our current journey across the landscape, our more immediate experience of the conflict, has brought us into the vicinity of a destructive attractor and thus into its gravitational pull.

3. How do attractors become stronger or weaker? Through coherence and incoherence. When the different components of an attractor start to support and reinforce one another (when they all move in the same direction), then the attractor becomes stronger and more coherent. This is what we see in mob behavior at soccer games when competition, heat, alcohol, intergroup rivalries, politics, and the foolishness of youth combine into a violent cocktail. It is also what we saw emerge just prior to WWI. Then, the pieces of the attractor are said to be connected mostly through *reinforcing feedback loops,* where the various components simply fuel each other.[3] But when some of the components go against the tide of the attractor (like when a sense of guilt or a law stops you from physically harming an opponent), then they are said to provide *inhibiting feedback.*[4]

Attractors with mostly reinforcing feedback loops connecting their different elements will tend to grow and spread, sometimes exponentially, and can become very strong and coherent. At some point, they may reach a plateau where they strike more of a balance between reinforcing and inhibiting feedback, achieving a new equilibrium. This happens when a conflict escalates to a given point and then remains there in a stalemate between the parties. However, this also happens when two people fall intensely in love, marry, and then live in a society where divorce is strongly prohibited. In both cases, you have strong reinforcing loops that are still driving the initial processes (conflict or infatuation) as well as strong inhibiting loops that are resisting change (deescalation of the conflict or divorce by the couple). These tend to induce states of high coherence. Weaker and less coherent relational attractors tend to evolve from conditions where there is initially more of a balance between reinforcing and inhibiting feedback in the relational context.

4. Why do conflict attractors become positive and negative? The specific types of behavior that can occur in a relationship between two people or between two groups are infinite. But usually after people have known each other for a while, their behavior falls into two or three general categories: positive (feels good), negative (feels bad), and neutral (eh). It is straightforward: the more severe and abundant the negative experiences and encounters that accumulate in a particular relationship, the stronger the negative attractor; the more positive experiences that accumulate, the more positive the attractor. So, between any two disputants with some history, there are likely to be these general kinds of attractors—positive, negative, and neutral. However, the relative width and strength of these different kinds of attractors makes a difference in shaping the landscape of conflict dynamics in any relationship.

5. How long does it take to grow a conflict attractor? It usually takes a long time to develop a strong attractor, an ingrained pattern of response to another person or group that resists change. Think of how long it usually takes for a person to develop a particular personality trait over his or her lifetime, or for a couple to develop strong patterns for how they fight and make up. It took decades to establish the war machine for WWI. So, even though people's and groups' *behaviors* may change rapidly and dramatically from one moment to the next, their *pattern of consistent behavior,* which is evidence of an underlying attractor, usually takes much longer to form.

6. How come some attractors are visible and obvious and others are hidden? During a conflict, the destructive thoughts, feelings, and actions evident in the disputants' dynamics may represent only the most visible attractor for them. But if there is a long history of interaction between the disputants, there are likely to be other potential patterns of thinking, feeling, and acting between them, including those that foster more positive interactions. These are considered to be *latent* (hidden and inactive) until the situation changes and a more positive pattern emerges and shapes the overt conflict dynamics. This is what the world witnessed during the Cold War between America and the USSR. Hostile relations had been

obvious for decades between the two countries, but after perestroika, their relations moved rapidly into a more tolerant and constructive attractor, which had been present but latent during the Cold War. During destructive conflicts, negative attractors are usually visible and positive attractors are latent. During more peaceful times, positive attractors are visible and negative attractors become latent.

7. How do we move from one attractor to another? When a conflict system has more than one type of strong attractor, almost anything, even very small things or random events (a comment, a kind gesture), can shift the conflict from one attractor to the other. This is most likely to occur when the current state of the conflict is near a tipping point between two attractors. We see this when there is a tense cease-fire between disputants that reignites into war, or when a drawn-out conflict between battle-weary parties collapses into peace. And these changes are often dramatic. Such as when former enemies become lovers, or when former lovers become archenemies. These are big shifts between attractors. What is critical to know, however, is that when a shift occurs from one attractor to another, *it does not mean that the latent attractor is gone.* It simply means that, for now, it is latent. Conditions can change again and bring latent attractors back to life.

8. What is a repeller? A repeller is the opposite of an attractor. It is a type or pattern of behavior rarely seen in a conflict situation (think of laws or norms or social taboos that prohibit certain types of behavior in disputes). And if such rare behaviors do occur, they are very unlikely to be repeated. However, at times taboo behaviors (like blowing yourself up) can become normative (terrorism), and then they can become attractors for particular groups. This type of transformation from repeller to attractor takes considerable time and a significant realignment of many forces.

9. And how does all this help us understand 5 percent conflicts? The 5 percent problem represents a special kind of hazardous attractor landscape for conflict that has its own set of unique dynamics and rules. These are landscapes with very strong and coherent current attractors for destructive interactions and weaker, less coherent, latent attractors for more constructive types of interactions. The negative attractors are made up of many elements, from feelings and beliefs to group rules for conflict to national holidays and institutions. These elements are all tightly linked through reinforcing feedback loops that intensify and spread the negativity and pull of the conflict over time. Additionally, they possess a set of loops that provides inhibiting feedback, which discourages or prohibits deescalation or other changes in more constructive directions.

When attractors develop considerable coherence resulting from an imbalance of reinforcing-to-inhibiting feedback loops growing and spreading over time, they can become *self-organizing*. This means they will continue to grow and spread, no matter what anyone tries to do to stop them. They become virtually impervious to outside influence. This is a relatively rare event, but when it does occur, conflicts cross a threshold into intractability. *This is the essence of the 5 percent.*

10. Why do intractable attractors endure? To outside observers, intractable conflicts are illogical. They seem to go against everything we know about motivation, like the fact that most people usually act in their own self-interest. After all, a conflict with no end in sight serves the interests of very few people, drains both parties' resources, wastes energy, and diminishes human capital in service of a futile endeavor. Despite this, attractors satisfy two basic psychological motives. First, *they provide a coherent view of the conflict,* including the character of the in-group (good) and out-group (evil), the nature of the relationship with the antagonistic party, the history of the conflict, and the legitimacy of claims made by each party. Second, attractors *provide a stable platform for action,* enabling each party in a conflict to respond decisively to a change in circumstances or to an action initiated by the other party. These are not trivial things, especially for disputants engaged in exhaustingly difficult conflicts. So, in addition to the technical reasons for intractability (imbalanced feedback leading to exponential growth and self-organization), they also serve these two important psychological functions that make them even more likely to persist. In this sense they have logic of their own. A deep logic.

So that is our story of the intractability of particularly treacherous attractors we face on some of our more dangerous conflict expeditions. And that is essentially what came to pass between Kasha and Anthony, Domenic and Charlie, the pro-life and pro-choice advocates in Boston, and Hindus and Muslims in Kashmir after years of being estranged and deadlocked in their dispute. At some point, any random thought about the "other," not to mention an actual encounter with them, would propel the disputants into the depths of the negative thinking, feeling, and acting of the destructive attractor for their relations—no matter what the other party actually did or didn't do and whether or not the disputants really wanted to respond that way. It felt impossible to do otherwise. And when outsiders tried to intervene in these conflicts, it only made things worse.

The power of these attractors are bolstered by many different things, but our experience of them is simple: they are bad and we are good. At this point, our sense of options in the situation is extremely limited (fight or flight), and our responses tend to build an even stronger attractor for destructive conflict between us and them.

WHAT THE ATTRACTOR LANDSCAPE MODEL MEANS FOR ADDRESSING 5 PERCENT CONFLICTS

We are *not* helpless in the face of the 5 percent.

A Bronx Tale

A few years ago, our research team was asked to work on a problem of ongoing gang violence in a public school in the South Bronx in New York City. The school had been dealing with recurring cycles of vandalism, theft, and intimidation by gang members for years. The problem would come and go but was never completely gone. For example, the school had recently been given a new, fully loaded computer center by a corporate donor, but couldn't use it.

When the center's doors were unlocked and students allowed in, everything would get stolen. Violent incidents occurred daily.

At some point, tensions among some of the gangs got really bad, and the school was afraid of violent retaliations. It was a bad situation that kept getting worse. Families, teachers, and administrators at the school felt totally burned out and hopeless about it. So we started talking to people in the community to try to get a sense of the main causes of the problem, to try to map it. Our maps looked like this.

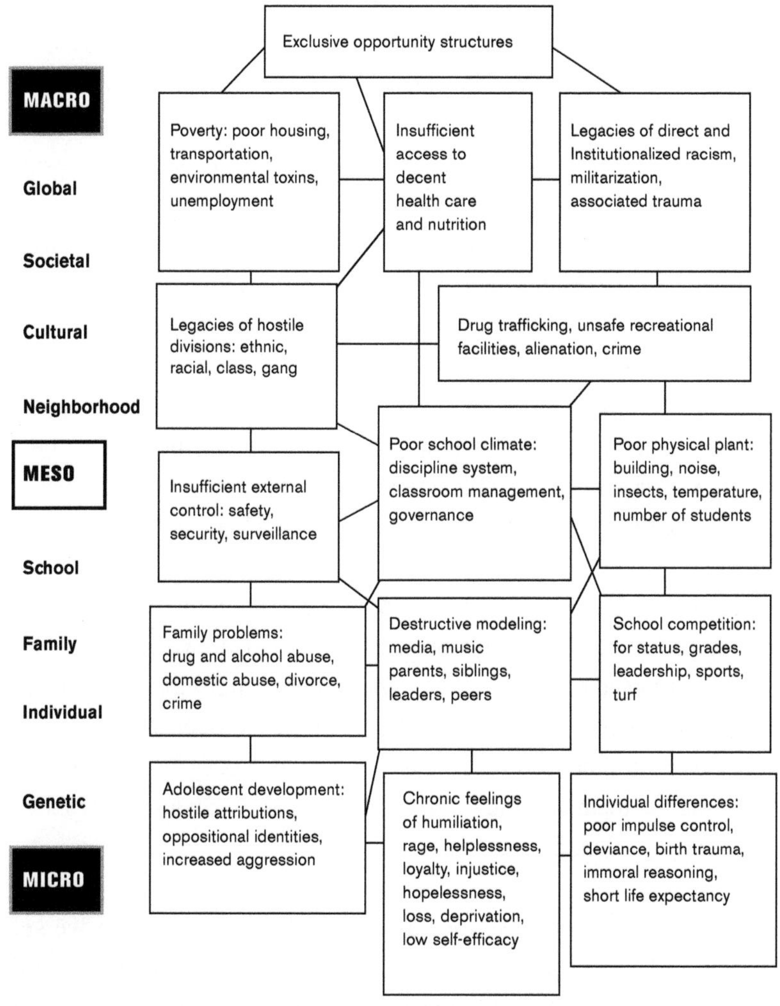

Ecology of Urban School Conflict and Violence

Immensely complex. The more we talked to people in the community, the more overwhelmed and depressed our team felt. We too felt ourselves getting sucked into the dark sense of helplessness and despair the community was experiencing. We fell hard into their attractor.

Then we noticed something interesting. When we talked to people familiar with the violence, but not *in it*—the principal and the local youth officer, social workers and a priest who was involved—there was a clear sense of how complicated the problem was. It was not just one thing that drove these kids into gangs and violence; many different kinds of problems were leading to the troubles. These kids were poor and lived in miserable housing; they had too many brutal role models and violent video games; they had been around drugs since they were infants; they had grown up exposed to environmental toxins like lead paint, which reduces impulse control; and they were often exhausted from being up all night in the ER with their sick siblings, because their family had no other access to health care.

But when we talked to the people *in* the conflict—the youth themselves and the gang leaders and even some of the parents and teachers who had gotten caught up in it all—the problem was very simple. *They* were the problem. The others. *They* were the punks and idiots and murderers who made *our* life hell. *They* were crazy and sick and were the ones the cops and the school needed to deal with—or else. For these people, the ones *in* the conflict, it was all very simple. Our side was just responding to their hostility and craziness. *We* were just trying to survive a bad situation. That was the simple truth.

What we realized is that to some degree they were right. They were all right. These situations were very complicated and did involve many different problems that fueled each other and were getting increasingly more complex the longer they lasted. But it was also true that the more tense and threatening these situations became to the people directly involved, the more obvious it was to them that the problem was simple: *they* were the problem. *We* were simply victims of their hate.

WHAT WE FOUND at this school in the South Bronx is what we see in most if not all 5 percent problems. The longer they last the more they tend to spread and intensify, recruiting more and more people and issues, which in turn makes them last longer. *And* the more intense and threatening the 5 percent become, the more the people in them will tend to perceive them as simple; they will see all the complicating issues as linked to the real source of the problem: "them."

Five percent conflicts represent a particular kind of systems dynamic, one that has been studied in other domains in order to help address particularly knotty problems. The attractor perspective offers a new way of thinking about and addressing these conflicts, as they are clearly more than conflicts of interest. Below, we present the implications of this new perspective as a set of basic *principles* for addressing the 5 percent. These principles summarize the main ideas and insights offered by the Attractor Landscape Model, and will set the stage for the practices outlined in the next section.

WHEN FACED WITH AN IMPOSSIBLE CONFLICT

1. Respond to dynamics, not events. Five percent conflicts are complicated, interlinked, evolving problem sets that change over time. Typically, when we are faced with such problems, we tend not to respond to the flow and pattern of the changes unfolding; instead, we respond to different stages of the situation, especially when it is in crisis. In other words, we are guided by the presenting situation and blind to the dynamics unfolding across its different phases. This is like trying to understand the arc and theme of a movie by viewing a few still shots taken from the most dramatic moments in the film.

At our school in the South Bronx, the authorities were often back on their heels, reacting to each incident on a case-by-case basis. In addition to being largely ineffective, this strategy occluded their understanding of the patterns unfolding at the school, and of how their responses might have played a role in perpetuating them.

Our mapping of the many aspects feeding the violence at the school in the South Bronx provided a collage: a snapshot of different perspectives on the many interrelated problems unfolding in the community. These evolving problems were affecting the levels of violence at the school at different times and at different timescales. In other words, some of the troubles bubbled up daily, others were evident once or twice a week, and other more severe incidents simmered for months before erupting. When we approach such fluid, multilevel problems in a reactive or piecemeal fashion, the impact of our actions are often counterintuitive and surprising. No wonder we got depressed!

Remember that the direction a 5 percent conflict takes is largely influenced by the *internal dynamics* of its elements. It is *self*-organizing. When we intervene, we are not directly inducing change; instead, we are perturbing a system that has its own strong dynamics. The conflict may react to our efforts by (1) *not responding at all:* completely resisting the action and maintaining the status quo; (2) *overresponding:* showing an exaggerated response to a seemingly insignificant action, although the response may be in the desired direction; (3) *freaking out:* evolving in a completely unpredictable, even opposite, direction seemingly independent of the intervention; or (4) *responding predictably:* behaving in a manner consistent with and proportional to our actions and plans. Any of these effects are possible and may be too strong, too weak, or even spawn entirely new dynamics and problems.

It is important to learn to recognize and respond to the dynamic flow of conflicts occurring over time, not just to discrete events.

2. Think in loops, not lines. Understanding 5 percent problems as evolving systems means we have to suspend our cherished linear cause-and-effect thinking about problems and solutions. Instead, we must see how different components of conflicts are linked together through loops.

Most thoughts, feelings, actions, and outcomes in a conflict will tend to either stimulate and/or constrain other components of the conflict through *feedback loops.* These are process loops connecting the different elements that either stimulate or inhibit one another in an ongoing manner. It can be compared to the way the network of the human nervous system operates, through a constant flow of energy among nerves and tissue to compel and constrain behavior. So instead of thinking about how someone's action in a conflict caused a reaction from someone else, it is important to start thinking about how various aspects of the people and the situation *mutually affected one another over time* to increase or decrease the likelihood of a certain outcome from happening.

In other words, it's vital to go from this . . . **X → Y**

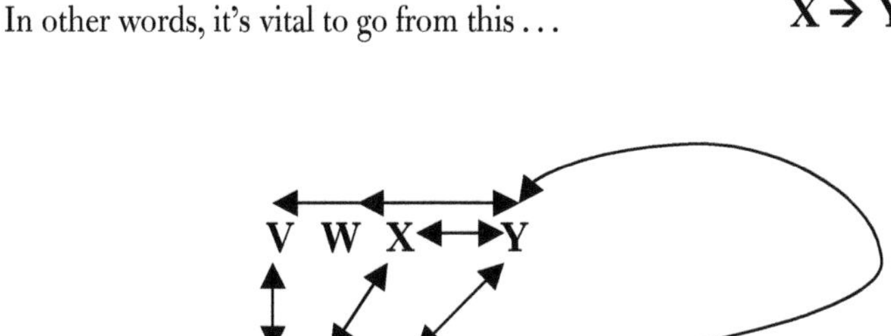

. . . to this:

This is *nonlinear* thinking. Although it looks scary, all it means is that instead of thinking that X caused Y to happen, it helps us to understand how many other factors linked together to influence both X and Y in the conflict. This type of thinking not only increases the accuracy of our understanding of the situation but also gives us more options for initiating change. Instead of just addressing X to change Y, we may be able to work with S, T, U, V, W, X, and Y to change Y.

Nonlinear thinking has many implications for rethinking conflict dynamics, but here we'll stress just a few that are directly relevant to the 5 percent: the role of *balanced feedback* in conflict, the difference between *incremental and catastrophic change* dynamics, and the importance of *initial conditions* in complex nonlinear systems.

Balanced feedback matters. Effective conflict instigation and conflict regulation involve a combination of reinforcing and inhibiting feedback loops. In a *reinforcing feedback loop,* one aspect of a conflict supports another along its current path. More leads to more and less to less. It is an important mechanism for generating and maintaining an initial conflict action, like when a series of negative encounters with someone mount up, eventually leading to overt expression of the conflict. Without this reinforcing process there would be no overt conflict, no learning, innovation, or personal or social change. In an *inhibiting feedback loop,* one element constrains, stops, or reverses another. It is necessary for terminating action once the conflict becomes sufficiently extreme, like when a parent steps in to stop a fight between siblings that is about to become violent.

As long as a conflict system includes both reinforcing and inhibiting feedback loops, instigating, mitigating, and terminating conflict remains possible. Conflicts can therefore be temporary and constructive learning experiences rather than unnecessarily tense and destructive ones. But conflicts escalate to uncontrolled levels when reinforcing feedback between destructive thoughts, feelings, and actions grows too strong at the same time that inhibiting feedback between these elements recedes. The regulatory process is then reversed and situations spiral out of control.

Our internal moral sense of right and wrong typically acts as a source of inhibitory feedback for us. It restrains our overly aggressive impulses and reactions to our opponents in conflict. But if our opponents begin to employ more aggressive, or even "immoral," tactics against us in conflict, the constraining influence of our moral sense can diminish and may even reverse. This phenomenon has played out recently as U.S. policies for interrogating terrorists became less constraining and more aggressive after 9/11. What had been an inhibiting feedback loop limiting coercion became a source of reinforcing feedback supporting aggression. Once such an increase in aggression is perceived as immoral by one's opponents, as seen in the Muslim world after photos of prisoner abuse in Iraqi Abu Ghraib prison surfaced, it completes the reinforcing loop—and catastrophic escalation may ensue.

Five percent conflicts typically evolve from conditions where strong networks of unconstrained reinforcing feedback loops among different hostile elements fuel destructive behaviors. This was clearly the case with our school in the South Bronx. There, many of the elements included in our map reinforced one another, leading to a quagmire of fear and violent conflict. The more reinforcing feedback loops instigating destructive conflict and the fewer inhibiting loops mitigating it, the higher the probability that the conflict will intensify and spread exponentially. The destructive conflict attractor in these situations becomes particularly strong and coherent.

When the conflict reaches a state of high coherence, bolstered by a combination of reinforcing feedback driving the conflict and inhibiting feedback prohibiting deescalation, the higher the likelihood that it will become self-organizing—virtually self-perpetuating. Thus, *feedback loops are crucial to the architecture of conflict attractors.* These loops are key targets for intervention and change in the amelioration of 5 percent conflicts.

Incremental versus catastrophic change. Some conflicts escalate slowly and steadily over time. Others burst open like a volcano. Why?

When conflict systems are made up of weakly linked elements with a relative balance of reinforcing and inhibiting feedback, they exhibit very different types of behavior than those with more tightly coupled, predominantly reinforcing feedback loops. The former conflicts are more complex and incoherent; the latter are *less* complex and therefore *more* coherent.

In a more complex attractor landscape, conflicts will tend to escalate gradually in an incremental fashion, with disputants responding proportionally to their opponent's tactics. This is because there is enough reinforcing feedback (like the opponent's provocations) to drive the conflict, but enough inhibiting feedback (common goals with the opponent, a sense of personal ethics) to limit the severity of response. In more coherent conflict landscapes, where other parties are either clearly with you or against you, conflicts will increase in intensity at a relatively slow rate (when others are seen as with you) until they reach a tipping point into a destructive attractor (when they are instantly seen as against you). Once this happens, the intensity shows a dramatic, catastrophic spike. This is evidence of nonlinear dynamics.

For example, this type of nonlinear shift from one attractor to another was observed in the dramatic outbreak of genocidal violence that occurred in Rwanda in the 1990s, where almost one million people were killed in a hundred days. This followed years of more gradual increases in interethnic hostilities between Tutsis and Hutus, which had primed the system for catastrophe. Once conflict has evidenced such a radical shift in intensity, decreasing the forces that drove it to such a state is unlikely to reduce the intensity to its original level: Not until another threshold representing a considerably lower level of forces is reached, which can propel the system back to the initial, more complex and constructive attractor.

This kind of incremental-versus-catastrophic escalation has been explored in the Intractable Conflict Lab as well. Under conditions promoting weak linkages between cognitive and affective elements of a conflict (the ties between participants were weak; they shared few associations in beliefs or feelings regarding each other), there was a linear relationship between antagonistic behavior from one person and the other person's antagonistic response. The participants responded in a proportional manner to antagonistic actions directed toward them, and the escalation and deescalation of conflict intensity happened slowly and incrementally.

However, in conditions promoting stronger reinforcing feedback loops (strong interpersonal ties between participants, which fostered close links between their thoughts and feelings regarding each other), participants experiencing antagonistic behavior from another at first chose to ignore the conflict and responded in a relatively mild fashion. But after a critical threshold of antagonism was reached, they responded in a highly aggressive manner. The transition from one type of response to the other was abrupt and extreme. These are the kind of change dynamics typically seen in more coherent (low-complexity) 5 percent conflicts.

Beginnings matter most. Research on conflicts in complex, nonlinear systems (in other words, conflicts in important human relationships) consistently shows that they are particularly sensitive to the initial conditions of the system. What does this mean? It means that beginnings matter.

Intractable Conflict Lab studies have found that how people feel during the first three minutes of their conversations about moral conflicts sets the emotional tone for the remainder of their discussions.[5] John Gottman has found similar effects: the first few minutes of a couple's emotions in conflict are up to 90 percent predictive of their future encounters.[6] These initial differences in emotional dynamics can be the result of various things: strong attitudes of the people coming in; how the conversations are set up and facilitated; history of the disputants' interactions together. But what is clear is that the initial encounters tend to matter more than whatever follows.

Computer simulations of these conflict dynamics go even further in their claims. They suggest that even *very slight* differences in initial conditions can eventually make a big difference.[7] These might consist of minor differences in the mood of participants, or their openness to dialogue, or the level of complexity of their thinking. The effects of these small differences may not be visible at first, but they can trigger other changes that trigger other changes and so on over time, until they pounce and have a huge impact on the dynamics. If these slight differences in mood and openness matter so much, just imagine the type of impact major differences in mood and affect—influenced by poverty, chronic illness, and rage—could have on initial conflict dynamics in a place like the South Bronx. The lesson for the 5 percent is clear. Tread carefully (or at least with intention) in the beginning stages of conflict.

3. Aim to alter patterns, not outcomes. It is almost impossible to predict any specific outcome in the complex, nonlinear systems of 5 percent conflicts, except that they are likely to persist. There are far too many variables interacting and affecting one another in unpredictable ways. As an instructive example, you need only recall the optimistic predictions made by several high-level Bush administration officials when the United States invaded Iraq in 2003 to get the point.

Fortunately, if we are able to observe a conflict over the long term, we are usually able to see patterns or attractors developing in the system, which we may then begin to understand better and even predict. Over time, almost every ongoing conflict system—be it in a marriage or a labor-management relationship or an ethnically divided community—will evidence some general patterns of interactions between the parties that are more predictable and stable than others.

From this perspective, we should be less concerned with bringing about specific outcomes in a conflict (generating particular insights, agreements, behavior change). Instead, we should focus on altering the parties' general patterns of interaction in a more constructive direction. This requires a substantial frame change, away from a focus on short-term wins and toward transforming the more stable patterns of thinking, feeling, and behaving in the system as a whole.

This frame change is hard because the immediate crises and pain associated with intractable conflicts tend to be considerable. They demand attention to the here and now. But it is equally important that we look at past behaviors and try to identify trends. We must try to anticipate how what we do today will affect what is and is not possible tomorrow. Unfortunately, crises rarely allow for long-term thinking, and today's goals often work at cross-purposes with those of tomorrow.

To illustrate: Operation Impact was a tough, targeted response to school violence in New York City, introduced by Mayor Bloomberg's administration in 2003. The program proposed a "bolstering of police resources" in schools and communities as the centerpiece of the plan. Although the application of security and deterrence measures to schools with poor safety records can be effective in the short term, such policies suffer from several drawbacks. They discourage accurate reporting of school violence; they oversimplify the problem of violence by focusing only on crime; they offer broad, general solutions to poorly defined, local problems; they highlight containment and deterrence while neglecting prevention, support, and care; and they emphasize short-term solutions to long-term (and shifting) problems.

Crisis responses to particularly dangerous school environments make good sense. However, they do not begin to address the types of systemic causes of violence and intimidation evident in our mapping of violent schools. Heightened surveillance and security measures are therefore a necessary but insufficient response. Too often, our political leaders are attracted to short-term, hard-line solutions to complex problems. The likelihood is that the solutions will show some immediate effect and signal to their constituents that they are in control of a difficult situation. However, such effects are only sustainable when they are accompanied by more considered responses that target the complex, underlying causes of school violence.

Consider, for instance, an alternative approach to community violence prevention. Fed up with piecemeal approaches to chronic patterns of violence and poverty in poorer neighborhoods in New York City, Geoffrey Canada and the Harlem Children's Zone (HCZ) have taken a different tack. Recognizing the complex ecologies of such intractable urban problems, they work systemically and comprehensively within a hundred-block radius of one neighborhood.

The HCZ approach is both simple and complex. First, the most at-risk children in the zone are identified by finding the lowest scorers on public school readiness tests. Then HCZ attempts to provide these children with everything. That's right, with virtually everything they need—medical care, good nutrition, safety, tutoring, committed teachers, you name it—to make it from kindergarten through college. The theory is that if HCZ can rescue and support the most vulnerable kids, the ones that get trapped by the attractor of the streets and fuel the drop-out/drug/violence/poverty syndrome, in time they will transform the community. This is a targeted but complex, long-term approach that is promising but still unfolding. Currently 90 percent of high school students who attend their after-school programs make it to college.[8]

From the perspective of the Attractor Landscape Model, it is critical to distinguish between short-term and sustained changes in the dynamics of conflict and violence. Short-lived oscillations in conflict intensity are likely to be observed in any relationship characterized by attractor dynamics, but they can provide a misleading sense of the trends of the conflict. They are not indicative of lasting changes as long as the underlying structure of the system remains in place. For lasting change to occur, the structure of the system must be modified in such a way that the attractor landscape is reconfigured. Such reconfiguration in turn requires changing the relations among system variables in a way that restores complexity and, in the case of the HCZ, hope.

4. Privilege emotions. Nelson Mandela once said that when trying to motivate people, we should speak to their hearts, not their heads. This is exactly what those who study the long-term dynamics of conflict have found. Emotions, although famously neglected in the scholarship on conflict, are not simply important considerations in conflict. They fundamentally *are the issue,* in that they set the stage for destructive or constructive interactions. In fact, research on emotions and decision making with patients suffering from severe brain injuries found that when people lose the capacity to experience emotions, they also lose their ability to make important decisions. Emotions are not only relevant to our decisions in conflict; they are *central* to them.

The laboratory research on emotions and conflict dynamics tells a pretty consistent tale: it is the ratio that matters. It is not necessarily how negative or how positive people feel about each other that really matters in conflict; it is the *ratio* of their positivity to negativity *over time.* Studies show that healthy couples and functional, innovative workgroups will have disagreements and experience some degree of negativity in their relationships. That is normal, and in fact people usually need to experience this in order to learn and develop in their relationships. However, these negative encounters must occur within the context of a sufficient amount of positive emotion for the relationships to be functional. And because negative encounters have such an inordinately strong impact on people and relationships, there have to be significantly more positive experiences to offset the negative ones.

Scholars have found that disputants in ongoing relationships need somewhere between three and a half to five positive experiences for every negative one, to keep the negative encounters from becoming harmful.[9] They need to have enough emotional positivity in the bank. Without this, the negative encounters will accumulate rapidly, helping to create wide and deep attractors for destructive relations. At the same time, the positive encounters will dissipate and have little effect on future positive relations. This can result in a conflict attractor landscape with overwhelming negative attraction. In other words, intractability.

5. Think different. For a person in the throes of a powerful, long-term conflict, misperception and misunderstanding rule. The pressure to view the conflict and the opposing disputants through a narrow, filtered lens is great. The filters are bias, selectivity, short-term crisis focus, and the prevention of loss. These filters will largely determine what we feel, think, and do.

Remember, at this point our thoughts and feelings are likely to be self-organizing, essentially immune to new or contradictory information. Typically, once we have gotten to this stage, we have already wandered far from concerns over obtaining accurate information regarding the substantive issues in dispute. Instead, we are focused on defending our sense of the Truth and what is Right. These may of course be valid concerns. But when everything makes perfect sense in a complicated conflict, when who the good guys and the bad guys are is perfectly clear, we must be all the more vigilant.

Life, so full of contradictions and surprises, rarely ever makes complete sense. The pieces of the puzzle seldom fit together perfectly. When they do—beware. Know that the press for certainty and coherence is a basic tendency in life greatly intensified by conflict, especially 5 percent conflict. And it often contributes to our total misreading of events. This tendency of course is nearly impossible to be mindful of when we are caught up in a 5 percent conflict.

A similar challenge faces the conflict expert. Whatever the area of training—political science, social psychology, law, education, communications, anthropology, linguistics, public health, economics—each expert frames his or her work in a manner consistent with that training. Our frames help to organize our thinking, yet they also constrain our understanding of the full complexity of the situations in which we engage. In fact, one of the most compelling findings from cognitive science in the last thirty years is that our cognitive frames can become physically present in the synapses of our brains, resulting in a total disregard for information inconsistent with our dominant perspectives.[10]

While an expert's reading of any conflict depends largely on the specifics of the situation, it is also usually heavily influenced by the cognitive frames he or she brings to the analysis. This is particularly true when the situations are difficult to comprehend: vast, complex, volatile, and replete with contradictory information. Like the 5 percent.

So what can be done to increase the accuracy of our understanding of the 5 percent? Get more information, especially *different* information. Recall that in our studies, providing people with multiple perspectives on the issues surrounding abortion led to more constructive conversations between people with opposing views.

Take another example from American history. After the 1961 Bay of Pigs disaster between the United States and Cuba, President Kennedy realized that his cabinet members had fallen prey to chronic consensus in their decision making. There was too much similarity and coherence in their views. So in order to challenge this tendency toward consensus, he instructed his brother Attorney General Bobby Kennedy to take up the role of devil's advocate in all their future decision-making meetings. This form of structured group dissent (inhibiting feedback) proved critical in fending off bad decision making and nuclear disaster later in October 1962, during the Cuban Missile Crisis.[11]*

There are myriad ways to introduce different, contradictory information into important decision-making processes. However it is accomplished, it should be a primary responsibility of third parties and other interveners in order to keep the pull toward certainty in the 5 percent at bay.

6. Know that conflict and peace coexist. Although most people feel pretty certain that peaceful relations are the opposite of contentious ones, research tells us that they are often *simultaneously present* in our lives. Even though we can usually only attend to one or the other, the potential for both exists in many relationships. In fact, they tend to operate in ways that are mostly independent of one another. In other words, conflict and peace are not opposites. They are two prospective and independent ways of being and relating—two alternative realities. This suggests that people can be at war and at peace at the same time.

Even during periods of intense fighting between divorcing couples, work colleagues, ethnic gangs, or Palestinians and Israelis, there exist hidden potentials in the relationships—latent attractors—that are in fact alternative patterns and tendencies for relating to one another. We see evidence of this when people move very quickly from caring for each other to despising one another, as happened with the work colleagues in the March to Silence case. Or when the opposite occurs, like the recent flip in Polish-Ukrainian relations, which had been mostly hostile since

*Similarly, in the documentary *Fog of War,* former U.S. defense secretary Robert McNamara describes how America's inability to truly understand the motives of the North Vietnamese during the Gulf of Tonkin incident led to runaway assumptions, poor decision making, and U.S. involvement in a tragic and unwinnable war. Here again the decision makers lacked different information.

WWII; they transformed dramatically into one of solidarity during the Orange Revolution in Ukraine. This boils down to movement from the current attractor to a latent one.

Our actions in a conflict can therefore have very different effects on three distinct aspects of the conflict landscape: on the current situation (the level of hostility in the conflict right now), on the longer-term potential for positive relations (positive attractors), and on the longer-term potential for negative relations (negative attractors). All three can have a life of their own.

This idea suggests that we need separate but complementary strategies for (1) addressing the current state of the conflict, (2) increasing the probabilities for constructive relations between the parties in the future, *and* (3) decreasing the probabilities for destructive future encounters. Most attempts at addressing the 5 percent target numbers one and three, but often neglect to increase the probability for future positive relations. They are aimed at stopping present suffering and avoiding future pain. But without sufficient attention to the bolstering of attractors for positive relations between parties, progress in addressing the conflict and eliminating future conflict will only be temporary.

7. See latent potential. Although our day-to-day experiences in impossible conflicts tend to be overwhelmingly negative with regard to the other side, and will often have very predictable scripts, we should pay attention to anomalies that occur. To things that surprise us. These cracks in the foundation of our understanding of the conflict and of the other parties are often important sources of *different* information: evidence that there are alternatives operating below our radar. These latent attractors, if we can spot them, may prove to be our best avenues for escaping or otherwise addressing the 5 percent.

For example, an unexpected finding of ours from a study we conducted with Palestinians and Israelis, during a high-intensity phase of the conflict in 2002, was the impact on participants of early, positive, serendipitous encounters with members of their out-groups.[12] Just as early traumatic losses were etched powerfully into the minds of individuals, often leading to deleterious psychological effects, these positive, spontaneous encounters described by participants tended to have an equally powerful effect for the good. One participant recalled:

> Now I met the first Jewish man in my life when I . . . like a real encounter . . . was when I was ten years old . . . it was in a Jewish moshave, a Jewish village, my teachers and students decided to go on toubashbat . . . it is a holiday of planting trees, we went to the neighboring Jewish village which is only ten minutes away from us . . . and what connects our village to theirs are the olive trees . . . we went there holding pine trees to go say hello to our neighbors . . . and that was the first real encounter and that was when I first realized that the Jews are actually not bad . . . you know . . . this man was very friendly who looked like we did and who wasn't . . . he had a beard . . . he was lovely . . . he gave us chocolate-chip cookies . . . he was yeah . . . it was a pleasant visit . . . that I felt wow there is something wrong here . . . I heard that Jews always had guns . . . that guy didn't have a gun. I thought Jews had horns . . . that guy didn't have horns. The fact that he . . . I always heard that Jews are stingy . . . he was offering us chocolate-chip cookies . . . how better could he get . . . I was ten years old. You know, we played with their kids . . . we had a lovely visit . . . you could tell that man was warm . . . was very warm to us . . . so I felt something was wrong in the picture . . .

These encounters had a lasting impact, even during times of open conflict. The spontaneous nature of these encounters seemed to capture individuals when their psychological defenses were down, thereby allowing the experiences to impact them both emotionally and cognitively. These are not easy experiences when embroiled in conflict. But they can make a powerful difference.

8. Respect the logic of the conflict. The 5 percent should not be seen as aberrations, but rather as the result of mostly normal psychological processes. It is perfectly natural, for example, for people to want coherence (perceive patterns, develop generalizations, demonstrate confirmatory bias) and to defend their coherent views against contradictory information (selective attention, reinterpretation, discounting, suppression). The negativity bias operating in all threatening situations ("bad is stronger than good") is also a natural and ubiquitous cognitive bias. The point is that bad outcomes (like unending conflict) do not necessarily reflect bad processes, just as bad behavior does not necessarily reflect bad character.

Often, for those inhabiting the world of the 5 percent, these conflicts are perfectly logical. In the South Bronx school, we met many dedicated but exhausted people who were caught in a trap fighting for their school, for their dignity, for a sense of belonging and voice, and for survival. These individuals and groups are often doing everything they can to respond to extraordinarily difficult circumstances. It is critical that interveners see this and do what they can to understand the local logic of any 5 percent.

9. Open it up. As discussed in chapter 3, research shows that more constructive conflict relations are characterized by relatively high levels of emotional, cognitive, behavioral, and structural complexity. High complexity is particularly advantageous when people and groups encounter new conflicts with others. Communities that maintain more complex, crosscutting structures and social networks have been found to be more tolerant, less destructive, and less violent when conflicts do spark. And they engage in a more constructive manner when conflicts become difficult. The same applies to people who hold more complex social identities and display more complex cognitive, emotional, and behavioral patterns.

Research also supports the idea that more constructive relations are often associated with an increased capacity for *movement.*[13] When people and groups get trapped in narrow attractors for social relations—whether in strong patterns of destructive conflict, oppressor-oppressed dynamics, or even in patterns of isolation and disengagement from others—their well-being tends to deteriorate and their level of resentment tends to build. These traps may be created by physical structures like segregated spaces and ghettos or by sociopsychological constraints like strong norms, attitudes, and ideologies. South Africa's period of apartheid represented both.

When trapped in such a narrow well, people can be very creative at becoming ever more destructive, oppressive, or isolated. This acts to deepen the current attractor and makes it less likely they will be able to escape its pull. These patterns can become ingrained and dominant, so that when the situation changes it is difficult for people to *adapt:* to take up different patterns of behaviors appropriate to the various new situations they face. From this perspective, sustainable solutions to difficult, long-term conflicts require establishing conditions that allow for sufficient openness: complexity, movement, and adaptation.

This is essentially what occurred during the years of dialogue between the pro-choice and pro-life leaders in Boston. In time, the sense of safety provided by the facilitators of the dialogue allowed the women to move psychologically; to begin to see, feel, think, and act in ways that they hadn't been able to for years. This increased movement didn't "solve" their differences on abortion, but it did free them from the constrained, overly simplistic good-versus-evil dynamic in which they had been trapped. It opened them up to experience the humanity of their "enemies" in more nuanced ways.

10. Look for simple solutions informed by complexity. My colleague Andrzej Nowak wrote: "The discovery that complex properties may emerge from simple rules is one of the most important discoveries of modern science . . . If simple rules can produce complex phenomena, then complex processes and structures can be explained by simple models . . . [but] only if these rules interact with each other or with the environment."[14] This is an idea Nowak calls *dynamical minimalism.* It suggests that very complex things, like epidemics, hazardous weather patterns, or mob behavior at sporting events, can sometimes be understood by a few simple rules that demonstrate how the basic components of a problem interact over time. The objective of this approach is to see through the complexity of a phenomenon to find the minimal set of mechanisms that can account for that complexity. Its goal is *simplicity informed by complexity.* In essence, this is the approach taken by the Harlem Children's Zone in focusing its resources on a relatively small number of children in order to transform a very complex system: Harlem.

Obviously, identifying the few mechanisms or processes responsible for something as complex as intractable social conflict is no small feat. As we've seen, at one level the 5 percent are immensely complex, involving something like fifty-seven different variables all linked and interacting with one another and changing over time. But at another more basic level, these conflict dynamics are quite simple. We have found that intractability can be understood as essentially this: *a self-organized, closed attractor landscape with an imbalance of types of feedback, low complexity, little movement, and insufficient positivity.* The focus of our practical techniques will be largely on addressing these few factors.

11. Employ evidence-based practices. This principle is straightforward: use methods scientifically proven to be effective. Why? Because it increases your probabilities of success.

Virtually any method of resolution may prove effective in addressing one or two situations of conflict. But we often do not know why. It might be because they are sound methods, because the particular method happened to work well with a particular conflict, because the intervener was particularly skillful or artful, or because of random luck. Given the high durability of the 5 percent, stakeholders often suffer from intervention burnout: too many cycles of promises and hope that prove ineffective and disillusioning. This simply contributes to a sense of futility and hopelessness.

So it is simple: use methods that have been proven to work to address the current state of the conflict, increase the probabilities for constructive relations between the parties in the future, *and* decrease the probabilities for destructive future encounters.

12. Anticipate unintended consequences. The German psychologist Dietrich Dorner has conducted research on decision making in complex environments. His findings suggest that well-intentioned decision makers who set an early course for improving organizations and communities *but fail to adjust their decisions in response to critical feedback* not only fail, but often do more harm than good. The most effective decision makers in his studies were those able to continually adapt; they stayed open not only to feedback, but also to reconsidering their decisions and altering their course. The implications of this analogy for analyzing and responding to feedback in situations of ongoing conflict are straightforward. Anyone attempting to implement change strategies with the 5 percent must *embody dynamics:* that is, remain prepared to change strategies, tactics, key indicators, and even members of the intervention team as the system evolves.

THESE PRINCIPLES AND INSIGHTS into the 5 percent derive from the Attractor Landscape Model. Like the leap from structuralism to Gestalt psychology, or that of Newtonian mechanics to field theory in physics, this model represents a paradigm shift in the conflict resolution field. A shift away from standard micro, atomistic, short-term, mechanical perspectives toward more holistic and dynamic views of conflict processes and sustainable solutions.

To illustrate, let us return to the pro-choice versus pro-life conflict in Boston. The approach taken by Laura Chasin, Susan Podiba, and the Public Conversations Project (PCP) was very much in-line with our Attractor Landscape Model. The PCP members were all local actors familiar with the context, major players, and issues in the case. They consulted with local leaders about the value of conducting top-level talks before reaching out quietly to several key leaders and inviting them to engage in *something different.* They explained that the process they were proposing was not business as usual; not a lawsuit or community meeting or even mediation or negotiation. *It was a very different type of experience where they would not try to "solve" the abortion debate.* This would be a new journey. They were all guaranteed safety, anonymity, and confidentiality and informed that they would only be asked to meet four times.

Then the process began. It was essentially *a gradual process* of *disentangling* fears, assumptions, misinformation, and faulty beliefs from the facts on the ground—and from the deeply held values of the women, values that had collapsed into one monolithic worldview. It was *a highly emotional* set of encounters involving two processes: *breaking down* negative assumptions, beliefs, and feelings regarding the "other," and *build-*

ing up new constructive, compassionate, cooperative relationships. Discretion and clear, respectful *ground rules* for the discussions were critical to success. After the fourth meeting, the participants agreed to extend their sessions to the one-year anniversary of the shootings. Subsequently, they chose to extend the sessions again. In all, *it took six years.* The meetings were all conducted in secret to protect the members of this expedition from the extreme dangers of the local terrain.

And then when they were ready, they went public. On January 28, 2001, the six women participants in the dialogue—Anne Fowler, Nicki Nichols Gamble, Frances X. Hogan, Melissa Kogut, Madeline McCommish, Barbara Thorp—copublished an article in the *Boston Globe* called "Talking with the Enemy." In it they documented the concerns over violence that had brought them together, the extraordinarily difficult challenges inherent in their work together, and what they had ultimately learned. They emphasized that "much had been transformed," despite the fact that they had not resolved the pro-life, pro-choice issues in their communities and had actually become more polarized in their views. Here they explain why they persisted in talking together.

> First, because when we face our opponent, we see her dignity and goodness. Embracing this apparent *contradiction* stretches us spiritually. We've experienced something radical and life-altering that we describe in nonpolitical terms: "the mystery of love," "holy ground," or simply, "mysterious."
>
> We continue because we are stretched intellectually, as well. This has been a rare opportunity to engage in sustained, candid conversations about serious moral disagreements. It has made our thinking sharper and our language more precise.
>
> We hope, too, that we have become wiser and more effective leaders. We are more knowledgeable about our political opponents. We have learned to avoid being overreactive and disparaging to the other side and to focus instead on affirming our respective causes.
>
> Since that first fear-filled meeting, we have experienced a *paradox.* While learning to treat each other with dignity and respect, we all have become firmer in our views about abortion.

> We hope this account of our experience will encourage people everywhere to consider engaging in dialogues about abortion and other protracted disputes. In this world of polarizing conflicts, we have glimpsed a new possibility: a way in which people can disagree frankly and passionately, become clearer in heart and mind about their activism, and, at the same time, contribute to a more civil and compassionate society.

The dialogue group members' decision to go public, particularly given their roles and status in their communities, *had a powerful positive impact on the larger system.* Today, despite the fact that the abortion controversy rages on in the United States and abroad, the violence and vitriol of the debate in the Boston community appears to have subsided. As one journalist reported in 2009: "The reduction in angry rhetoric that resulted from the dialogue may have helped assign to history that ugly chapter in the abortion controversy."[15]

The point is this. It is not disagreement over any moral or political or ideological issue that is bad. It is the generalized negative view of one another, and its collapse into good and evil, that is destructive; it has driven countless generations of people to perpetually plot to destroy one another, just like the inhabitants of the House of Atreus. But it is also this collapse that can be remedied by focusing on the dynamic properties of a conflict.

The events and processes in the Boston case are illustrative of the type of alternative thinking and approaches we suggest can help address the 5 percent. However, the dialogue approach of PCP is only one of a variety of methods available for increasing complexity and reconfiguring attractor landscapes. In order to make these ideas and methods more useful, more grounded and practical, we have translated them into a set of basic *practices* to develop and to employ in addressing intractable conflicts. These practices are the subject of the remaining chapters.

part three

THE METHOD

RESOLVING IMPOSSIBLE CONFLICTS

chapter 5

GETTING UNATTRACTED TO CONFLICT: THREE PRACTICES

RESOLVING INTRACTABLE CONFLICTS is never going to be quick or easy. But it doesn't need to be impossible. It basically requires three things:

1. **A *good enough* conceptual framework** for understanding what's going on.
2. **A set of evidence-based practices** for addressing the 5 percent.
3. **A core set of skills** for developing the capacity to employ the practices effectively.

The general objectives of the approach to 5 percent conflicts prescribed by the Attractor Landscape Model (ALM) differ fundamentally from the objectives of more standard models of constructive conflict resolution that are concerned with the other 95 percent of conflicts. The ALM does not aim to identify and satisfy underlying interests and needs in order to resolve the presenting conflict. Rather, the ALM looks to *transform the dynamics of the system maintaining the status quo.* Specifically, its objectives are to regain a sense of *accuracy, agency,* and *possibility* in the conflict; to achieve *sustainable solutions* by first opening up the closed system of the 5 percent to different information; and to then reconfigure the attractor landscape for the relationship.

This is done by employing a set of practices aimed at constructively managing the current state of the conflict, while increasing the probabilities for constructive relations between the parties in the future *and* decreasing the probabilities for destructive future encounters. This takes time.*

STANDARD AND DYNAMICAL MODELS

Problem-solving Model	**Attractor Landscape Model**
Assumptions	*Assumptions*
• Short-term, outcome focus (agreements)	• Dynamic, long-term change in patterns
• Rational decisions	• Emotional context of decisions
• Linear change processes	• Nonlinear dynamics
Orientation	*Orientation*
• Identify presenting conflict issues and underlying needs	• Map links and feedback loops between elements
	• Identify actionable hubs
	• Visualize manifest and latent attractor landscape
Objectives	*Objectives*
• Satisfy underlying needs, resolve conflict	• Accuracy, agency, possibility, sustainability
	• Reconfigure attractor landscape
Approach	*Approach*
• Conflict analysis, intervention, and agreement	• Case study (loop-mapping), visualization, address probabilities and read feedback
Tools	*Practices*
• Problem solving, negotiation, mediation, consensus building, compensation, log-rolling, pressure, coercion	• Complicate to simplify
	• Build up and tear down
	• Change to stabilize

THE PRACTICES

There are three basic practices for addressing the 5 percent constructively. These practices are all informed by the ALM model, principles

*John Paul Lederach once said that he almost got thrown out of a meeting in Northern Ireland regarding the conflict there when he suggested it might take them as long to get out of the conflict as it had to get into it (centuries). This is of course not always the case, but it is a prudent consideration.

and research presented in part 2 of the book. Together they constitute both an ancient and modern approach to conflict. Ancient in that they are rooted in thinking on complexity, coherence, dynamism, and conflict first presented by the Taoists in the third or fourth century BC. Modern because they are informed by contemporary research and methods in psychology and complexity science.

Like most everything associated with conflict, these practices involve tension and process. They are not tools or techniques for intervention. That would reflect linear cause-and-effect thinking. They are dialectical practices that incorporate the psychological principles of change, contradiction, and holism outlined in chapter 4.[1] They are ways of thinking and acting that can enhance our capacity for addressing the 5 percent and thereby increase the probability for constructive change. Each practice addresses basic contradictions: *complexity/simplicity, creation/destruction,* and *change/stability,* which are opposing human needs, tendencies, or processes.[2] At their core, the practices involve an iterative process of managing tension, contradiction, inconsistency, and change.

1. Complicate to simplify. This entails breaking through the press for coherence and oversimplification that is so forceful and constraining with the 5 percent, while attempting to identify the actionable hubs, gateways, and patterns otherwise disguised by the complexity of the conflict.

2. Build up and tear down. This is the practice of stirring or creating a sense of hope and possibility for more constructive relations in a conflict, while simultaneously deconstructing the traps for enmity and destruction that lie in wait to recapture the dynamics of the system.

3. Change to stabilize. This practice views adaptation and change as critical to stability and sustainability. It is about leveraging opportunities for change in a manner mindful of long-term dynamics and the need for adaptation in nonlinear systems.

ALL THREE PRACTICES WORK TOGETHER in a *cyclical fashion.* The first, **complicate to simplify,** constitutes a framework for *conflict analysis and mapping;* it can allow for new understandings and insights to emerge for addressing difficult conflicts. The second, **build up and tear down,** is the main category of *strategic action;* it involves an array of tactics, both old and new, for altering the conflict attractor landscape over time. The final practice, **change to stabilize,** highlights the importance of leveraging change and adapting effectively to changing circumstances in order to achieve sustainable solutions. Of course, any conflict could benefit from these practices. However, the 5 percent, which drag us, often unwittingly, into the depths of their attractors, require them.

What follows are more detailed discussions of each of the practices and their associated actions and skills. Whether or not you find value in any particular action for addressing conflict, remember it is the *practices* and the *science* behind the practices that really matter. This is what you should take with you and use as you see fit. In other words, think of these practices as the basic equipment you need when setting out on your own expedition to discover your 5 percent solution.

The Conflict in the Middle East—at Columbia University

For years, students in the Middle Eastern and Asian Languages and Cultures Department (MEALAC) at Columbia University had complained about what they saw as intimidation of Jewish students by pro-Palestinian professors in the department. The university, for a variety of reasons, had been generally unresponsive to these complaints. Everything changed when an Israeli advocacy group released a documentary film called *Columbia Unbecoming,* presenting student testimonials alleging incidents of academic abuse and intimidation by MEALAC faculty.

Students flocked to see the film in which several professors were identified by name. The testimonials claimed that Jewish students had been mocked and marginalized by these and other "pro-Palestinian" Columbia professors. The faculty members implicated in the film denied the allegations, but nevertheless events escalated.

The accusations grew, from initial complaints about the actions of a few professors at MEALAC, to claims of pervasive bias in the university curriculum and a general anti-Israeli and pro-Palestinian culture among university faculty. The debate also spread to the news and editorial pages of several newspapers and to the blogs of several prominent Israeli and Palestinian commentators. The *New York Daily News* published a special report headlined "Poison Ivy: Climate of Hate Rocks Columbia University." It stated: "Dozens of academics are said to be promoting an I-hate-Israel agenda, embracing the ugliest of Arab propaganda, and teaching that Zionism is the root of all evil in the Mideast." In response, one of the implicated faculty responded by writing: "This witch-hunt aims to stifle pluralism, academic freedom, and the freedom of expression on university campuses in order to ensure that only one opinion is permitted, that of uncritical support for the state of Israel."

Columbia's president, Lee Bollinger, responded by establishing a high-level faculty committee to investigate the claims of bias put forth in the film. But members of a student group immediately protested this move. They charged that the committee itself was biased because of personal and professional connections to the implicated professors, and due to some of the committee members' own prior anti-Israeli statements. Nevertheless, the committee continued its investigation and tensions spread. One of the professors named in the film abandoned his signature course for that term for fear of reprisals (he was pre-tenure). There were several instances of nonenrolled hecklers attending the implicated faculties' courses, and insults and death threats were left on their answering machines. It was also reported that the conflict began affecting alumni funding and student admissions. Then the Israeli ambassador to the United Sates withdrew under protest from an international conference scheduled to take place at Columbia.

When the faculty committee released its report, it issued a harsh condemnation of university grievance procedures, but offered little clarity on the many other issues linked to the dispute. While the report was clear on the need to reform grievance processes, the initial allegations of bias and intimidation remained unresolved, and the student, faculty, and public response was indignant. The controversy has continued for years. It has been particularly contentious around tenure decisions for the implicated faculty, and around related issues of classroom behavior and the limits of academic freedom. Further, the conflict was touted by some as merely one example of a problem that festered at many other campuses as well, and the filmmakers expressed their intention to release new documentaries made at other colleges and universities.

PRACTICE I: COMPLICATE TO SIMPLIFY

Imagine you are the president of Columbia University when the exposé documentary *Columbia Unbecoming* premieres at Columbia's Lerner Cinema, accusing your university of flagrant anti-Semitism. Within minutes the calls and emails start flooding in. Angry parents, furious faculty, student activists, the media, bloggers, the mayor of New York City, the New York Civil Liberties Union, alumni donors, members of your own family, you name it, call and demand action. But of course the actions they demand are all over the map, extreme, and often in direct contradiction to one another, or completely irrelevant to the issues as you see them. The pressure on you to act decisively is extraordinary.

Alternately, imagine that you are one of the students at Columbia. You feel you were publicly humiliated by a faculty member for asking a straightforward question in class. You were thrown out of class and later told by your peers that your professor called you a "Jewish spy." Said professor then reportedly went on a "paranoid rant" about people like you. And you know all too well that this is not an isolated incident. Other students have been treated this way by Columbia professors and subsequently complained to the university. Yet they got a less than satisfactory response from the administration. You are also aware that this is happening not only at Columbia, but at other colleges and universities as well.

Or imagine that you are one of the accused faculty members implicated in the MEALAC case at Columbia. For years now, despite being cleared of any wrongdoing by the university's investigatory panel, every paper you publish, every comment you make, every glance toward a student, even the things you do not say are scrutinized, documented, and taken as more evidence of your obvious anti-Semitism. You know that a well-organized network of pro-Israel activists outside the university is working tirelessly against you; manufacturing falsehoods, inflaming opinions, and lying in wait for you to misspeak.

What's a disputant to do?

The attractor has you. You are now lying on your back at the bottom of a wide and deep crevice of conflict. Whether you are the beleaguered university president, or the aggrieved student, or the accused faculty

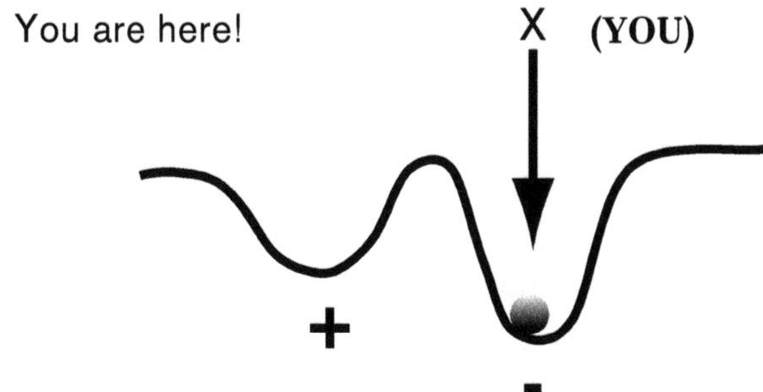

member in this scenario matters, of course. But *everyone* is now constrained and controlled by a powerful constellation of mostly unseen forces.

Of course, our natural impulse in these situations is to fight or flee. To lash out, blame, attack, or challenge someone, or otherwise try to *get out* and avoid the situation altogether. These responses make perfect sense in the short term, but likely will have little effect on the 5 percent. In fact, they may make matters worse in the long term.

So *if escaping or resolving this conflict is your goal* (and we do not assume this is always the case), we suggest a different approach. And it begins with complicating your life.

CONFLICT-MAPPING 1: COMPLICATE THINGS

See the System

When you find yourself stuck in an oversimplified polarized conflict, a useful first step is to try to become *more* aware of the system as a whole: to provide more context to your understanding of the terrain in which the stakeholders are embedded, whether they are disputants, mediators, negotiators, lawyers, or other third parties. This can help you to see the forest *and* the trees; it is *a critical step toward regaining some sense of accuracy, agency, possibility, and control in the situation.*

At the moment, the 5 percent conflict is in charge. It is shaping what you and others see, think, feel, and do. So it is important to first regain some sense of accuracy in your perceptions. This is not easy. It is swimming upstream against what you and others in the conflict feel to be certain. However, because of the dramatic pull of the 5 percent attractor, achieving a better sense of the different independent but interrelated elements of the conflict is an essential fist step. As Columbia president Lee Bollinger stated at the time of the MEALAC crisis, "Many people, perhaps understandably, do not grasp what's at stake. They see one side of it, one aspect of it. This can't be reduced to a single line of thought."[3]

Recall that the collapse of complexity that accompanies 5 percent conflicts happens along many dimensions:

- A very *complicated* situation becomes very *simple.*
- A focus on concrete *details* in the conflict shifts to matters of general abstract *principle.*
- Concerns over obtaining *accurate* information regarding substantive issues transform into concerns over *defending* one's identity, ideology, and values.
- The out-group, which was seen as made up of many *different* types of individuals; now are all *alike.*
- The in-group, which was seen as made up of many *different* types of individuals; now are all *similar.*
- Whereas I once held many *contradictions* within myself in terms of what I valued, thought, and did; now I am always *consistent* in this conflict.
- Whereas I used to feel *different* things about this conflict—good, bad, and ambivalent; now I feel *only* an overwhelming sense of enmity and hate.
- I've shifted from *long-term* thinking and planning toward *short-term* reactions and concerns.
- Where I once had many action *options* available to me, I now have *one:* attack.

This is the bad news about the 5 percent, but it's also the good news. The collapse of complexity occurs on so many levels, all leading a similar state of "us versus them" thinking, that *reintroducing a sense of complex-*

ity and agency can also be achieved in a wide variety of ways. There are therefore many places to find points of leverage to rupture the certainty and oversimplification that rules in these situations.

The question is how to find them.

Most standard approaches to conflict analysis begin with making lists for this very purpose. They start with a negotiator, lawyer, mediator, or other third party who listens to the disputants, identifies the main issues, lists them on a piece of paper, prioritizes them, and then gets to work. This is exactly how I was trained by the New York State criminal courts to be a community mediator. The standard lists look like this.

UNIVERSITY ADMINISTRATION	UNIVERSITY STUDENT
Inflammatory accusations	Public humiliation
Importance of free speech	Importance of free speech
Protection of CU's reputation	Protection of personal reputation
Respect grievance procedures	Unresponsive procedures
Faculty's and students' rights	Students' rights
The plight of Palestinians and Israelis	The plight of Israelis

Although listing issues can be a useful tool for organizing the discussion, and has proven helpful with many types of disputes, it presents two problems in addressing the 5 percent.

Problem 1: Subjectivity, bias, and spoilers. Analyzing conflicts is an *active* cognitive process where the analyst perceives, interprets, shapes, and articulates the pattern of events in question. This flies in the face of traditional notions of third-party *neutrality* and *objective fact-finding* in conflict resolution, which are pervasive in the field today.[4]

Typically during analysis, conflict interveners make a set of critical choices, often under severe constraints, which help determine the future pattern of conflicts. For instance, if invited to intervene in the Columbia University conflict, we would typically have a say in determining which stakeholders, out of the multitude of possibilities, are especially relevant to the conflict and therefore need to be included in assessment and resolution processes.

Immediately, several questions arise. Shall we work with key group representatives or with all stakeholders in a large-scale consensus-building process? Shall we involve more radical agitators inside and outside the university community, or focus on mainstream insiders with broad spheres of influence? These are often necessary and practical choices that carry powerful symbolism; they signal which parties are legitimate and central and which are not. This legitimization can ultimately contribute to the unintentional development of "spoilers": parties who become motivated to undermine what they perceive to be an exclusive and misguided peace process.[5]

A similar process occurs when identifying and prioritizing the issues and grievances in a conflict. As certain problems gain in salience (such as concerns over the university's grievance procedures), they tend to capture the attention of the intervener and main stakeholders, often at the expense of other issues. Over time the neglected issues and parties can regain importance and challenge the integrity of prior agreements. (This, incidentally, is what many believe led to the collapse of the Oslo Accords in the Middle East conflict.)

The point is that the choices interveners first make help to set the *initial conditions* and subsequent *pattern of conflicts.*

Problem 2: Linearity and premature simplification. The second problem with using simple lists of issues as a way of organizing the conflict resolution process is that it once again compares fluid things to fixed things. It typically involves a process of listening to complex, contradictory stories—multiple, nuanced, subjective narratives of ongoing escalatory dynamics—and then using terms or short phrases to capture the main points.

So what is an alternative? Loops.

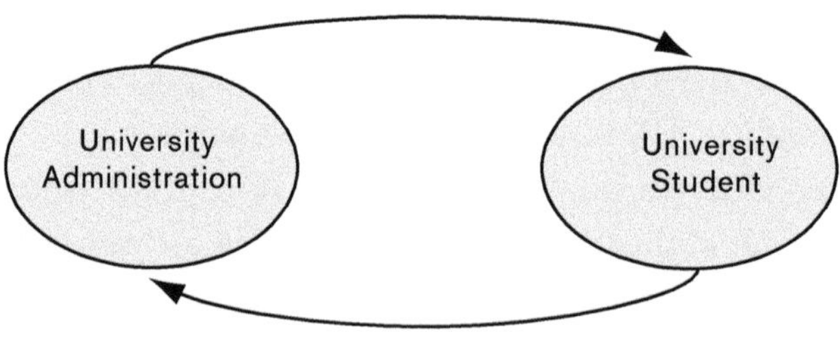

Conflict Feedback Loop-Mapping

Rather than making lists, it can be fruitful to sketch the evolving system of 5 percent conflicts through a series of feedback loop analyses. Loop analysis was developed decades ago by the mathematician and cultural epistemologist Magorah Maruyama.[6] It is particularly useful for mapping different aspects of a conflict and identifying reinforcing and inhibiting feedback loops that contribute to the escalation, deescalation, and stabilization of destructive conflicts.

This method not only helps to *recontextualize* our understanding of a conflict, but also helps to identify central hubs and patterns in the conflict unrecognizable by other means. This is achieved by capturing the multiple sources, links, and complex temporal dynamics of such systems.

Mapping any of these aspects of an evolving conflict can help to tease out and disentangle the morass of grievances and misperceptions that make up the coherent and oversimplified world of the 5 percent. It can help to simply take the time to see how complex these problems can become, which is one reason mapping is used increasingly by conflict practitioners working on the ground in complicated situations.

However, I must offer one caution. It is *very* important when using a conflict-mapping methodology that everyone involved be clear about the degree of *objectivity* versus *subjectivity* of the exercise, and of whatever elements are being mapped. This can be thought of along a continuum.

OBJECTIVE-SUBJECTIVE CONTINUUM

Objective	**Subjective**
(Externally verifiable elements of conflict)	(Psychologically perceived elements of a conflict)

Mapping Objective Structures. On one end of the continuum are conflict maps that can be generated of actual, empirically verifiable entities, structures, processes, and events. For example, the communications networks—phone traffic, email correspondence, Internet traffic, physical visits together and time spent speaking—of disputants and stakeholders in a conflict setting could be mapped, as could the physical locations of

CONFLICT MAPS ARE VERSATILE TOOLS

A variety of different aspects of conflict can be mapped.

- **People and social networks.** How allies and opponents relate to one another in conflict situations. Who talks to whom in the conflict? Who avoids whom? Are there possible communication links through various parties for linking negotiations between key adversaries? Are the social networks stable or changing over time?
- **Cultural beliefs, social norms, and community institutions.** How macro elements of the conflict work together or against one another to perpetuate destructive (or constructive) intergroup relations. For example, how group beliefs in the utility of violence, political rhetoric about past atrocities committed by the out-group, cultural norms dictating distrust of outsiders, school curricula that present biased historical accounts of a conflict, and the presence of rituals and monuments honoring slain warriors operate together to reinforce the need for ongoing group struggle. Or alternatively how strong advocates for human rights, a free press, an attentive and responsive international community, and an impartial judiciary system can operate to inhibit destructive dynamics.
- **Issues, needs, and interests.** How the different concerns and goals of the disputants relate to one another. Are they a set of relatively unrelated and loosely coupled issues, or a tight constellation of needs and interests? Which issues are more basic and pivotal to each party? Are these concerns shared by different stakeholders? Have the primary concerns shifted in importance over time?[7]
- **Visions, hopes, and dreams.** What does an ideal solution to this conflict look like for each stakeholder group? What are the activities, events, and structures they would like to see in place that would help resolve the conflict and sustain more tolerant or constructive relations? How do the different stakeholder maps compare and contrast? What potential problems or unexpected consequences may result from these activities, events, and structures?
- **Individual thoughts, feelings, and actions.** How different aspects of any individual stakeholder's experience of the conflict link together and collapse into a coherent attractor or not. These aspects may include its past history, perceptions of the in-group and out-group, feelings of loss, guilt, and so on. Where are the strongest and weakest links?

And most important:

- **A chronology of events.** How a series of events transpired over time to increase the intensity and destructiveness of a conflict to maintain it in its current state and/or to deescalate it. What are the specific events? When did they occur? How did they reinforce or inhibit the escalation, stalemate, or deescalation of the conflict? Did any elements in fact do both: escalate and deescalate the conflict simultaneously or over time?

events, such as crimes or conflictual encounters or group violence. These maps can employ sophisticated network analysis and visualization tools; they can be very helpful in visualizing temporal and spatial patterns of relationships and events. This type of mapping is less common in the conflict and peace field today (with the exception of police and peacekeeping activities, disaster relief, and covert intelligence gathering), but its use is increasing in emergency situations. For example, humanitarian observers of the political violence in Kenya in 2009 used GPS tracking of cell phone data from hundreds of locals to pinpoint and communicate the location of hotspots of political violence.

Mapping Subjective Aspects of Conflict. On the other end of the spectrum, conflict maps can also be generated of disputants' and other stakeholders' *perceptions* of relevant parties, issues, norms, institutions, etc. in a conflict. This is typically known as *concept-mapping* or *mind-mapping.* It is an excellent exercise for unearthing assumptions, perceptions, and misperceptions in understanding; for providing context and nuance to the perceiver's sense of a conflict; for exploring temporal dynamics in people's understanding of the chronology of events; and for identifying areas of shared or contradictory meaning for different stakeholders.

This more subjective version of conflict-mapping is used more frequently by peace practitioners today. However, even though this exercise can generate complex conceptual maps of important and relevant aspects of a conflict, and show the reinforcing and inhibiting links between these elements, it must be understood to be *a purely subjective tool.* These maps are not maps of external structures or of objective facts; they are simply expressions of each individual's or group's perception of what has transpired in the conflict, which is typically biased in the 5 percent.

This distinction is not meant to devalue subjective conflict-mapping; on the contrary, it can be immensely useful. However, it is important to be clear that there are significant differences between the value and utility of more objective conflict-mapping exercises and more subjective mapping processes.

This is one reason why we recommend beginning with stakeholder mapping of the *chronology* of events of the 5 percent. Although the *reason why* particular events occurred is often hotly disputed in 5 percent conflicts, the facts of *where, when,* and sometimes *how* they occurred are usually *somewhat less* so. That means that conflict event chronology-mapping falls somewhere between purely objective (fact finding) and purely subjective (perceptions, memories, and interpretation) exercises. This is because some events will be documented formally and may be easier to agree upon (for example, *Columbia Unbecoming* had its first public showing on Columbia's campus on Friday, January 18, 2003), while others may be much more ambiguous and contested. Thus, event chronologies are usually good starting points for stakeholder mapping. They can help disputants unpack and visually express their shared and contradictory understanding of the history of events and of how each event may have affected the next set of events.

Conflict Event-Mapping: Four Steps. The process of event-mapping involves four basic steps.

Step 1: *The stakeholders clarify which dynamic they are trying to understand.* Do they want to know why a conflict *escalated* so quickly and so aggressively? Do they want to understand why the conflict is *stuck* and has remained at a stalemate for years (key to the 5 percent)? Or do they want to understand why the conflict seems to follow a *periodic pattern* of escalation and deescalation over time without ever really changing course? This point of focus must be defined at the start of the exercise, as each of these dynamics may require mapping somewhat different aspects of the conflict.

Step 2: *The stakeholders identify the chronology of events relevant to the dynamic of interest, as far back as they feel is important, leading up to the present circumstances.* Again, what is seen as "relevant" will be determined subjectively by each stakeholder involved and by the specific focus of the exercise (mapping escalation, stalemate, periodicity, etc.). We suggest this step first be conducted with independent stakeholders or small constituent groups; in-group differences in perceptions and values can then be explored before moving on to compare and contrast maps with members of out-groups.

Step 3: *The stakeholders begin to map and connect the different events in chronological order.* They use two criteria: (1) how each event triggers, feeds, or *reinforces* other events in such a way that more leads to more, or less leads to less (reinforcing feedback), and (2) how each event constrains, *inhibits,* or reverses other events so that changes in one direction are associated with changes in the opposite direction (inhibiting feedback). This activity can be done most simply using flip-chart paper or a whiteboard, or by using PowerPoint or any simple concept-mapping software available online, like Mindjet or iMindMap.

Step 4: Once the event maps are drafted, we have several options. One option is to work with each individual stakeholder or group to explore their map; we identify missing elements and links, surprising connections, and generally work to enhance the diversity and complexity of their understanding of the conflict. A second option is to compare maps across stakeholder groups with the expressed goal of *thinking different,* of seeing the conflict from a fresh point of view. A third option is to go on to the next phase of practice 1, which is to simplify things before engaging stakeholder comparisons or discussions.

Conflict Event-Mapping: An Illustration. Below we illustrate this exercise by walking through a preliminary subjective event-mapping of the exponential escalation of the Columbia University MEALAC case over five phases of its escalation. These events were compiled from several newspaper accounts and personal communications.[8]

Phase 1: The MEALAC conflict at Columbia seemed to escalate quite rapidly in 2002–2003. Whether or not it was a coincidence, reports of bias and abuse at MEALAC first surfaced around the time of the intensification of the second intifada in Israel; they also came in the wake of a quashed movement by students and faculty at Columbia to divest from companies that manufactured and sold weaponry to Israel. The MEALAC department had been formally constituted at Columbia in 1965 and some of the accused faculty had been there for decades. However, the 2001–2002 escalation of events in the Israel-Palestine region may have triggered past traumas, resentments, or guilt of Columbia faculty and students, contributing to their actions at this time.

Events probably went like this. Reports of discriminatory behavior at MEALAC became associated with reports of similar acts of bias at other universities (for example, at the University of Chicago in 2002). The

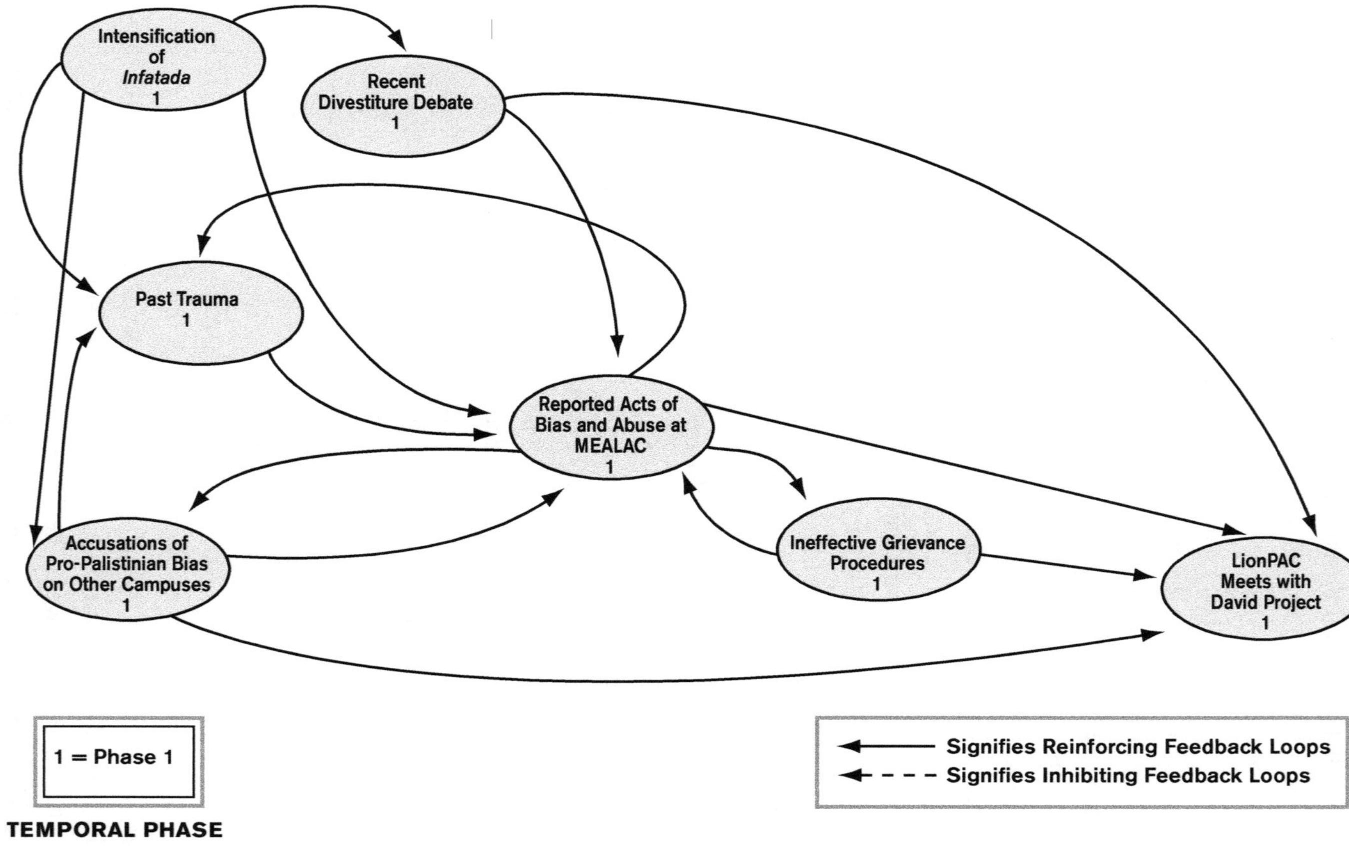

TEMPORAL PHASE

Initial Phase of the MEALAC Conflict at Columbia

existing grievance procedures at Columbia offered a limited response to the grievances. The sense of outrage among students intensified. At this point members of Columbia's LionsPAC student organization were likely motivated to approach the David Project, a pro-Israeli advocacy group. The film *Columbia Unbecoming* was conceived, setting the stage for escalation. Note how all the mapped events are connected by reinforcing links, with no inhibiting loops to slow things down. This contributed to the rapid escalation of the conflict on and around campus.

Phase 2: In December 2003, the David Project released *Columbia Unbecoming,* which presented student testimonials of academic abuse and intimidation in MEALAC. The documentary named three professors: George Saliba, Hamid Dabashi, and Joseph Massad. Students claimed that in recent years they had felt mocked and marginalized by these and other "pro-Palestinian" professors. Two allegations received the most attention. One involved a sidewalk encounter between a former student and her professor at the time, Saliba. The student claimed that Saliba told her that because she had green eyes, she was not a Semite and could therefore not claim ancestral ties to Israel. The second allegation was made by a student who had served in the Israeli army. He said that when he tried to question Massad during an off-campus lecture, the professor responded by asking him, "How many Palestinians have you killed?" The implicated faculty members denied the accusations. The allegations became officially public in October 2004, when Barnard College president Judith Shapiro referenced the film in a speech at an alumni event.

These events began to link together, reinforcing one another in the minds and conversations of the Columbia community and beyond. They intensified the conflict, connecting directly with peoples' varied experiences of the long and troubled history of the Israeli-Palestinian conflict. During phase 2, once again no significant events that served to dampen the escalation of tensions were identified.

Phase 3: Soon after President Shapiro's comments, the *New York Sun* printed the first of many inflammatory articles about the events at Columbia; within two weeks hundreds of students packed Columbia's Lerner Cinema to view the film. Then, early in December 2004, a group

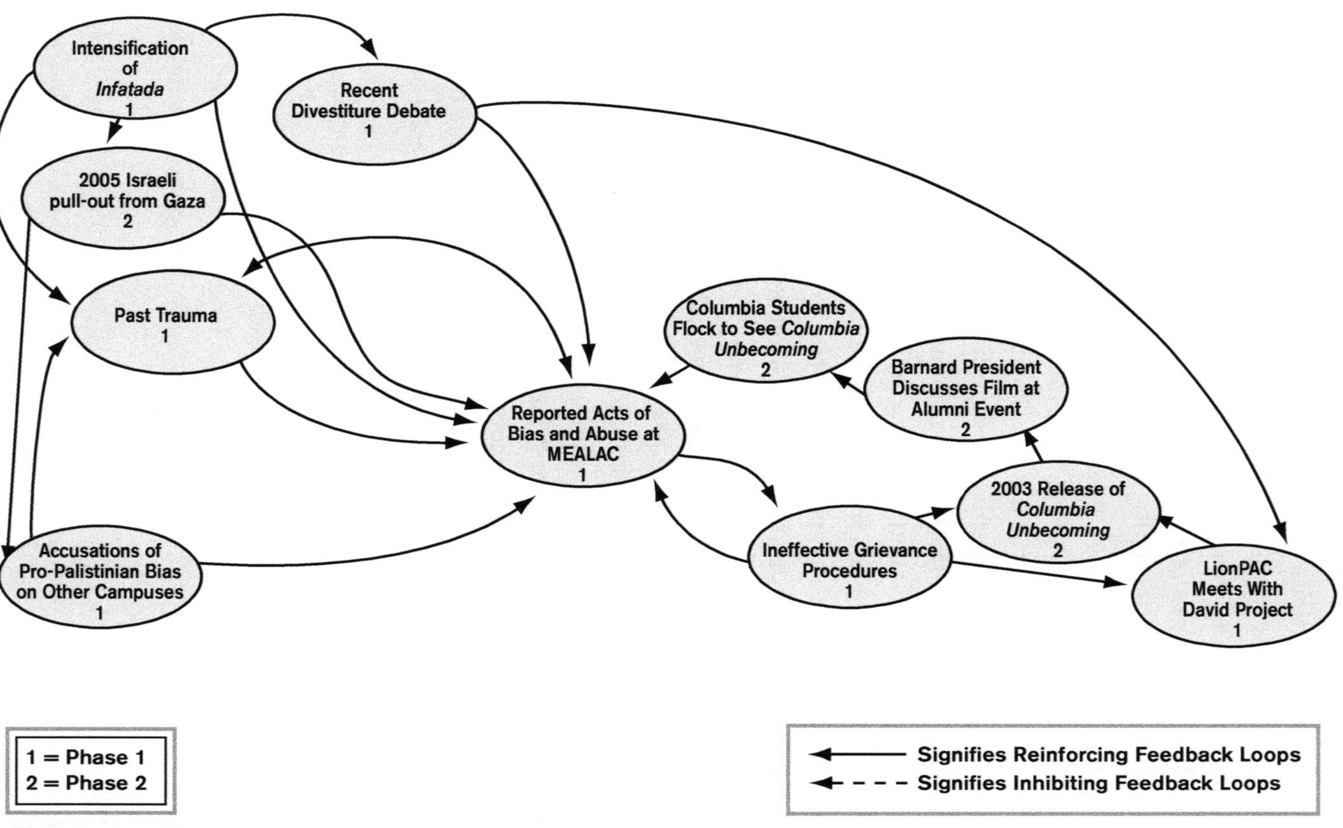
Intensification of *Infatada* 1
Recent Divestiture Debate 1
2005 Israeli pull-out from Gaza 2
Past Trauma 1
Accusations of Pro-Palistinian Bias on Other Campuses 1
Reported Acts of Bias and Abuse at MEALAC 1
Columbia Students Flock to See *Columbia Unbecoming* 2
Barnard President Discusses Film at Alumni Event 2
2003 Release of *Columbia Unbecoming* 2
Ineffective Grievance Procedures 1
LionPAC Meets With David Project 1
1 = Phase 1
2 = Phase 2
Signifies Reinforcing Feedback Loops
Signifies Inhibiting Feedback Loops

TEMPORAL PHASES

Phases 1 to 2 of the MEALAC Conflict

of fifty students, faculty, alumni, and community members held a press conference to protest what they felt was the stifling of voices critical of Israel. This group, the Ad Hoc Committee for the Defense of Academic Freedom at Columbia, accused the university of failing to protect freedom of speech; it also accused the David Project of misrepresenting facts. These accusations may have lessened the escalatory impact of *Columbia Unbecoming* by questioning its legitimacy (a rare inhibitory link), but they also sparked increased tension and controversy evident in editorials and blogs (which served as reinforcing loops).

Events swiftly escalated further. Accusations expanded to include claims of anti-Israeli bias in the MEALAC curriculum and a general anti-Israeli, pro-Palestinian bias among the entire Columbia faculty. The debate continued to spread through the news and editorial pages of several newspapers and to the websites of several prominent pro-Israeli and pro-Palestinian commentators. The New York Civil Liberties Union and the Foundation for Individual Rights in Education issued strongly worded statements.

It wasn't just the media—things were becoming personal. One professor in Columbia's medical school sent an email to Professor Massad, saying "Go back to Arab land where Jew hating is condoned. Get the hell out of America. You are a disgrace and a pathetic typical Arab liar."[9] Professor Massad was compelled to abandon one of his signature courses, Palestinian and Israeli Politics and Societies, that spring term. There were several instances of classroom heckling, and insults and death threats were leveled at the faculty. Concerns that the conflict would affect Columbia's alumni funding and student admissions arose.

Phase 4: On December 8, 2004, Columbia president Lee Bollinger responded to the controversy by announcing the creation of a high-level faculty ad hoc committee to investigate the claims of bias put forth in *Columbia Unbecoming*. This strategy might have temporarily mitigated the conflict. However, members of a student group then sent a letter to Bollinger charging that the ad hoc committee was itself biased: there were alleged personal and professional connections among members of the committee and some of the implicated professors from MEALAC, and some of the committee members had allegedly made anti-Israeli

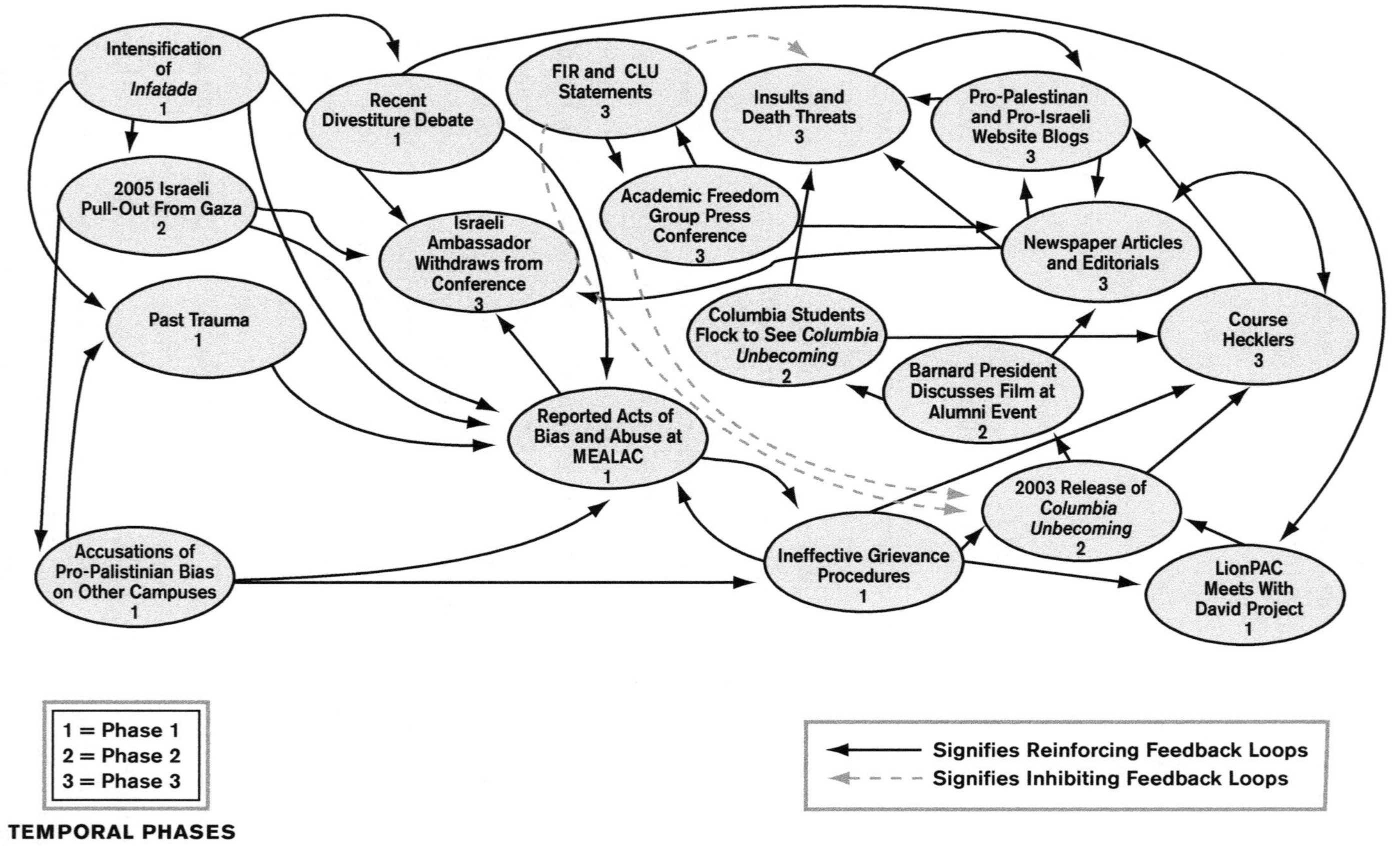
Intensification of *Infatada* 1
2005 Israeli Pull-Out From Gaza 2
Past Trauma 1
Accusations of Pro-Palistinian Bias on Other Campuses 1
Recent Divestiture Debate 1
Israeli Ambassador Withdraws from Conference 3
FIR and CLU Statements 3
Academic Freedom Group Press Conference 3
Reported Acts of Bias and Abuse at MEALAC 1
Insults and Death Threats 3
Columbia Students Flock to See *Columbia Unbecoming* 2
Ineffective Grievance Procedures 1
Pro-Palestinan and Pro-Israeli Website Blogs 3
Newspaper Articles and Editorials 3
Barnard President Discusses Film at Alumni Event 2
2003 Release of *Columbia Unbecoming* 2
Course Hecklers 3
LionPAC Meets With David Project 1
1 = Phase 1
2 = Phase 2
3 = Phase 3
Signifies Reinforcing Feedback Loops
Signifies Inhibiting Feedback Loops

TEMPORAL PHASES

Phases 1 to 3 of the MEALAC Conflict

statements. For instance, one committee member had advised Professor Massad on his PhD thesis, and two others had signed the 2002 divestment petition demanding that Columbia withdraw economic support from Israel. This sparked even more outrage. Nevertheless, the committee proceeded as originally constituted, hearing testimony and deliberating for two months. Then in January 2005, in response to the controversy, the Israeli ambassador to the United Sates, Daniel Ayalon, withdrew from an international conference scheduled to take place at Columbia.

On March 31, 2005, the ad hoc committee released its conclusions in a twenty-four-page report, issuing a harsh condemnation of Columbia's grievance procedures but offering little clarity on the many other issues in dispute. The report stated that, for years, students' complaints about Middle East studies professors in MEALAC had been ignored or mishandled. In this climate, the report continued, the complaints festered and the department became riddled with "suspicion, incivility, and an unhealthy, highly politicized atmosphere."[10] The report also said that the committee found no evidence of anti-Semitism, although it did find that Professor Massad had on one occasion violated "standard norms of acceptable professorial conduct."[11] The report served to validate many of the complainants' concerns (reinforcing loop) and ameliorate some of the due process issues (inhibiting loop). However, it was seen as an insufficient response by many (once again, a conflict-reinforcing loop).

Phase 5: In April 2005, a group of students claiming they were in Professor Massad's class on the day of the alleged misconduct wrote a letter denying the incident had taken place. Also in April, the *New York Times* editorial board wrote that Columbia had "botched" the investigation by involving professors on the panel who were perceived as biased; it also accused Columbia of limiting the committee's mandate so narrowly as to constrain the implications of its findings.[12] President Bollinger was assailed by some faculty members for defending the rights of professors too weakly and failing to contain the controversy. All these are conflict-reinforcing elements. Mr. Bollinger responded by saying that he found the dispute "very painful"[13] and that he was trying to protect both faculty and student rights.

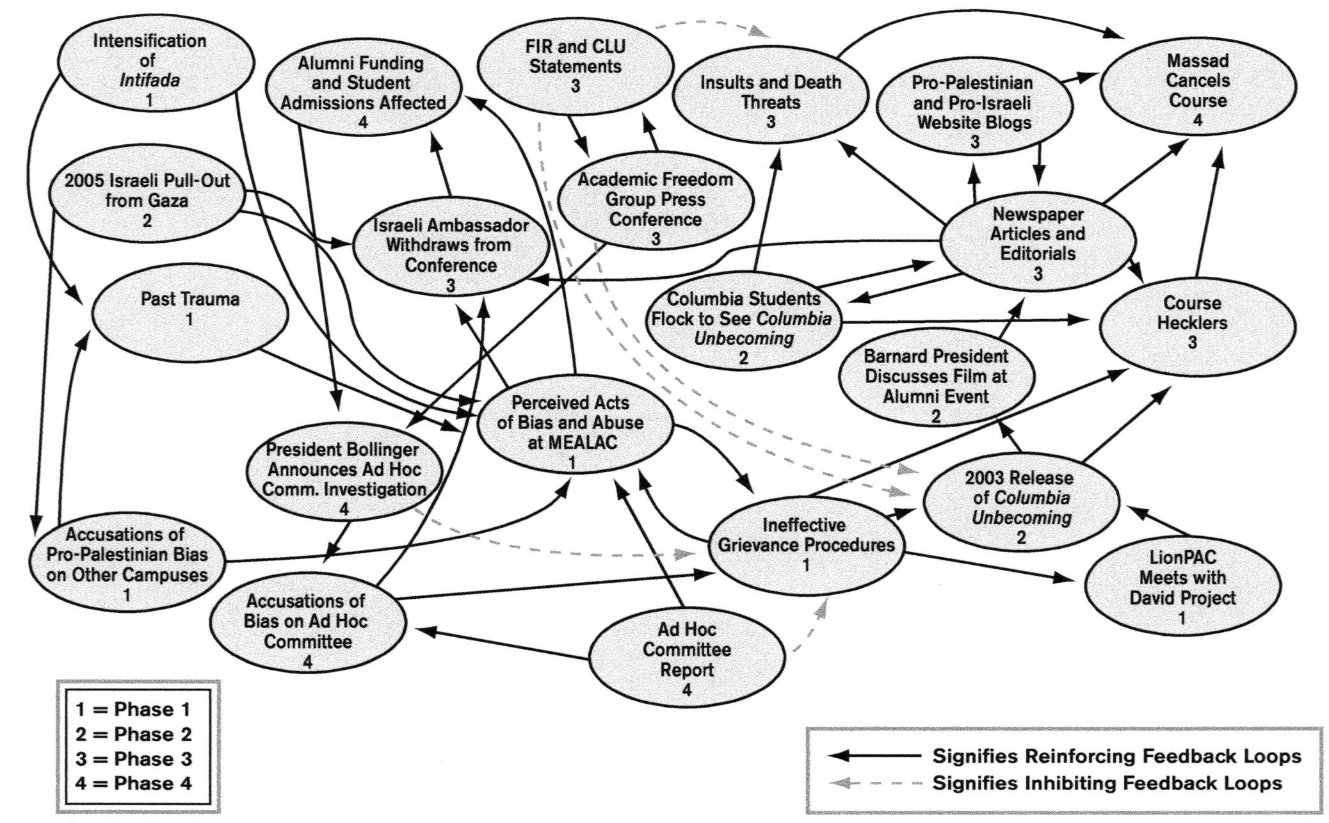

Intensification of *Intifada* 1
Alumni Funding and Student Admissions Affected 4
FIR and CLU Statements 3
Insults and Death Threats 3
Pro-Palestinian and Pro-Israeli Website Blogs 3
Massad Cancels Course 4
2005 Israeli Pull-Out from Gaza 2
Israeli Ambassador Withdraws from Conference 3
Academic Freedom Group Press Conference 3
Newspaper Articles and Editorials 3
Past Trauma 1
Columbia Students Flock to See *Columbia Unbecoming* 2
Course Hecklers 3
Barnard President Discusses Film at Alumni Event 2
Perceived Acts of Bias and Abuse at MEALAC 1
President Bollinger Announces Ad Hoc Comm. Investigation 4
2003 Release of *Columbia Unbecoming* 2
Accusations of Pro-Palestinian Bias on Other Campuses 1
Ineffective Grievance Procedures 1
LionPAC Meets with David Project 1
Accusations of Bias on Ad Hoc Committee 4
Ad Hoc Committee Report 4
1 = Phase 1
2 = Phase 2
3 = Phase 3
4 = Phase 4
Signifies Reinforcing Feedback Loops
Signifies Inhibiting Feedback Loops

TEMPORAL PHASES

Phases 1 to 4 of the MEALAC Conflict

In the midst of the controversy, despite campus programs like Turath's and LionsPAC's joint Project Tolerance and an announced million-dollar grant to start dialogue to increase multicultural awareness (inhibiting feedback loops), the campus remained divided. While the ad hoc committee's report brought a measure of closure to the need to reform Columbia's grievance procedures, the initial allegations of bias and intimidation remained unresolved. The accused MEALAC professors all took leaves of absence in 2005–2006. High faculty turnover and a climate of cautiousness and gloom reportedly continued to mark the department. One student called the professors' absence "a brilliant political move" and remarked, "People are naive if they think we're just going to kind of let things lie."[14]

The MEALAC controversy continued for years and is likely latent today. At times it has become particularly contentious over tenure decisions regarding one of the implicated faculty members and around related issues of classroom behavior and the limits of academic freedom. As mentioned, the controversy at Columbia is regarded by some as only one example of a problem that festers on many other college and university campuses.

As this exercise illustrates, conflict event-mapping allows us to begin to capture how a complex set of events in a conflict unfolds over time. We can then see how this set acts in concert to trigger and reinforce other events and/or to constrain and inhibit other events. It all works together to escalate, perpetuate, or deescalate conflict. These maps can be generated alone as a prenegotiation exercise (with minimal training), with the help of facilitators or mediators, or in small groups of stakeholders. Again, with concept-mapping the goal is not necessarily to get it right. The goal at this stage is *to get it different:* to try to reintroduce a sense of nuance and complexity into the stakeholders' understanding of the conflict. The goal is to try to *open up the system:* to provide opportunities to explore and develop multiple perspectives, emotions, ideas, narratives, and identities and foster an increased sense of emotional and behavioral flexibility. To rediscover a sense of possibility.

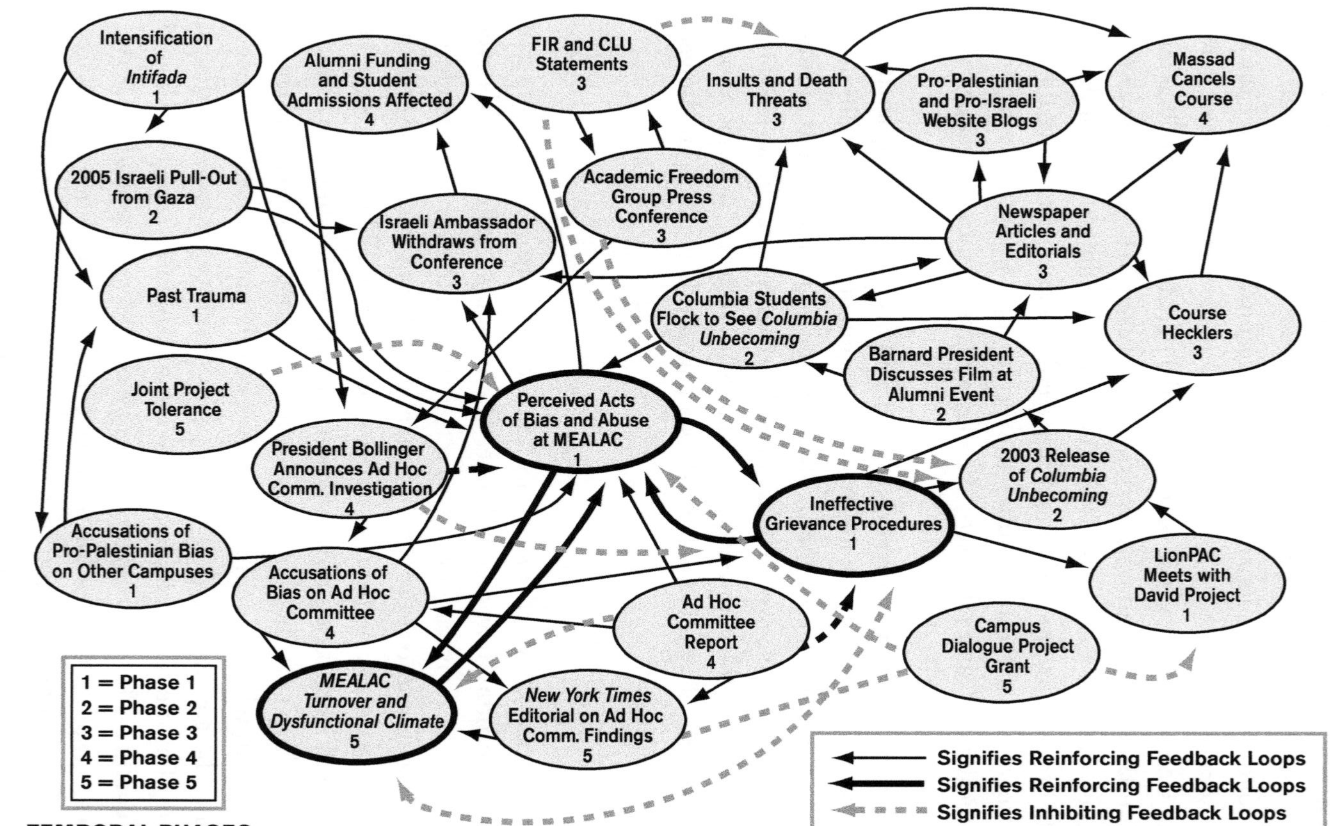

TEMPORAL PHASES

Phases 1 to 5 of the MEALAC Conflict

A note to third parties: It is important for the conflict specialist to be mindful of her or his own dominant frames when helping to construct these maps. Which perspectives does the specialist tend to use and not use, and is anything important missing? A political scientist might focus primarily on what roles politics and power play in establishing the current attractor at MEALAC. To what degree is Columbia being played as a pawn by external political groups to bring attention to their cause? Are internal groups playing up ethnic differences to mobilize altogether different agendas?

Alternatively, a social psychologist would likely emphasize how social conditions on campus contribute to malignant relations between groups such that they maintain the problem. Given that some Jewish and Arab faculty and students may have been raised to hate, fear, and suspect the other, has Columbia done enough to establish conditions for respectful tolerance and dialogue on campus? Specialists with training in communications or linguistics might emphasize meaning-construction around the events, suggesting that we pay special attention to the stories being told about MEALAC in newspapers, official documents, and coffee houses on campus. Those trained in epidemiology might focus on the often overlooked roles that the individual and collective trauma of Israeli and Palestinian faculty and students, exacerbated by current threats of violence, play in the unfolding patterns at Columbia. How does past exposure to atrocities and human suffering affect their current responses to the situation at Columbia?

Of course, any of these perspectives on the problems at Columbia may be accurate and useful. That's not the point. The issue is that they are all *aspectual;* they focus attention on some aspects of the problem and away from others. So whatever their training, it is often helpful for specialists to actively seek out varied and contradictory sources of information, to aim for increased accuracy in their understanding, and to try hold the temptation for premature simplification at bay.

In summary, complexity matters. And learning to effectively map 5 percent conflicts is one approach to capturing their complexity. It requires us to both see the problems in new ways *and* to attend to aspects of the problems we are not used to seeing. Of course, the degree of complexity of 5 percent conflicts defies comprehensive analysis. But that is not the objective of practice 1. Feedback loop–mapping can allow contextualization, discovery, and insight to emerge; our sense of the issues and events in a conflict can take on new meaning when seen from such a "field" or relational perspective. These exercises also highlight the value of cross-disciplinary collaboration; we need distinctly trained individuals working together with stakeholders in these settings in order to better comprehend the problem sets, both specifically and systemically.

CONFLICT-MAPPING 2: SIMPLIFY THINGS

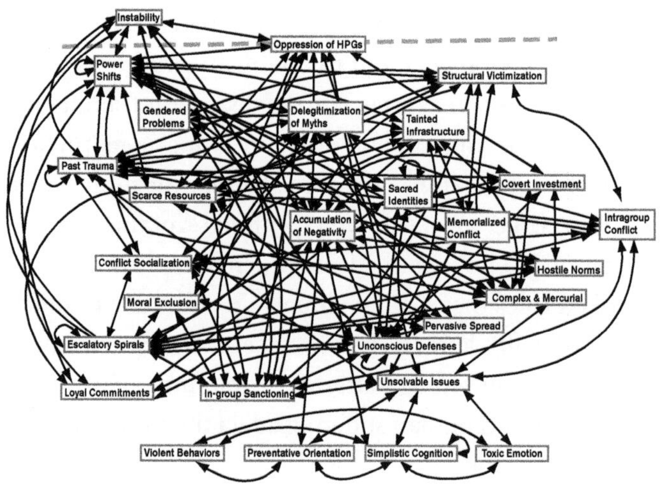

Help!!!

In early 2010, NBC reporter Richard Engel uncovered a wildly complicated PowerPoint map depicting U.S. strategy to increase popular support for the Afghan government. It involved over 100 elements, each with multiple links or loops to other nodes. It was characteristic of the U.S. military's current approach to counterinsurgency and what some officers refer to as a "fur ball." Upon first seeing the map, General Stanley A. McChrystal, leader of American and NATO forces in Afghanistan at the time, remarked, "When we understand that slide, we'll have won the war."[15]

At the heart of much of what we've discussed so far is the double-edged sword of complexity. If the story of a conflict has lost complexity and become overly simplistic and polarized, we must reintroduce nuance into our understanding of the situation. But adding too much complexity can easily make an already complicated situation overwhelming, even immobilizing. Or it can lead to increased resistance and an even stronger push to *oversimplify* and choose sides.

It's vital to employ a few general tactics for *managing complexity.* This will permit us to see both the forest and the (more important) trees in the 5 percent. Each tactic is informed by our model and in particular by the approach of *dynamical minimalism,* whose goal is to make use of the complexity of a problem in order to find the minimal set of mechanisms that can account for its evolving pattern, its character. Once again, the goal of dynamical minimalism is *simplicity informed by complexity.*[16]

In this section we outline five actions for harnessing the complexity generated in phase 1 of conflict-mapping; they will help us to develop more focused strategies and insights for understanding and leveraging change in 5 percent conflicts. They are (1) identify hubs, loops, and energy in the system, (2) identify local actionables, (3) locate what is already working, (4) identify integrative agents, and (5) visualize the attractor landscape.

1. Identify hubs, loops, and energy in the system. Once you sufficiently map a conflict system, you can begin to employ basic ideas and tools of network analysis to further explore the dynamics. *Network analysis* comes from work on network theory and has applications in areas of study including particle physics, computer science, biology, economics, operations research, and sociology.

Formal network analysis tools are most appropriate for conflict maps of a more objective nature: mapping communications networks, social networks, formal authority structures, and so on. However, the feedback-loop structure of subjective concept maps can also benefit from the application of network analysis tools. This is especially true when the maps have been generated and therefore validated by different stakeholder groups representing diverse points of view on the conflict.

There is value in focusing in on a variety of different aspects of conflict maps. For example: identifying central *hubs* of activity, elements that link with many other elements; key *reinforcing loops,* elements that stimulate themselves through links with other elements in an ongoing fashion; and the *ratio,* or balance, between conflict-reinforcing and -inhibiting feedback, which can determine whether a conflict is escalating, deescalating, or stuck in a stalemate.

Or you can look to see differences in levels of *in-degree* of different conflict elements, as in how many links feed into each element; *out-degree,* which elements serve as key sources of stimulation or inhibition in the conflict for other elements; and *betweenness,* which describes the degree to which elements are located between and therefore link other elements. These are all useful lenses that can focus our attention and clarify our understanding of complex maps.[17]

Identifying central hubs and strong feedback loops in the system is particularly important for locating *centers of energy in the system, gateways for high-impact intervention, strategic targets for introducing conflict-inhibiting feedback* (such as early-warning systems that deter escalation), and *peace-reinforcing feedback* (like high-stakes common interests that motivate reconciliation). They also help to focus the analysis of conflict-mapping and to manage the anxiety associated with the overwhelming sense of complexity of the system. *However, they do so in a manner informed by its complexity.*

In mapping our analysis of the Columbia conflict, I highlight the *reinforcing feedback loops* that operate to intensify the conflict in an ongoing fashion (with solid lines) to illustrate two reinforcing loops: one between the reporting of acts of bias and the ineffective grievance procedures, and the other between the reporting of bias and the high level of turnover and dysfunctional work climate in the department at the time of the analysis.

When students' complaints about bias at MEALAC were left unaddressed by officials at Columbia, it fostered student resentment and hypersensitivity to future abuses at MEALAC, leading to more complaints to the university, which when neglected increased resentment and so on. This is a conflict-reinforcing loop.

Similarly, word of the complaints of bias at MEALAC negatively affected the morale and work climate in the department, which led to higher turnover of experienced faculty and staff, resulting in fewer well-trained personnel and therefore a higher potential for student dissatisfaction, leading to more complaints against MEALAC and so on. Another loop.

Alternatively, I use dashed lines to highlight the various sources of *inhibiting feedback* operating to lessen the intensity of the conflict in the system. This map would be of particular interest to those invested in deescalating tensions and maintaining relative calm on campus. (Of course, it might be equally interesting to activists, anarchists, and other agitators interested in fanning the fires at Columbia as well.) This focus can help identify the current sources of conflict-inhibiting feedback as well as possible targets for introducing new sources.

For instance, strongly worded statements issued by the New York Civil Liberties Union and the Foundation for Individual Rights in Education challenging the accuracy of the accusations made in *Columbia Unbecoming* and in the *New York Daily News* reporting, contributed to an easing of the initial hysteria triggered by the film. The press conference held by the Ad Hoc Academic Freedom Group had a similar impact. Of course, the investigatory panel's report helped mitigate tensions over the ineffectiveness of grievance procedures at Columbia, but it triggered other concerns due to the narrow nature of its mandate and findings. Most important, ongoing initiatives like the Joint Project on Tolerance and the campus dialogue project likely provided the strongest inhibitory feedback loops for decreasing the intensity and negativity trends of the conflict.

Another alternative is to highlight the many *in-degree links* that feed conflict intensity with dotted lines to support the sense that there is considerable energy and tension associated with the reporting of bias, and also to help provide a more detailed understanding of the myriad sources of this energy, in addition to the acts themselves, feeding these tensions.

Various factors worked in concert with local concerns of inadequate grievance procedures and biased investigatory panels to intensify not only the significance but also the likelihood of perceptions of bias at

MEALAC. It was a multiply determined phenomena that culminated in high levels of tension at MEALAC. This is not to suggest that acts of bias did not occur at MEALAC. It merely accounts for the level of sustained tension surrounding the events.

This analysis simply provides more options. It suggests that it may be more than ineffective grievance procedures driving the conflict, and that much more could be done to address these tensions—for instance, by addressing the climate at MEALAC, working across universities to stem acts of bias, and broadening the mandate of the investigatory panel beyond the grievance system.

The point to stress here is that the burgeoning area of network studies has begun to provide us with a *new grammar* for characterizing, exploring, analyzing, and ultimately learning from the science and art of conflict feedback loop-mapping. These maps and analyses can help us to become more aware of the context of problems—and to work within their complexity to identify key levers for change. Such an approach can help stakeholders regain a sense of efficacy in situations that tend to elicit hopelessness.

Once dynamics are identified, it becomes possible to home in on what's most important: increasing probabilities for resolving the conflict.

2. Identify local actionables. Once you have mapped and explored the broader view of the feedback structure of the conflict, it can be immensely helpful to focus in on more local elements and links that are *actionable.*[18] This means those things that can feasibly be addressed. If you are the president of Columbia University, there isn't much you are going to be able to do about the intifada, the Israeli pullout from Gaza, or the actions of the Israeli ambassador. So it simplifies your task if you eventually drop the nonactionable elements (dashed-line ovals) and focus in on those you might be able to do something about, such as directly refuting untruths and inflammatory claims in editorials, blogs, and the documentary; enhancing tolerance through support of new and ongoing campus projects; joining with other university presidents to address these issues nationally; and cracking down on class hecklers and issuers of death threats. These are all feasible actions, informed by the complexity of events, that can affect the probabilities of constructive change on campus.

But they should only be targeted after a fuller mapping of the system has provided a sense of the context in which these elements are operating.

3. Locate (carefully) what is already working in the system. Laura Chasin is former director of the Public Conversations Project and facilitator of the Boston dialogue over abortion. When she enters a new community she is working with, which is deeply divided over a difficult conflict, she first tries to identify the existing "networks of effective action." These are the individuals and groups that somehow manage to stay connected to parties on the other side of the conflict; they work effectively and constructively to keep relationships and dialogue going, even under stressful and dangerous circumstances. These social networks can often be found in conflicts within families, communities, and between nations. In more threatening environments, they may be forced to go underground. But typically they are there, despite the danger, working carefully to keep communications open.

From the perspective of complexity science, these individuals and their networks are evidence of latent attractors for constructive relations operating within these families and communities. Given that they are usually locally motivated, well networked, and typically well informed, they often present a vital resource for bolstering alternative approaches to destructive conflict in the system; they provide hope and possibilities in an otherwise impossible situation. However, they must always be identified, approached, and supported carefully, as their covert status is often a necessary defense against alienation or direct attack, typically from members within their own groups or communities.

But these constructive networks are merely an illustration of a larger point—that *there are usually processes and mechanisms already operating in every conflict system, no matter how entrenched, that are functional and constructive.* Think of them as antibodies in the body of the conflict, quietly fighting against the spread of the 5 percent infection. These constructive forces can often be overlooked in conflict analyses, as the suffering and crises associated with the 5 percent grab our attention and make the *problems* salient, usually at the expense of existing buffers or remedies. But a thorough scan of the system can help to locate its more functional components; these include local norms and practices that prohibit aggression and violence beyond certain levels, indigenous grievance systems or other regulatory mechanisms considered impartial and fair, or widely respected members of families or communities that might be able to play a more actively constructive role in addressing disputes.

Returning to the MEALAC case, we can now see that the Columbia community had many constructive resources already operating around the time of the initial intensification of the conflict. The Office of the Ombuds, the Office of Student Affairs, two well-known conflict resolution centers on campus,[19] student-based conflict resolution groups, interfaith religious figures and organizations, and interethnic tolerance-focused student organizations are just some of the well-known entities functioning at Columbia during this time. And it is likely that a more thorough scan of the social-political networks in the community would identify many other less obvious resources. Identifying, engaging, and supporting such groups and resources, even in a low-key manner, takes advantage of the existing infrastructure for enhancing constructive dynamics and respects the local knowledge and expertise of these actors.

4. Identify integrative catalysts. Another tactic for managing the overwhelming nature of complicated, evolving conflict systems is to attempt to identify *integrative catalysts.* Typically these are individuals who, for reasons of their own personal or professional development, somehow embody the different conflicting identities and tensions inherent to the conflict. They may simply be trusted friends or family members, or have multicultural or multiethnic identities, but typically they hold a special status that allows them to stay above the fray and not get forced onto one side or the other. Here is a quote from one such individual:

> I decided to go to the march to protest the complicity of the Israeli government in that massacre and the complicity of the Israeli army and calling for a commission of inquiry . . . As I got down to the march . . . there were a lot of Arabs that were marching with signs that said "Jewish star = swastika" and had pictures of the massacred babies that said "Israel has blood on its hands." Now I felt all of the sudden, "whoa—I cannot join that march." I really feel something wrong has happened here, that

it should be investigated, I feel that students have a right to speak out, but that message didn't resonate with me. It went right to the place of blame without even looking for facts or collecting information. I can't go there. On the other side of the street were all the Jewish student groups protesting the Arab student groups and responding to their messages saying "Israel right or wrong" and "Israel shouldn't come under anyone's scrutiny" and "Israel is above the law" and I thought "crap, I can't go over there either. I have nowhere to walk." And so at that moment some friends and I formed a third group.

—a Jewish Israeli, 2002

These integrative agents can present important opportunities for boundary spanning and peacemaking. They personify an integrative solution. In the history of the Middle East peace process, individuals like Yitzhak Rabin (a military hero and general in the Israeli army who turned peacemaker as prime minister), Anwar el Sadat (Egyptian president, Arab, former revolutionary, and peacemaker with Israel), and Amos Oz (Jewish Israeli writer and journalist, founder of the "land for peace" NGO Peace Now) have played such integrative, boundary-crossing roles. In intractable identity-based conflicts these roles are vital. They are at times fraught with danger—Rabin and Sadat were both assassinated by members of their own groups—and so need to be engaged and supported with proper caution and care.

5. Take time seriously: visualize the attractor landscape of the conflict. The many different conflict elements and networks of reinforcing and inhibiting feedback loops that make up the 5 percent ultimately work together to constitute the conflict's attractor landscape. In other words, the conflict maps provide a sketch of the *process architecture* of the conflict: how the skeleton, tissue, circulatory, and nervous systems of the living, evolving body of the conflict operate together. Conflict-mapping is like taking an X-ray of the internal workings of the body, an excellent tool for diagnosis and treatment planning.

Ultimately, however, we have found it useful to move from mapping to working with a simple visualization software program to begin to see how the different elements of a conflict interact together *over time*. This is critical for focusing our understanding on how the conflict system evolves and establishes temporal patterns or attractors across time.

THE ATTRACTOR SIMULATION: OVERVIEW

As described, a conflict system can be characterized on three dimensions: its current state, its potential for positive interactions, and its potential for negative interactions. But characterizing conflict on these three dimensions is not straightforward for most people. Moreover, any factor influencing a conflict system may affect each of the three aspects in different ways. For example, an increased police presence during a student protest at Columbia may decrease the momentary state of violence on campus. But it may also decrease the strength of the attractor for future positive interactions between the administration and the community, and at the same time increase the strength of the attractor for future negative interactions. Therefore, understanding the multiple consequences of an action can be a daunting task for anyone involved in a dynamic conflict.

The Attractor Software platform has been developed to assist disputants, conflict practitioners, policy makers, and other stakeholders in addressing conflicts without neglecting the dynamic properties and complexity of the systems in which they work. It allows them to see how all the pieces of their 5 percent puzzles fit together and evolve, and ideally how they can be changed.

The Attractor Software is a visualization tool designed to help users see the three dimensions of systems described above. It prompts the user to specify the key factors influencing the conflict (ideally generated from their mapping exercises), the actions that can be undertaken, and to estimate the consequences of these actions with respect to three types of outcomes (current state, potential positive, potential negative). By evaluating each factor, the user estimates the strength and the direction of the influence of each factor on the *whole conflict system*. The software merely visualizes the understanding of the user; it is a tool for describing what parties and interveners have identified, based on their own expertise, experience, and mapping of a case.

Research on the use of Attractor Software in conflict resolution trainings has shown promising effects.[20] Two studies conducted at the University of Warsaw in Poland compared the effects of training in Attractor Software to standard integrative negotiation training. All participants were trained in integrative negotiation; however, only one group learned to negotiate with the help of Attractor Software and the integrative negotiation model. Participants who worked with Attractor Software found it much easier to communicate with their negotiation partners and reported a better understanding of the negotiation process. But the most interesting finding was that although the groups did not differ in terms of their sense of satisfaction with the resolution of the conflict, there were significant differences in the long-term stability of the agreements the groups generated. In fact, each pair that negotiated with the help of Attractor Software achieved durable long-term solutions, whereas the majority of the other pairs failed to achieve such results. These findings speak to the fact that even a highly satisfying outcome may be not be durable; this fact may go unnoticed by the parties until the consequences of their actions come back to haunt them. Attractor Software can serve as a nontrivial yet simple tool that potentially increases the durability of agreements.

To date, the Attractor Software has been used in a variety of settings, including in New York City public schools, at the West Point military academy, at a state-level genocide prevention institute at Columbia University (Engaging Governments in Genocide Prevention), and in negotiation and mediation trainings in communities and at universities and conferences around the world. It is also being used by Dutch UN peacekeepers and FARC leaders in the Colombia conflict.

But don't let that intimidate you! The software was developed to be easy to use. Thousands of individual users have logged on to our website (http://www.iccc.edu.pl/as/introduction.html) to access and work with the program. I invite the reader to go to the appendix to read more about working with the Attractor Software.

In the next two sections we discuss the actions available for shaping the long-term potential patterns in conflicts. We move from the discussion of *understanding* the past and the present in a conflict to *acting* on the future. We do so by describing the practices and actions involved in working incrementally to transform the attractors themselves.

PRACTICE II: BUILD UP AND TEAR DOWN

Finding and implementing *sustainable solutions* to intractable conflicts essentially comes down to altering the system's attractor landscape. This may sound abstract, but it simply means thinking and working long term.

The film *American History X* provides an excellent illustration of some of the key principles of the Attractor Landscape Model, and in particular the role the future plays in changing intractable mindsets. It presents a disturbing yet compelling portrayal of a young man, Derek Vinyard, a brutal and charismatic neo-Nazi skinhead. Derek is a rising leader in the skinhead movement in the Venice Beach area of Los Angeles.

The film shows us how a constellation of factors—trauma from the early loss of his father, adolescent angst, inadequate parenting, racism, hard economic times, unemployment, peer modeling, idle time, manipulative adults, and a strong neo-Nazi ideology and propagandistic rhetoric—can combine to send a youth down the path of extreme hate and violence.

It also effectively portrays how the youth's attitudes, in-group and out-group perceptions, identities, politics, and behaviors collapse together; they form into simple, all-encompassing "us versus them" worldviews that focus on the annihilation of out-groups (minorities, gays, and immigrants are seen as insects that deserve to be exterminated). Most important, it artfully captures Derek's transformation. He suffers severe ruptures in his ultracoherent worldview; in prison, Derek is attacked by a group of skinheads, and later he is rescued from another gang by a young black man. Coupled with a *latent alternative identity* and a raison d'être—his deep love for his younger siblings and mother, who need his protection and leadership—these experiences lay the groundwork for his transition from a violent attractor to a man leading a dramatically more constructive life.

This laying of groundwork for constructive relations and peace is the primary aim of practice II. The main objectives here are to support and enhance latent positive attractors and make them *more attractive,* and to inhibit and deconstruct negative attractors to make them *less attractive.* To build up and tear down.

BUILD UP: GROWING HIDDEN POSSIBILITIES

Here the idea of *latent attractors* discussed earlier comes into play. We have found that the malignant thoughts, feelings, and actions that characterize a person's or group's dynamics in a 5 percent conflict represent only the most obvious attractor for the conflict. In particular, where there is a long history of interaction between people or groups, likely other potential patterns of mental, emotional, and behavioral engagement exist, including those promoting positive relations.

Take Ukraine and Poland. Relations between these countries had been hostile and tense for decades, going back to atrocities committed by both sides during World War II. However, their dealings go back many decades before the war, during which time they shared mutually beneficial trade and cultural relations. In fact, the strained relations that developed during and after World War II can be considered the exception rather than rule. Presumably, then, there existed an attractor for positive relations between Ukraine and Poland that was supplanted by a negative attractor during the war. It is therefore not completely surprising that the mutual antagonism, which had lasted for decades, gave way in a dramatic fashion to mutual solidarity during Ukraine's Orange Revolution in 2004–2005. In social relations, these types of "flips" from one attractor to another are more common than one might think. But they require the

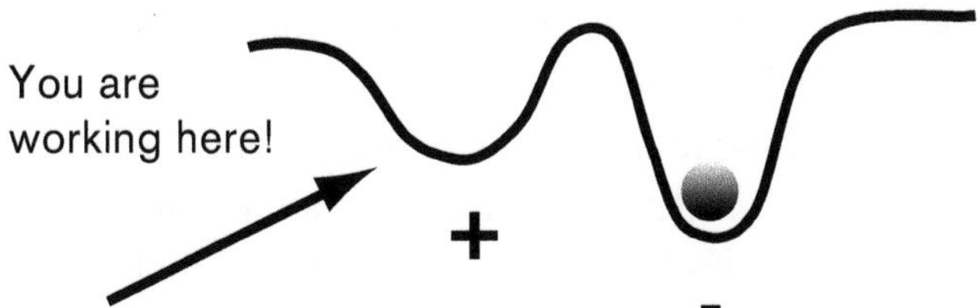

presence of a sufficiently robust latent alternative for the relational dynamics.

But latent dynamics are hard to see. Some changes in a system can be easily observed because they affect the current (overt) state of the system. Other changes, however, may only affect the *possible* states of the system and thus not be immediately apparent. Such changes may remain latent for extended periods of time, yet manifest rapidly in response to external influences and events that seem relatively minor. Although movement between attractors may be rapid and abrupt (back and forth between constructive and destructive patterns), *the change of attractors themselves is likely to be far slower and more gradual.* Thus, when a specific policy or intervention does not produce a visible effect, this does not mean that it is futile. Rather, such activities may be creating, deepening, or destroying latent attractors in a system. In other words, they may affect the range of possible states rather than the current state.

With this in mind, identifying and reinforcing latent positive attractors—"traps" for peaceful or constructive relations—should be among the principle aims of both conflict prevention and intervention. With the 5 percent, the identification, support, and initiation of constructive forces within the system (common projects, citizen exchanges, dialogues, etc.) are critical for increasing the long-term chances that peaceful relations will resurface—*whether they show short-term results or not.*

Below we outline a few of the many actions available for creating and bolstering positive latent attractors. They include (1) stop making sense, (2) alleviate constraints on constructive networks, (3) circumvent the conflict, (4) employ weak power, (5) construct chains, (6) build on serendipity, (7) identify superordinate goals and identities, (8) rebuild social capital, (9) protect experiments and prototypes, (10) leverage the irony in impossible conflicts.

1. Stop making sense. As discussed earlier, rational decision making and game theoretical strategies for maximizing outcomes typically have little to do with the long-term tendencies of enduring conflicts. Certainly, vested interests and calculated decisions play a role, but it's nothing like the bedrock role that affect (feelings of fear and hate, of loyalty and loss) plays in establishing the context for conflict dynamics. Emotions are the glue: the cement that holds attractors together. Some emotions also constitute a primary source of reinforcing feedback for the 5 percent. Feelings of anger and disgust, for instance, have been found to enhance a sense of certainty (coherence) in situations, thus bolstering attractors and future feelings of enmity.[21] Therefore, rational appeals for peace and tolerance will often fall well short of their objectives with the 5 percent.

With this in mind, we suggest that the main task involved in creating or enhancing latent positive attractors in the 5 percent is to help develop, foster, and trigger positive feelings between the parties. This may seem simplistic, but it's everything. In fact, the more distant these attempts are from rational persuasion, from obvious attempts at swaying emotions, the better.*

The good news is that if the parties had any type of constructive relationship prior to the conflict, or if they have had opportunities to experience each other's' humanity under better circumstances, likely there is some reservoir of positivity for their relationship, albeit latent. The bad news is the *negativity effect:* the finding that negative emotions have something like a five-to-one stronger impact than positive emotions on relationships.[22] This usually makes it much, much harder to foster positivity in a 5 percent relationship.

In his Love Lab, one of the methods psychologist John Gottman employs with couples in conflict is to assign positivity exercises.[23] He will give one partner in an estranged couple the task of noticing ten positive things the other partner does during a week. This tends to elicit positive behaviors from one partner, and make them salient and noticeable to the other. By reminding both partners of this potential in their relationship, this activity triggers and reinforces the positive attractor latent in their dynamic. Of course, this method assumes that parties are willing and able to engage in the task, which is often not the case in the 5 percent. Nevertheless, simple initiatives like cultural and citizen exchanges, sharing of

*Consider that confidence men and intelligence operatives often develop a wide range of subtle tactics for getting people to like them and their group, like leaving cartoons and comics around that portray their group in benevolent ways—seriously!

medical technologies, and disaster relief programs can go a long way in increasing positivity in an otherwise hostile relationship.

2. Alleviate constraints on constructive networks. As mentioned, virtually every conflict system, even the most dire, will contain people and groups who, despite the dangers, are willing to reach out across the divide and work to foster dialogue and peace. There are countless examples of this in the international arena: among Germans and Jews during the Nazi campaign in Europe during WWII; blacks and whites in South Africa in the 1980s; and today in places like Darfur, Somalia, Iran, and North Korea. These networks are often the centerpiece of latent constructive attractors for people and groups. However, the actions of these constructive agents are usually tightly constrained by the dynamics of the conflict. During times of intense escalation, these people and groups may become temporarily inactive; they may even go underground. But they are often willing to reemerge when conditions allow, becoming fundamental players in the transformation of the system. Thus, early interventions should engage with these individuals and networks, carefully, and work with them to help alleviate the constraints on their activities in a safe and feasible manner.

3. Circumvent the conflict. Recognizing that players in a conflict who have strong, negative 5 percent attractors often view peacemakers themselves as also being players in the theater of conflict, some interveners attempt to work constructively in these settings by *circumventing the conflict.*

The idea here is that a main reinforcing feedback loop of 5 percent conflicts is the *conflict trap.* This is a situation where the destructiveness of the conflict exacerbates the very negativity and strife that created the conflict conditions in the first place, and thereby perpetuates it. However, attempts to address these circumstances directly, in the context of a peace process, typically elicit resistance; they are seen as affecting the balance of power in the conflict (usually by supporting lower-power groups most affected by the conditions). Interveners recognizing this will work to address these conditions of hardship, without making any connection whatsoever to the conflict or peace processes. To some degree, this is what many community and international development projects try to achieve. The difference is that this tactic targets the conditions seen as most directly feeding the conflict, and requires that every attempt be made to divorce these initiatives from being associated with the peace process.

This approach is employed in some of the work of the Ashoka Fellows, social entrepreneurs working in zones of armed conflict. Typically, they are local people working in innovative ways to help rebuild social capital and provide a sense of efficacy in struggling communities. They address basic needs destroyed or neglected during a conflict, such as building community latrines in slums, organizing dances for idle youth, providing local phone networks to allow isolated people to better communicate with neighbors, etc.[24] This *unconflict resolution* strategy can help address some of the negativity and misery associated with conflicts, without becoming incorporated (attracted) into the polarized "good versus evil" narrative of the conflict. This is an important idea that has widespread implications for our understanding of peacemaking in settings with ultracoherent destructive attractors.

4. Employ *weak power*. Sometimes more direct intervention into a conflict is necessary. Employing *weak power* has proven effective at fostering positivity and eliciting less resistance.[25] Strong conflict systems, with wide and deep attractors for destructiveness and narrow and shallow attractors for peace, will often reject out of hand most strong-arm attempts to force peaceful relations. History provides countless examples of strong outside parties' failure to forge peace in such systems. Consider the relatively ineffectual role of the United States in brokering Middle East peace.

Nevertheless, sometimes peace does emerge out of long-term conflicts, and we suggest that one reason may be the power of powerlessness; that is, the unique influence people and groups with little formal or "hard" power (physical strength, military might, wealth) but effective "soft" power (trustworthiness, moral authority, wisdom, kindness) can have in these settings.[26] Weak-power third parties are at times able to carefully introduce a sense of hope for change in the status quo; a sense of doubt or dissonance in an ultracoherent "us versus them" meaning system. And they can also begin to model and encourage other more constructive means of conflict engagement (shuttle diplomacy, mediation, negotiations).

This is the extraordinary role that Leymah Gbowee and the Women's International Peace Network (WIPN) played in the early 2000s, when they helped end Liberia's decades-long civil wars.[27] This ordinary group of women—mothers, aunts, and grandmothers—organized amid the grueling armed conflict in Liberia, with no formal authority and few "hard" resources, and helped mobilize and shepherd the peace process between the government of strongman Charles Taylor and the rebels. For example, at one point in the war, UN peacekeepers were stuck in a protracted gun battle with rebel forces in the jungle and could see no way out. They contacted the WIPN, who arrived at the scene in their white T-shirts and headdresses. The women then entered the jungle with hands raised, dancing and singing. After spending two days there, feeding and speaking with the rebels, the women brought the rebels out of the jungle, ending the stalemate. Weak power can be powerful.

5. Construct chains. An increasingly popular tactic, designed to break through deadlocks and initiate peace talks in protracted conflicts, is the use of negotiation chains. This practice involves a sequence of actors in the exploration of more formal talks. Actor A speaks directly to actor B; A is not politically constrained against speaking to B, but B has contacts further down the chain with the other side. Talks transpire through a series of encounters that allow for communication between parties who (1) need to be able to maintain deniability in the talks, and (2) would otherwise not be able to communicate.

Such chains have been employed in a variety of 5 percent conflicts, including with Nelson Mandela in South Africa during apartheid and between leaders of Sinn Fein and the Unionist Party in Northern Ireland.[28] They are clearly one way of fostering or bolstering latent, positive potential under threatening conditions.

6. Build on serendipity. Sometimes good luck helps. Despite the effectiveness of some planned interventions, sometimes unexpected encounters can be much more effective. This is what we found in our research on attitudes of Palestinians and Israelis regarding the Middle East conflict: the lasting impact of early, serendipitous positive encounters with members of out-groups. It seems that the unexpected nature of these encounters made them distinct from planned encounters. For example:

> . . . but what happened when I went to Natanya I saw a different face of the Israelis than I saw from the ones at the bridge . . . I mean on the bridge all I saw was soldiers who searched me and humiliated me and made me wait and then like, you know, you have female soldiers who strip searched me and made me totally naked and leave the cubicle where I am . . . she wouldn't close the curtain . . . like I'm not even a human being . . . you now humble enough to be seen by everyone . . . so for me that is the only image I know. But when I went there it was a normal life people were sitting at the beach, you know, teenagers kissing and mothers babysitting and scholars sitting by the café so I've seen a different face and so I said no matter how I feel and no matter what it means to me I'm not going to but I'm not going to hate something that was done to us. I don't think I want to resolve a problem by creating another. There are some people here who are already established and I don't see them leaving . . . but now am looking for a solution that gives people the right to exist side by side. That's my first time to think about a two-state solution, before that time I always thought Palestine, the whole country is for Palestinians and nobody else but . . . so this was a transformation for me in 1972, and since then I have been working towards a peaceful solution that gives the rights of both people to live in their own separate states . . .

These surprising incidents were described as providing constructive motivation over long periods of time. Such experiences provided a buffering effect over the long term because they resided in the emotional memories of our participants and were a lasting reminder of the diversity and humanity of the enemy.

7. Identify superordinate goals and identities. This is a classic approach to addressing intergroup conflict. It involves the identification or introduction of joint goals or superordinate identities between parties in conflict, in an attempt to establish a foundation of cooperation and eventual trust between them. In fact, this strategy was the centerpiece of UNESCO's Culture of Peace Project, a notable initiative aimed at establishing peaceful relations in pre- and post-conflict settings like El Salvador, Mozambique, Burundi, Congo, Guatemala, and Nicaragua.

Seen from the perspective of attractor landscapes, finding common ground between parties, emphasizing shared goals and concerns, facilitating trust-building activities, and incentivizing cooperative conflict resolution initiatives—although they may appear to be largely ineffective in situations locked in an ongoing protracted struggle—may in fact be acting slowly and indirectly to establish a sufficiently wide and deep attractor basin for moral, humane forms of intergroup relations. One day, these initiatives may provide the foundation for a stable, peaceful future.

8. Rebuild social capital. Five percent conflicts affect a broad swath of families and communities, often pervading even mundane aspects of their lives. This can include affecting decisions about where to shop and eat, who to play and visit with, and when it's safe to travel or even go outside. This degree of impact impairs the basic conditions for trust, cohesion, support, and functioning in family and community life.

Thus, in contrast to the formal peace-building strategies of track-one diplomacy (official negotiations), or even the less formal track-two initiatives (semiofficial activities), track-three activities have been developed to work from the bottom up in conflict zones. They involve working with the most directly affected members of groups and communities to address the day-to-day consequences of the ongoing conflict. As Louise Diamond, originator of the concept of multitrack diplomacy, has suggested, it is these types of local bottom-up initiatives that must occur if an infrastructure for peace is to be built and sustained.[29]

9. Protect experiments and prototypes. One strategy for cultivating and sustaining positive systemic change is through the identification or establishment of strong but isolated prototypes of the desired change; prototypes that can survive long enough to test and then facilitate the transfer of changes throughout the broader system.[30] These experiments can be used as systemic probes to explore and learn about a system's reactions to the proposed change.

For instance, it could serve Columbia University to identify and communicate its best examples of departments on campus, where interethnic relations are constructive and healthy, emphasizing the specific conditions and processes that maintain such relations. Alternatively, Columbia could provide support and political cover to groups of Palestinian and Israeli students and faculty able to design and implement innovative or exemplary approaches to coexistence. (Turath's and LionsPAC's joint Project Tolerance is a likely candidate.) These types of experiments, when successful, can help create a new sense of possibility.

This is essentially what Laura Chasin and her organization, PCP, were able to do with the pro-life and pro-choice dialogue group in Boston. The initiative was launched in secret, and PCP was able to protect the anonymity of the group for several years, until the members themselves felt confident enough about their process and outcomes to go public. What was critical here was the facilitator's capacity to *protect the boundaries of the experiment* (and in this case the lives and livelihoods of the participants) as long as was necessary.

10. Leverage the irony in impossible conflicts. Finally, we suggest that the growth of latent positive attractors may in some cases be an inevitable consequence of developing a strong, negative 5 percent attractor. That's right. In other words, the stronger the dynamics of self-organizing intractable conflict, the higher the likelihood that a latent potential for peace is growing. Why? Because in emphasizing the negative aspects of a relationship while ignoring or downplaying its more positive elements, people often have to suppress or discount particular thoughts and behaviors. These suppressed elements may themselves become self-organized to promote their own more positive attractor. Under certain conditions, the latent attractors formed in this way may suddenly become manifest.

Research on thought suppression supports this idea. It has found that many types of thought become hyperaccessible after attempts to suppress them.[31] In one study, people were asked to write essays about a day in the life of a skinhead; some were to use stereotypes and others not. The participants instructed *not* to use stereotypes were found later to have these stereotypes more in the forefront of their minds.[32] Scholars believe this occurs because of a mental monitoring process that scans our conscious thought for the presence of unwanted content: for instance, "That was a lovely gesture my enemy just made." As this thought-suppression process occurs, it repeatedly activates this information in our memories, making it even more pronounced.

This scenario has some surprising consequences. Very strong attractors will often exclude a wide variety of information discrepant from our main point of view. An explicitly peaceful overture by an out-group, for example, is difficult to reconcile with the in-group's negative attitude, and thus may be discounted as an anomaly. Should enough incidents like this occur, however, they may begin to coalesce into a new or latent attractor reflecting benign or positive attitudes toward the out-group. At this point, if an event or intervention temporarily defuses the conflict, the newly formed latent attractor could suddenly become manifest and redirect the in-group's thoughts, feelings, and actions vis à vis the out-group. More research needs to be conducted to investigate this potential.

To summarize, if a 5 percent conflict represents a strong attractor for a system, then any deviation from this state of conflict will result in the system activating its mechanisms to return to the attractor. This is especially likely if the system lacks or has lost attractors for positive interaction. So while the *severity* of conflict may be related to the intensity or amount of violence between individuals or between groups, the *intractability* of conflict may be understood as *the loss of alternative sustainable states of positive interaction.* In complexity-science terms, an intractable conflict landscape lacks attractors for stable positive relations.

However, the gradual and long-term construction of positive attractors may be occurring imperceptibly, preparing the ground for a future stable positive state. Of course, short-term emergency programs often need to focus on eliminating the triggers that fuel catastrophic conflict or violence in the system. However, these types of initiatives will be insufficient and ultimately ineffective if they are not supported by long-term incremental work on growing latent positive attractors.

TEAR DOWN: DISMANTLING DESTRUCTIVE TRAPS

This is the mirror opposite of building up. It emphasizes the importance of working actively to break down destructive conflict attractors, which are usually still operating in a latent manner even after more constructive relations have re-emerged. The objective here is to make negative attractors *less attractive.*

Of course, the most obvious need in difficult conflicts is to quell the hostilities or violence and do what you can to contain destructive processes. This is often done by separating the disputants by introducing authority figures, third parties, or, in the case of large-scale community disputes, police or peacekeeping troops or other forms of regional or international military support.

However, even when conflict intensity diminishes and disputants appear to move into a state of relative calm, it is critical that we recognize that the lure of destructive interactions still exists. Attractors often remain as potent and alluring as ever when latent, even at times increasing in strength. It is critical, then, that we recognize when coming out of a conflict that the current state of peace is most likely temporary and therefore work actively to deconstruct and dismantle the infrastructure of negative attractors.

There are a variety of actions useful for dismantling negative attractors, including (1) work down below, (2) honor emotion, (3) decouple reinforcing feedback loops, (4) introduce inhibiting feedback loops, (5) awaken the third side, (6) institutionalize more nuanced conflict narratives, (7) limit the spread of negativity through movement, and (8) foster repellers for violence.

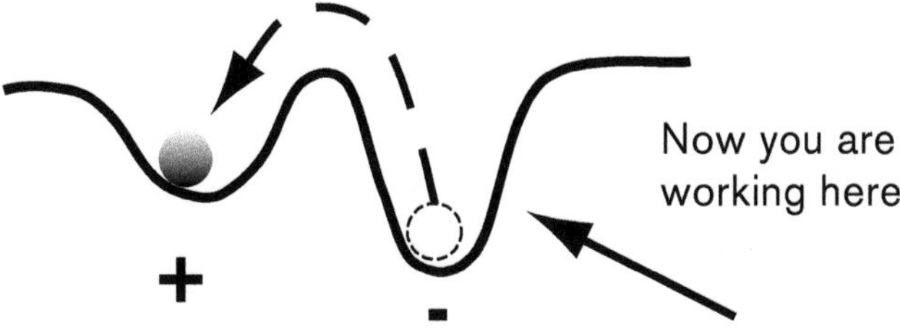
Now you are
working here
+
-

1. Work down below. Generally speaking, breaking down attractors most readily occurs from the bottom up. Social psychological research shows that global mental states such as strong identities or attitudes, or even fervent beliefs regarding "truths," can be effectively disassembled into their lower-level elements; that is, into the different component parts that constitute the attitude or belief. Doing so can create the potential for a wholesale change in people's understanding of their own and others' actions.[33] For example, pointing out multiple exceptions to a negative out-group stereotype can degrade the influence of the stereotype on behavior. We call this *reverse engineering*.

With conflict, this means calling attention to specific actions, events, and pieces of information without making the connection to the global pattern in which they are embedded. When decoupled in this fashion, these lower-level elements can become reconfigured into an entirely different pattern (e.g., a more positive view of the out-group and benign interaction pattern). It is like making small adjustments in the mechanics of a tennis stroke or a golf swing that lead to radical changes in the player's overall game.

Psychological research provides clues regarding this "disassembly process." It suggests that disruptions to ongoing action tend to make people sensitive to the overlearned details of the action, as do instructions to focus on the details of a narrative rather than on the narrative's larger meaning. For instance, the instruction "Drive the car" will elicit a more automatic, global response from experienced drivers. But when asked to "Grasp the steering wheel, turn the ignition key, place the car into drive, put slight pressure on the gas pedal with your right foot," the driver will have a less familiar or coherent experience, and become more vulnerable to reconsidering how best to drive.

This occurred in the abortion case in Boston, when the shock of the violent shootings at family-planning clinics forced pro-life and pro-choice leaders to carefully reexamine their rhetoric and actions, and to forge new approaches to their activism. They moved from their global action of "fighting for a righteous cause" to a more careful consideration of the consequences of their specific actions. When habitual actions are made salient in this way, people become vulnerable to new interpretations that can lead to a different, coherent perspective. In effect, the tack is to recapture the complexity of a conflict attractor and reconfigure the elements to promote a more benign form of coherence.

For instance, assume that Columbia University's administration had been prepared early on to publicly refute, with data, each new "anti-Israel bias" accusation, showing each to be false. This type of specific information, unlike general claims of innocence, might have inhibited the links political agitators were attempting to forge in people's minds: links between individual actions (a classroom altercation) and a broader political agenda (a concerted anti-Israel campaign at Columbia). But as the details of each incident were left unaddressed, it became easier for them to add up in people's minds and link to broader conspiracy theories.

In a similar vein, the deconstruction of what had become a one-dimensional conflict at Columbia (pro-Palestinian versus pro-Israeli) into a multitude of smaller issue-specific conflicts (regarding professional respect, freedom of speech, grievance processes, and so forth) would be another approach to breaking down the attractor by increasing complexity from the bottom-up. For instance, round-table negotiations could be implemented that center on a large set of independently defined issues, with "subtables" for each of the many issues in dispute. This growth of complexity, brought about by decoupling important issues, may not only provide solutions for the specific issues at stake, but also start a self-organizing process that lowers the intensity of the conflict and paves the way for the development of a more constructive attractor for the parties.

The important point is that attacking a destructive (global) pattern in the 5 percent directly is likely to intensify rather than weaken the pattern, because of the tendency for attractors to resist change. Therefore, one should focus instead on isolating and addressing lower-level elements, thereby weakening or eliminating the reinforcing feedback loops between them and matters of general principle.

2. Honor emotions. Establishing conditions that enable people *to accept and navigate intensely negative emotions is pivotal to deconstructing destructive attractors.* Being able to move on with one's life after experiencing traumatic losses due to conflict is a daunting task. The inability to forgive oneself and others, as well as becoming psychologically paralyzed by feelings associated with conflict are common. However, research has identified a few adaptive strategies for managing such emotions in the context of ongoing conflict, including *compartmentalization* and *channeling.*[34]

Compartmentalization entails psychologically separating one's potentially disabling emotions from one's current actions and reactions. For example, one Palestinian-Israeli remarked:

> I mean, it is really unreal what is happening . . . I don't know how people under curfew, no food for children, people can't go to work, people even who have money can't go to buy . . . can't go to buy food . . . Well, regardless of how I feel about this . . . I'm really being just open and frank and giving my . . . this is a study and I don't want to just gloss it over . . . so this is how I feel, these are my feelings . . . but at the same time I'm working to establish an equal solution and that is where I am at . . . Like I say, sometimes I give a metaphor . . . it's like if I have in my house a piece of furniture that are my family heirlooms but they don't fit anymore in my living room, I may put them in the attic but it doesn't mean I'm going to throw them away . . . I could go up there and visit them and remember them, but you know I settled to the fact that they are not in my living room and that it is how it is . . .

Alternatively, channeling involves tapping strong emotions as a source of motivation for constructive change. For example:

> Mostly because I don't do well with hopelessness. It doesn't sit well with me. It's a theme in my life. I definitely go there sometimes, but I don't want to live there. I think my antidote to hopelessness is to figure out ways to take action . . .
>
> Okay, so you get angry . . . what you do with it, that is the question I always ask myself . . . lately I have been trying to gather this energy of being angry and channel it into productive steps and measures, and that is very difficult to do . . . you know we are all human beings . . . I'm no Dalai Lama here . . . okay, I'm not the Dalai Lama . . . there is a lot of compas-

sion but I'm not somebody who reached a point that when every time he is angry can do something positive about it. It's a tough process . . .

Respecting the emotional terrain of 5 percent conflicts must be the centerpiece of change initiatives. These strategies are not without their own long-term consequences, but they are often necessary conditions for destabilizing destructive traps.

3. Decouple *reinforcing feedback loops* that feed destructive conflicts. Conflict attractors develop as separate issues, events, people, and other aspects of conflict become linked by reinforcing feedback to promote a global perspective and action orientation. In the Columbia case, the global message was that "all Columbia faculty are anti-Israeli and must be exposed and thwarted." Reverse engineering entails decoupling some of the feedback loops, thereby lowering the level of coherence in the system.

There are a variety of strategies for delinking reinforcing feedback loops that contribute to complexity collapse and escalation. These are best determined through the initial mapping of the escalatory system. After identifying the relevant elements and the nature of their linkage, one is in a position to disrupt the most important linkages and thereby decouple the elements and issues. To some degree, this is what occurs in the context of many mediations and problem-solving workshops; although typically with a more narrow focus on the issues, not on how the issues and other elements in the conflict feed or inhibit one another. By itself, decoupling does not guarantee the solution to the conflict, but it does pave the way for disassembling the conflict structure so the issues can be addressed separately.

Depending on the nature of the conflict, disassembling its feedback structure may take different forms. Recall that the collapse of complexity associated with the 5 percent happens along many dimensions, and thus opportunities for decoupling are many.

- **From "this is all very *simple*" to "it is in fact a very *complicated* situation."** The National Issues Forum, a not-for-profit organization that works to ebb the tide of polarization over hot topics in communities, takes this approach.[35] It provides community groups with a variety of different perspectives on current hot-button social issues, and then facilitates small-group learning dialogues aimed at reintroducing nuance into overly simplistic discourse on the issue. Conflict mapping, counseling sessions, interethnic dialogue groups, and other methods of exposure to less simplified, polarized narratives and media reporting can also help here.

- **From a focus on matters of general *principle* to concrete *details* in the conflict.** The approach taken to the seeming intractable conflict between the Soviet-backed communist government and the pro-democracy Solidarity opposition in Poland in 1989 illustrates this tactic. Verging on civil war, the deadlock between these factions was broken by the implementation of the Polish Round Table Talks, which involved a variety of "subtable" talks focusing on specific elements of the negotiated new system, such as education, unions, the media, political institutions, the economy, and health care. These negotiations initiated the first free elections in Poland since World War II, the implementation of a new democratic system, and the collapse of the communist regime. Such a peaceful revolution was made possible by the transformation of the previous dynamic, where intractability over political rule was at a stalemate, to a new lower-level dynamic where in-depth discussions over the multitude of issues concerning the nation could be addressed. Significantly, this change did much to eliminate the conflict that had defined the political situation in Poland for almost half a century.
- **From concerns over *defending* one's identity, ideology, and values to concerns over obtaining *accurate* information regarding substantive issues.** Research shows that under certain conditions, important decisions will be made more *systematically* (thoughtfully) than *heuristically* (automatically), with a particular concern for obtaining as accurate information as possible.[36] These conditions include low physical threat, high psychological safety, low noise, few cognitive demands, comfortable temperatures, and little time pressure. These conditions are typically provided in ongoing citizen exchanges like the interactive problem-solving workshops

developed by John Burton, Chris Mitchell, Herb Kelman, and others[37] and the Dartmouth Conference, the longest sustained bilateral dialogue between American and Soviet citizens; the conference began in 1960 and contributed to a peaceful transition between their countries after the Cold War.[38]

- **From "they (out-group) are all *alike* (evil)" to "they are made up of many *different* types of individuals."** If the structure of conflict binds together perceptions of all the out-group members, then showing positive examples of specific out-group members (particularly more than one) can increase complexity, since a single judgment cannot accommodate all the out-group members. This is what occurred in the serendipitous encounter between a Palestinian boy and a kindly Jewish man described in chapter 4. Another tack is to identify a set of issues for which the structure of self-interest is shared by the in-group and out-group. Acceptance of a cooperative structure of interests is usually not consistent with the simplified assumption of overall out-group incompatibility.
- **From "we (in-group) are all *similar* (saintly victims)" to "we are made up of many *different* types of individuals."** On the other hand, if the structure of conflict binds together perceptions of all the in-group members, referencing questionable or negative examples of specific in-group members can increase complexity, since a single judgment will no longer be able to accommodate all the in-group members. This is one of the main factors that led to the awakening and transformation of the skinhead leader depicted in *American History X*. Another tack is to work with high-status in-group members who do not share the in-group's view of the conflict. If these individuals are sufficiently central that they cannot be marginalized within the group, the homogeneity of the in-group will be destabilized.
- **From "I am always *consistent* in this conflict" to "I hold many *contradictions* within myself in terms of what I value, think, and do in this conflict."** Under conditions of high psychological safety such as those facilitated by Laura Chasin and PCP during the Boston dialogues, people are much more able to reflect, explore,

and identify their own internal contradictions (I am pro-choice *and* I respect a pro-life leader). Recognizing their own discrepancies fosters more tolerance for out-groups; this can open disputants up to taking more responsibility for their role in the conflict and its solution.[39]

- **From "I feel *only* an overwhelming sense of enmity and hate" to "I feel many *different* things about this conflict: good, bad, and ambivalent."** The research from our Intractable Conflict Labs shows that even relatively minor cognitive interventions that introduce more complexity into disputants' intellectual understanding of difficult conflicts can create a dynamic where their emotional experiences open up; they experience more vacillation between positive and negative emotions, which is associated with more constructive encounters. This is one of the most surprising findings from this research: that minor changes in the complexity of information lead to substantial changes in the ratios of positive-to-negative emotional experiences in these moral discussions.
- **From immediate *short-term* reactions and concerns to *longer-term* thinking and planning.** There are several methods for reorienting disputants from immediate toward future concerns. One such practice, developed by Elise Boulding, is called *focused social imaging.*[40] It begins by identifying some of the social concerns shared by stakeholders regarding the conflict (such as reducing community violence or improving community health services). The participants are then asked to temporarily disregard the current realities of the situation and to step twenty to thirty years into the future, when their concerns have been effectively dealt with. As the participants begin to develop some sense of the social arrangements and institutions in this idealized future, discussion ensues. Together, they begin to create a vision for a community that has the institutions and relationships necessary to effectively address their shared concerns. Then the participants are asked to move slowly backward in time, and to begin identifying the steps that would precede the establishment of such institutions and relationships. This is both a creative and a critical process of examining the

achievement of their ideal future in the context of the circumstances likely to exist between the present and such a future. Ultimately, this process results in both a vision and a plan for making the vision a reality. It can also serve to open up the participants' awareness of options and approaches to the conflict that they previously found impossible to imagine.

- **From employing very *simple rules* (if X, then Y, period) to using more *nuanced, flexible rules* of conflict engagement (if X, then Y, unless A, B, C, or maybe even D are true).** In tightly coupled complex systems, rules rule. Very basic rules for behavior, if followed by most people, can have profound emergent effects on the system's dynamics. Our lab research has found that more simple and inflexible rules for conflict engagement (if you cross me, I must harm you) lead to much more destructive dynamics than more nuanced rules (if you cross me, I must harm you, unless it was unintentional, or you were forced to do it, or you were simply messing around, or . . .). Thus, identifying the underlying rules for conflict (such as honor codes, different rules for in-group versus out-group members, rules for responding to moral digressions) and working to introduce more nuance into them can have widespread long-term effects. Again, this is also what occurred in the Boston community between 1994 and 2000, as the leaders' rules for engagement and public discourse with the other side relaxed considerably, resulting in the emergence of more civil community discussions regarding abortion.
- **From *only* encountering members of the out-group in conflict or *never* encountering them directly to encountering them in many *different settings* (at work, at play, at worship).** Research shows that enhancing and increasing the number of integrated or crosscutting social structures is one of the most effective ways of making intergroup conflict manageable, because it creates structural conditions that make it difficult to collapse into "us versus them." These socials structures include ethnically integrated schools, playgrounds, houses of worship, business associations, trade unions, professional groups, political parties, and sports

clubs. A comprehensive study of Hindu-Muslim violence in India found exactly this. Interethnic communities in India that had separate institutions for employment, shopping, education, etc., for Hindus and Muslims were significantly more likely to engage in violence against members of the other group, when conflicts arose, than were communities that had more integrated groups and institutions.[41]

- **From "these conflicts are all linked" to "this one stands alone."** Studies of long-term international conflicts have shown their tendency to become strongly interconnected with other enduring conflicts, which increase their potential for escalation and intractability.[42] The delinking of these different conflicts has also been found to be related to the termination phase of these enduring rivalries. For instance, the decline in intensity of the Cold War between the United States and the USSR happened around the same time that tensions between the United States and China declined.
- **From having one action *option* available (escalation) to having *more*.** Sometimes simply modeling or introducing new action strategies—increasing a disputant's sense of options in a seemingly overly constrained situation—can go a long way in alleviating the stress associated with being trapped by a 5 percent; it can therefore open disputants up to more nuanced perceptions, emotions, and actions. This is essentially the strategy that Charles Osgood proposed in his GRIT theory (graduated reciprocation in tension reduction) for deescalating the arms race between the USSR and the United States during the Cold War. It simply presented unilateral deescalation, by way of offering good-faith initiatives to one's opponent, as another feasible option. This is also what reportedly occurred in the context of the Northern Ireland peace process, after observing how a negotiated settlement was reached in South Africa between the African National Congress and the De Klerk government. Options.

4. Introduce *inhibiting feedback loops* that interrupt escalatory spirals. Once the reinforcing feedback system of conflict escalation is mapped, it can help to target specific links for the introduction of inhibiting feedback mechanisms. This includes tactics such as establishing early-warning systems to notify officials when ethnic or racial tensions heat up, increasing the presence of "neutral" monitors or observers in areas where conflicts tend to be triggered (for instance, at school bus stops around urban schools where violence is prevalent), and increasing the number of crosscutting structures (such as joint sports teams, political clubs, and workgroups described above), which tends to discourage intergroup polarization.

At Columbia University for example, negative feedback could be institutionalized in the form of an early-warning system operated through the Ombuds Office. The office could monitor college-wide patterns of claims of disrespect, academic abuse, discrimination, and interethnic tensions on campus, and report back to the community in a timely and transparent manner. Many human rights groups use a similar technique of "naming and shaming"—publicly outing individuals, groups, and nations engaged in egregious violations of human rights—as a method of curtailing behaviors. This is a clear example of the use of data collection, public reporting, and shame to provide inhibiting feedback in order to decrease or end destructive policies or activities.

5. Awaken the "third side." William Ury of the Harvard Program on Negotiation coined the term *third side* to characterize the invaluable roles community members can play in preventing, resolving, and containing destructive conflict.[43] Too often, majorities in communities relegate peacemaking and peace-building to a select few: public officials, diplomats, mediators, and other conflict professionals. This is a fatal mistake with the 5 percent. The successful transformation of these landscapes requires all hands.

Engaging multiple sectors is a strategy also advocated by former U.S. ambassador John McDonald of the Institute for Multi-track Diplomacy.[44] He has worked for years to engage the business communities in India and Pakistan to become active proponents of peace in Kashmir. Ambassador McDonald emphasizes the bottom line for business; he presents cost-benefit ratios of the impact of violence on tourism and other aspects of the economy and offers evidence of what could be gained in a peaceful Kashmir. In a study we conducted, he stated:

> Historically the business community has always disassociated itself from the conflict . . . I said, what do you think about trying to get the business community of India and Pakistan involved? . . . if a business takes a longer-term vision of the whole thing, supports what we're trying to do over the next four or five years, they can then go in and invest in Kashmir because there will be a reduction in violence . . . and so we went there and did our training."[45]

And this is just one track of their nine-track approach to peace-building, which includes government, professional conflict resolution, business, private citizens, research and education, peace activism, religion, and funding organizations. They believe no single track, like diplomacy, can effectively sustain peace in these situations. It takes awakening and mobilizing a community.

6. Institutionalize more nuanced conflict narratives. Five percent conflicts typically result in (and are perpetuated by) biased narratives in families, schools, communities, and the media about the history of the conflict; who played the roles of hero and villain and what is still at stake. Mechanisms to monitor and revise such one-sided narratives are essential for preventing future generations from returning to the same destructive patterns.

Monitoring these institutionalized forms of bias is the primary activity of IMPACT-SE (Institute for Monitoring Peace and Cultural Tolerance in School Education). It examines school curricula worldwide, especially throughout the Middle East, to determine whether the material conforms to international standards, and to analyze what is being taught with regard to recognition and acceptance of the "other." Typically, it conducts annual analyses of the official-history curricula of schools in conflict zones, to identify the degree of bias in the presentation of polarizing historical events (wars, revolutions, freedom fighters versus terrorists, etc.). It then publicizes the findings in an attempt to put pressure on education ministry officials to correct biased or unnecessarily inflammatory accounts.

7. Limit the accumulation of negativity through movement. Negativity is a potent force. Possessing the impact of about five times that of positive experiences, it can have an overwhelming effect on social relations. Negativity resulting from violence will have an even greater impact. We have learned from trauma research that negative encounters have a tendency to accumulate, both psychologically and socially, over time. However, our research on conflict conducted through computer-based modeling of the spread of negativity in 5 percent conflicts has led to the paradoxical finding that *movement* is key to dissipating negativity in community relations.[46]

Typically, dominant powers will attempt to ghettoize their opponents during periods of open conflict, in an attempt to better monitor and control them. We have found that these are the ideal conditions for the intensification of malignancy in conflict; hostilities are more likely to fester and grow when groups are constrained in one location. This is exactly what occurred during the independence struggle in Algeria in the 1950s and 1960s, when the French limited the movement of non-French Algerians to the Kasbah. This constraint led to the festering of resentments and the organization of insurgents. Alternatively, systems where negativity is relatively unconstrained, and where members of groups are allowed to travel and disperse, will tend to show a dissipation of negativity over time. This is a counterintuitive finding with substantial implications for policy and practice.

8. Foster repellers for violence. Violent acts often represent a tipping point in conflicts, a threshold very difficult to return from. Fortunately, most communities have laws and other prohibitions against physical violence, establishing what we call *repellers* in complexity parlance. In fact, archeological research suggests that communal taboos against violence have existed for the bulk of human existence, and were a central feature of the prehistoric nomadic hunter-gatherer bands. Indeed, a key characteristic of peaceful groups and societies, both historically and today, is the presence of nonviolent values, norms, ideologies, and practices.[47]

Although nonviolent norms are practiced in many communities around the globe, they are often overwhelmed by more violent ideologies and social modeling. Yet there exists a wide variety of parenting and educational methods for fostering more nonviolent, pro-social attitudes and skills in children: violence prevention, tolerance, cooperative learning, conflict resolution, and peace education curricula, to name a few. The socialization and indoctrination of constructive, nonviolent methods of problem solving for both children and adults is a central force for dismantling the war-system of the 5 percent and sustaining peace.

To SUM UP: *work on building up and breaking down latent and manifest attractors is the cornerstone of the ALM approach.* This is the case for both negative (undesirable) and positive (desirable) attractors in a social system. Campus riots, for example, are usually initiated in a very rapid fashion, but are invariably preceded by a series of incidents, such as the humiliation of individuals, discriminatory acts, or the denial of basic rights. Since each of these specific instances is not necessarily dramatic in itself, group opposition to them (inhibiting feedback) may be fairly minimal and contained. Each incident, however, creates and deepens a latent attractor for hostilities that can subsequently determine the pattern of interaction. Once an attractor for destructive conflict has been firmly established, relatively small provocations may move the system into this attractor, thereby dragging the whole system into full-blown conflict.

At Columbia University, the screening of *Columbia Unbecoming* served as this trigger. But even more minor events may trigger a "tipping point," if they move the system into a different attractor. By the same token, positive acts by one group toward another (as is occurring in the joint tolerance initiative on the Columbia campus) may not have any immediate observable effect. Nonetheless, such acts can pave the way for the sudden escape from a negative attractor by building or bolstering a positive attractor into which the system can move. It is important to emphasize that latent attractors not only provide a foundation for conflict resolution, but also pose the risk of a rapid return to hostile feelings and actions. The resolution of a conflict, then, does not necessarily mean that no further effort is required. As long as the attractor of destructive conflict remains, it holds potential for recapturing the dynamics of the system.

PRACTICE III: CHANGE TO STABILIZE

But what about right now?

Practice II provides a wide range of actions for altering the *potential landscape* of the disputants' relationship and therefore can affect the *possible future states* of the 5 percent conflict. But what about today? What can we do now to get unstuck from the depths of an attractor and get on with our life?

Practice III is about change and stability. It is about the things we need to do in order to produce a *qualitative change* in the current state of the conflict (moving the conflict between attractors) or in the character of the landscape. It is about knowing when social conflicts are *ripe* for change; it is about discovering those *few things that change everything* (altering attractor landscapes). And it is about *understanding the difference,* in terms of time and impact, of various change strategies. But it is mostly about fostering stability through sustainable change. This comes from enhancing our abilities to adapt.

1. Leverage Instability. Remember that coherence and stability in social conflicts are not the enemy until they become the enemy. But when absolute certainty about "us versus them" and "good versus evil" take over in a conflict and provide *the* foundation for understanding and *the* platform for action, then you are likely operating in the grips of the 5 percent. And it's probably time to change things up. Here the challenge becomes what the organizational theorist Gareth Morgan calls "opening the door to instability."[48] This entails either capitalizing on existing conditions or creating new conditions that in fact *destabilize* the system.

For instance, imagine that you are a consultant called in to work with a company on the ongoing tensions and declining productivity of a

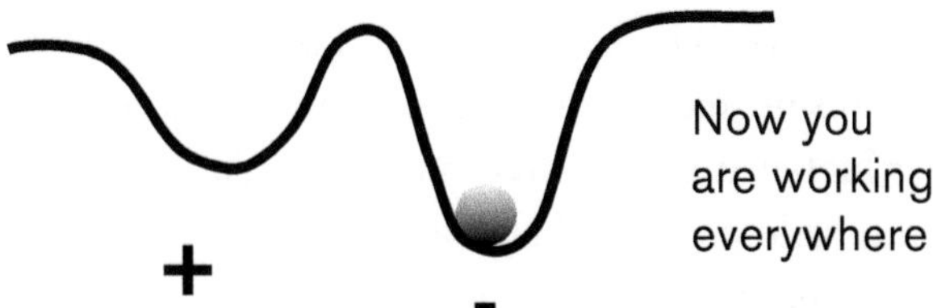
Now you
are working
everywhere
+
-

previously top-functioning R&D team. After an initial investigation, you learn that the team has been run for years by a very efficient but somewhat brutal boss, who typically enjoys berating and publicly humiliating members of the team and staff. As this is "business as usual" on the team and to some degree in the industry (entertainment), and as they were functioning as one of the more effective R&D teams in the firm, everyone went along with his style of leadership for years. Despite mounting resentment, this was the status quo of the attractor of this team.

Then something happened. One of the newer hires reported being sexually harassed by the team leader. And then it became clear this type of behavior had been going on for years. The other women had all simply been too fearful and concerned about losing their place on the team to go public with accusations. Once word got out, everything changed. Upper management came down on him, and the other members of the team began refusing to accept his hostility; in meetings, they started calling him out on his behavior. The climate of the team meetings became very contentious, and their productivity declined precipitously.

There are many ways to understand what happened at this firm—legal, moral, psychological—but from a complexity-science perspective, the leader broke the boundaries of the attractor. The entire team had been captured by a destructive attractor of conflict: abuse and fear at work that had become commonplace and seemingly tolerable for most. However, when the leader preyed on a new hire insufficiently socialized by the system, she blew the whistle. And when others on the team learned about the sexual harassment, they considered it outside the bounds of their (implicit) agreement of acceptable behavior. This transgression destabilized the system and sent it into free fall.

This was an opportunity to challenge the status quo of abusive work norms (the attractor) in the team and at the firm. Such challenges to "business as usual" will certainly meet with many forms of resistance: established mind-sets (this is the way it is and probably the best way to get things done in this business), ensconced power relations, vested interests (such as other higher-ups who may employ similar practices), even simply habits; automatic codes of behavior difficult to break. Nevertheless, this phase of instability presents an important opportunity for change.

And these destabilizing opportunities can be created as well as discovered. If you as a consultant investigate the team and uncover the business-as-usual abuses, you could act unilaterally to destabilize the system. For example, you could inform the leader's superiors that his abusive style is costing the company in turnover, absenteeism, and productivity. Or you could inform his employees of their right to protect themselves, as established by company policy, in order to change their understanding of the acceptability of his behaviors. If the acts you uncover are illegal, you could inform outside authorities. These are often difficult ethical and professional decisions. They are also risky choices, as the defensive forces operating in the dominant attractor may react by chewing you up and spitting you out. And you could also jeopardize the employees' positions as well. But destabilize, they would. The point is that whether they are happenstance or intentionally triggered, periods of instability can provide important opportunities to shift out of attractors and to begin to alter conflict landscapes.

2. Ride Shock Waves. One leading way that instability occurs in 5 percent conflicts is through major shocks to the system. In fact, research on international conflict has found that significant political shocks are associated with both the onset and the resolution of the 5 percent.[49] The shock may be a world war, civil war, a significant change in territory and power relations, regime change, an independence movement, or a transition to democracy. In the personal realm this translates to a loss of employment, a weather-related disaster, or a family crisis.

In a study of the approximately 850 enduring conflicts that occurred throughout the world between 1816 to 1992, over 95 percent began *within a ten-year period* following at least one major political shock.[50] From the ALM perspective, these shocks created fissures in the previous system, eventually leading to the establishment of the necessary conditions for the major restructuring and realignment of conflict landscapes—for catastrophic conflict.

But the reverse also occurred. Over three-quarters of the enduring conflicts ending within this period also did so within ten years of a major political shock. Again, such shocks destabilize conflict systems and allow for the deconstruction and reconstruction of the attractor landscape. This may take years to become evident, as the initial shock most likely affects factors that affect other factors and so on, until overt changes occur. It is important to note, however, that such ruptures to the coherence and stability of sociopolitical systems do not ensure radical change or peace. It must therefore be considered a necessary but insufficient condition.

3. Grow Ripeness. In standard conflict resolution parlance, *ripeness* is defined as the willingness of disputants to negotiate peace that is motivated by two conditions: a *mutually hurting stalemate* between parties, where both are losing and neither can win, coupled with a *mutually enticing opportunity* to gain a more favorable outcome in the conflict.[51] Ripeness has been the focus of much attention in the thinking about motivation and change in conflict and conflict resolution.

In our research, we found this perspective on ripeness to be only partially valid; it misses something important, especially when it comes to the 5 percent. That is the fact that the ripeness of a conflict is not only determined by the perceptions and motives of the parties, but also by the often vast constellation of forces that make up the attractor in which they are trapped. In fact, in 5 percent conflicts it is quite possible that all the parties are sufficiently hurting and hoping, yet find themselves so constrained by the attractor dynamics that their every attempt at resolution fails. Thus, we have suggested that the time is ripe for rethinking ripeness systemically.[52]

According to the ALM model, when intractable conflicts become organized into strong destructive and self-perpetuating attractors, ripeness, or the willingness to engage positively with the other side, appears absent. However, it is important to remember that in most conflict systems several attractors often coexist.

Conflict is only truly unripe for resolution if the attractor representing destructive conflict is very potent and *no alternative attractors exist.* A conflict begins to ripen for resolution when an alternative attractor develops, corresponding to some form of peaceful engagement that may eventually capture the dynamics of the system. As long as the state of a system remains in the domain of a destructive attractor, conflict will be maintained or will intensify. But if the system moves to a state close to a more peaceful attractor, it may capture the dynamics of the system. Such transitions can be triggered by rare events, as when natural disasters mobilize disputants to work together, or by intentional conciliatory initiatives from parties or third parties.

Thus, the conditions and processes that can *increase the probabilities of ripeness and constructive engagement* in long-term conflicts include (1) the many psychological, social, and structural factors that strengthen positive attractors for thinking, feeling, and acting between the parties, (2) the many factors that can weaken negative attractors, and (3) the factors that can tip the state of the system from the attractor of destructive conflict to the attractor of peace. Although these components of ripeness are somewhat interrelated, they must be understood as independent contributors to constructive engagement and sustainable peace.

4. Work the Edge of Chaos. Mathematicians and computer scientists have identified moments in complex systems when they are particularly vulnerable to *phase transitions;* that is, forks in the road that can lead to qualitatively different futures. For example, the moment when a very slight increase in temperature turns water to steam or a decrease turns water to ice. Similar phenomena have been called the "edge of chaos" because they are thought to be located in the area of a system somewhere between order (the pull of attractors) and chaos (high states of complexity). It is in these edge-of-chaos states that systems seem particularly sensitive to even very small changes.

A family system in crisis, for example, might find itself on the edge of chaos. The sudden announcement of divorce by the parents, a child's

The Edge of Chaos

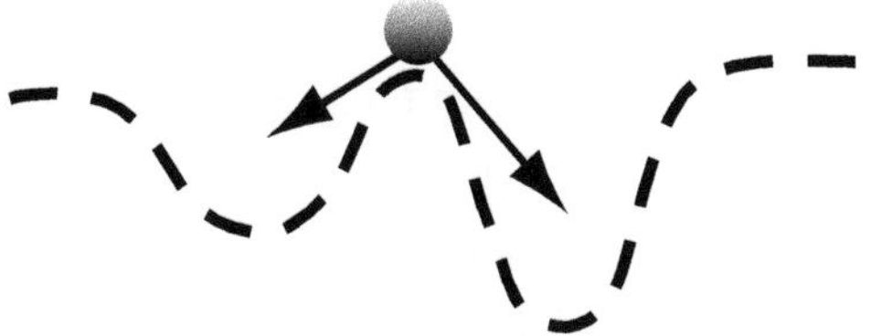

diagnosis of terminal illness, or the need to quickly uproot and move out of state for work could all place a family system into a tenuous, high-anxiety state. They might then be poised to either (a) revert to the same old patterns of behavior, (b) transition into a new, formerly latent pattern of interaction, or (c) remain in a state of confusion and disarray for a while, until a new attractor develops and restabilizes the system.

This idea has two main implications for leveraging change in 5 percent attractor landscapes. First, it's useful to learn to read and recognize these edge-of-chaos states. Anomalies in systems—unusual incidents of tension, hardship, stress, aggression, violence, success, luck, or despair—may all be possible indicators of the presence of such states. Pay attention to these. Second, as these states usually represent *bifurcation points,* transition states between two possible states or attractors, it would be important to be familiar enough with the system to have a sense of what the latent and manifest alternatives might represent, and then work to tip the system in a more constructive direction. This can be done by searching for feasible, high-impact initiatives that might help trigger the transition from one state or attractor to another.

For example, in 1989, South Africa stood at the brink of civil war. The Afrikaner government was being pressured to change its apartheid policies from many sides, and younger, more militant factions within the African National Congress were gaining strength and threatening to take to the streets. The country was at a bifurcation point between the status quo and the chaos of war. It was under these conditions that President De Klerk reached out to begin negotiations with Nelson Mandela for his release from prison after twenty-seven years of incarceration. Mandela's release was a profound gesture that signaled a new path for South Africa. This highly symbolic act helped to avert civil war and eventually led to the dismantling of apartheid and the establishment of a multiracial democracy in South Africa.

5. Identify the Small Things That Change Everything. This practice goes beyond altering the existing manifest and latent attractors of the conflict to trying to change the landscape; that is, the number and types of attractors in a particular relationship. In complex systems, many different factors interact to create attractors, but usually only a small subset of variables promotes really noteworthy changes in them. Even slight changes in these variables (called *control parameters*) can produce qualitative changes in the system's attractor landscape. These can take many forms, but the result is often dramatic changes in the conflict landscape.

But finding the control parameters in any specific conflict is no small matter. To translate this into a specific strategy for conflict resolution, it is necessary to identify the relevant control parameters with the potential to change the attractor landscape constraining the behavior patterns. They are typically determined by the specific form and history of a conflict, and identifying them usually entails both an intimate knowledge of the situation and a bit of trial and error.

For example, would constituting a standing committee of members of the Columbia community, elected by members of Jewish and Arab student associations at Columbia to address the broader issues in the conflict, qualify as an action that transforms the pattern of thinking and behavior of the community regarding the issues surrounding the MEALAC controversy? Or drafting a Columbia University faculty and student bill of rights? How about mandating a yearly multicultural training for all students, faculty, and staff? Or establishing an independent interuniversity grievance panel to hear serious disputes of an interethnic nature? And if these changes affected the patterns at Columbia, would they promote the emergence of a new attractor (e.g., more positive intercommunal relations), or would they introduce movement between very different attractors (e.g., oscillation between positive and negative relations)?

The identification of control factors and their effects on the attractor landscape of a system characterized by intractable conflict are daunting tasks, but the potential payoff can be substantial.

6. Take Change Seriously. Change comes in all shapes and sizes. And especially when working with complex, tightly coupled nonlinear systems, change is often perplexing and unpredictable. Nevertheless, when it comes to leveraging change, there are a few distinctions we have found useful for categorizing and understanding change initiatives in 5 percent conflicts.

Systemic Change Initiatives

	Episodic	Developmental	Radical
TOP-DOWN	• Peacekeeping • Legal Proceedings • Intelligence	• Policy Changes • Control the Ecology	• Frame • Breaking Outsiders • Issue Framing
MIDDLE-OUT	• Community Leader Crisis Support	• Midlevel Influentials • Procedural Changes	• Strategic Initiatives • Ashoka initiatives
BOTTOM-UP	• Direct Humanitarian Aid	• Teaching • Socializing • Treatment for Trauma	• Adjust Local Rules, Timing, Location

Change initiatives can have three basic types of *effects* in social systems: (1) *episodic* effects, which are direct and immediate but typically short term or superficial, affecting for instance the intensity, pain, or misery inherent in a particular situation but not necessarily altering the pattern; (2) *developmental* effects, which take time, perhaps years, to unfold in a system but can have substantial influence on the quality of the patterns of interaction (width and depth of attractors); and (3) *radical* effects, which are often dramatic, altering the attractor landscape or moving the state of a system from one established attractor to another.[53]

Change initiatives can also differ categorically by the *level* of change. Three general levels are (1) *top-down,* involving leaders, policies, and other elite decision makers; (2) *middle-out,* involving midlevel leaders and community networks, structures, and processes; and (3) *bottom-up,* relating to grassroots organizations or addressing the masses directly.[54]

Episodic initiatives at all three levels are typically responses to crises associated with conflicts that attempt to quell outbreaks of violence or suffering and reinstate a sense of safety and stability. These initiatives, such as military or police intervention, calling for calm from community leaders, or direct crisis aid, can lessen the intensity of the destructiveness of the conflict, but typically do little to interrupt the strong hostile patterns that characterize protracted conflicts. An investigation by police of the death threats to MEALAC faculty and a strong security presence employed at campus demonstrations over the controversy are examples.

Developmental initiatives can have an eventual impact on the pattern of a conflict, but such effects are typically gradual, particularly when they are introduced at lower levels of the system. One bottom-up strategy, *teaching,* is aimed at fostering changes in the fundamental beliefs and assumptions that form patterns of meaning for stakeholders in a conflict.[55] This is often accomplished by encouraging critical reflection, bringing to the surface taken-for-granted assumptions that constitute the basis of understanding of conflicts. Another approach is *socializing,* aimed at altering the character of relationships in a conflict. This targets behavioral and communication interactions, which can lead to new beliefs, values, and cultures.[56] Such strategies require a moderately long time to bubble up and impact the broader system, through lower-level interactions between local members of the community, but they can have a lasting impact on establishing new constructive patterns of interaction.

A popular midlevel developmental approach to initiating change in conflicts involves working with "middle-range leaders." These are influential, unofficial representatives (members of the media, former or potential officials, leaders of business, educational, religious, union, and other local institutions) from opposing sides of a conflict who represent the mainstream of each community.[57] Ongoing workshops are convened with these leaders, who attempt to reintroduce nuance, compassion, and complexity into their understanding of the other and the conflict, and then rely on their individual spheres of influence and social networks to affect change. If implemented at Columbia, such a strategy could involve representatives from different ethnic and religious student groups, university and local media, alumni, and other key stakeholder groups.

Finally, *radical* initiatives can trigger extreme shifts in attractor patterns through small but targeted changes. For example, Connie Gersick, professor at UCLA's Graduate School of Management, suggests that such changes can be brought on by the attraction of influential newcomers to a system. Typically, these are young or unsocialized outsiders who are drawn in by a crisis in a system; they are less resistant to change and thus better able to initiate *frame-breaking changes* in the mind-sets of stakeholders.[58] This is the role Mahatma Gandhi and Martin Luther King Jr. played in introducing strategies of nonviolent civil disobedience to their respective independence and civil rights movements. This type of radical leadership could emerge from anywhere within the Columbia community—new students, faculty, administrators, local community leaders—and reorient the discourse around MEALAC. In fact, the creation of a new Israeli Studies Chair in the MEALAC department provides an excellent venue for such leadership.

However, it is important to remember that simply triggering a change in pattern does not guarantee either positive or lasting change in dynamic systems. Change initiatives can result in anything ranging from no change in pattern, to a slight reorientation of the system's structures, to a radical recreation of the system where the "core values that govern decision premises are also transformed."[59]

7. Humility, Please. Given that complex systems are often highly unpredictable, that change initiatives can operate in different ways and at different time scales across an attractor landscape, and that 5 percent conflicts are in fact *defined* by the fact that they resist many good-faith attempts to change them, we encourage humility.

Remember, when intervening in a tightly coupled system, we are in fact perturbing a system that already has its own strong internal dynamics. Also, we rarely have just one effect in these systems. Almost anything we do will have multiple effects because the problems we are addressing are always embedded in the context of other problems. Our objective with practice III is to try to move the state of the conflict into a latent attractor, or to reshape the attractor landscape to increase the probabilities of constructive relations. Ultimately, however, the resulting attractor will find its own form. In other words, we can try to shape and guide attractor dynamics, but in the end they are in control. Which is why the next action is so critical.

8. Adapt to Change. In his influential book *The Logic of Failure: Why Things Go Wrong and What We Can Do to Make Them Right,* Dietrich

Dörner presents his research on decision making and initiating change in complex environments involving "simulated communities." Dörner created a variety of different computer-simulated planning games of community life. One community was the Moros, a seminomadic tribe in Tanaland, a small region in West Africa; another was a small town of 3,700 people in Greenvale, in northwest England. He equipped them with all the itinerant problems that come with small African villages (drought, disease, tsetse flies, sparse population) and small British townships (unemployment, insufficient tax base, demand for housing). Dörner then brought research participants into his lab and gave them ample resources and dictatorial powers over the inhabitants of the communities. He tasked them with the objective of promoting the well-being of the population. The participants were told they could essentially do anything without opposition—impose hunting regulations, fertilize fields, irrigate, electrify villages, improve medical care, introduce birth control, you name it. Dörner then observed the participants' activities over a period of ten years in the life of the computer simulation, where years sped by in minutes.

A typical scenario follows. A well-educated and well-intentioned participant gathers information about Tanaland; he then sets out to improve life there by increasing the food supply with new tractors, fertilization, and irrigation; he sets up vaccination programs and medical clinics to improve medical care. As a result, the food supply in Tanaland improves, the number of children grows and the number of deaths decline. Life expectancy improves. Problem solved. Except that long about the 88th month of the 120-month experiment, the population suddenly, exponentially outruns the food supply; an irreversible famine breaks out and eventually kills off the Moros population. This is a pretty standard dynamic found in Dörner's research: existing problems are solved with insufficient thought given to repercussions or new problems the solutions might create.

Dörner's research tells us a lot about decision making, change, and leadership in complex systems that raises important considerations for fostering *sustainable* solutions with the 5 percent. His findings suggest that well-intentioned decision makers working in complex systems typically commit a standard set of errors.

- They act without prior analysis of the situation, or clarification and prioritization of goals.
- They fail to anticipate the side effects or long-term repercussions of their actions.
- They assume that the absence of immediately obvious negative effects means their correct measures have worked.
- They let overinvolvement in subprojects blind them to emerging needs and changes on the ground.

Why? Because this way of thinking and acting is usually more efficient in the short run and helps bolster people's self-esteem by letting them feel in control. Human processes of systematic thinking and memory retrieval are slow, and we tend to neglect problems we do not see happening. We also tend to employ what Dörner terms *methodism,* seeing new situations through old paradigms, and *ballistic decisions,* making a decision and sticking to it, damn the consequences (these were also discussed in chapter 2). This tends to culminate in a self-organizing type of thinking, planning, and problem solving: basically, recapitulating the same decisions and behavior over and over regardless of their effects. Sound familiar?

The good news is that Dörner's research also sheds light on more effective methods of decision making and problem solving with complex systems. The research participants able to improve the well-being of the simulated communities did the following:

- **Made more decisions.** They assessed a situation and set a course, but then continually *adapted,* staying open to feedback and to reconsidering their decisions and altering their course. They were found to make more, not fewer, decisions as their plans unfolded. They found more possibilities for enhancing their community's well-being as the situation evolved.
- **Acted more complexly.** They seemed to understand that the problems they were addressing were closely linked with other problems and so their actions would have multiple effects. Therefore, they made many more decisions and actions when attempt-

ing to achieve one goal (I'll increase revenues in Greenvale by creating new jobs, investing in product development, and advertising). This was in contrast to those who failed, who would typically make one decision per goal (I'll raise taxes in Greenvale to raise revenues).

- **Focused on the real problems first.** They took the time to gather enough information to determine the central problems to address, and did not jump into action prematurely or simply focus on the problems they *could* solve because it felt good.
- **Tested hypotheses more.** They tested their solutions in pilot projects and assessed the effects before committing to them.
- **Asked *why?* more.** They actively investigated the *why* behind events: the causal links that made up the *network of causation* in their community.
- **Stayed focused on the prize.** Ineffective decision makers got easily distracted and diverted; they hopped around a lot from problem to problem as each arose. Effective decision makers identified the central issues early on and stayed focused on addressing them.
- **But not on one solution.** However, effective decision makers did not develop a single-minded preoccupation with one solution. If the feedback data informed them that a solution was too costly or ineffective, they altered their approach.

This approach to solving difficult problems is simply more open, flexible, and tolerant of ambiguity. It requires more reflection on *how* we are thinking and solving problems, as well as a keen recognition that data matters. It means recognizing that when feedback on the result of our actions comes in, that is the time to pay more attention, not less. And to make more decisions, not fewer. It involves starting wisely, making corrections in midcourse, and always learning from our mistakes. Because every situation is unique and circumstances are always changing, we must stay online in real time if we are going to continue to effectively navigate 5 percent problems. Especially when we think they are solved.

How can we do this? Complicate, simplify, build up, tear down, leverage change, and adapt.

part four

THE 5 PERCENT SOLUTION

PUTTING IT ALL TOGETHER

chapter 6

REALIZING THE IMPOSSIBLE IN MOZAMBIQUE AND BEYOND

IN THIS CHAPTER, WE CONNECT THE DOTS. We walk you through the ALM model and three practices by applying them to an actual case of a 5 percent conflict. It is a painful case from the international arena, of a country with a history of four hundred years of colonialism, ending with a ten-year war of independence. The war was followed almost immediately by sixteen grueling years of civil war and violence that witnessed a million deaths and countless atrocities. But it is also a place where something extraordinary happened—peace broke out when it was seemingly impossible.*

The Country That Never Was

Imagine a country that was never independent, united, and at peace. Where out of a population of 12 million people, a million died in a violent sixteen-year civil war. Where multitudes were made amputees by landmines. Where 4.5 million persons were either refugees or internally displaced people. Where the constitution did not allow multiparty political representation. Where its neighbors actively destabilized and continuously threatened the country's security. And where multiple good-faith attempts at peacemaking failed. Then you have a glimpse of Mozambique in 1990.

Mozambique is a breathtakingly beautiful but starkly impoverished country on the southeastern coast of Africa. Explored by Vasco de Gama at the end

*One of the contributors to this book, Andrea Bartoli, was directly involved in the peace process described in this case study, as a member of the community of Sant'Egidio and as a UN representative.

of the fifteenth century, it became a Portuguese colony for more than four hundred years, a part of the elaborate network of trade routes established by the Portuguese across the globe. After the end of World War II, when decolonization pressures led European powers to give up control of their colonies, the Portuguese resisted and engaged in a long and bloody war with the Mozambique Liberation Front (FRELIMO) in Mozambique. Although these forces controlled some territory, they were unable to fully liberate the country until a 1974 leftist military coup in Lisbon made the Portuguese change centuries' old policies and grant independence to Mozambique at last.

On June 25, 1975, Mozambique was free of Portuguese control. From the capital in the south to the northern border with Tanzania, the country was united in expressing joy and pride. Unfortunately, conditions in Mozambique, and in particular the nature of the transition, were far from auspicious.

Because Portugal had very tight control of the country's administration, most qualified labor left the country at the moment of independence. Rhodesia and South Africa, at that time ruled by white supremacists, immediately sought ways to destabilize the new black African Marxist government. When it won independence, FRELIMO reorganized into the governing party, with the aim of overcoming all traditional tribal and ethnic divisions, thus unifying Mozambique. However, the independence enthusiasm of the population was misinterpreted by the FRELIMO leadership as "revolutionary fervor," setting the stage for the implementation of harsh and demanding top-down governmental policies.

Two of these policies were especially problematic: the abolishment of private property through mass "villagization," the arbitrary relocation of 1.8 million Mozambicans into communal villages; and the eradication and disempowerment of local traditional cultures, authorities, and healing practices. The haste and violent implementation of the FRELIMO government's unifying policies provoked a defiant reaction from tribal groups that led to open rebellion by the Resistencia National Mocambicana (RENAMO). Actively supported by Rhodesia and South Africa, RENAMO's strategy was to make sure that a government controlled by FRELIMO would never be functional. They intentionally attacked infrastructure and civilians and forcefully recruited young children as soldiers.

The subsequent war ravaged the country for over sixteen years. The continual interference of the neighboring anti-independence countries, Rhodesia and South Africa, made the emergence of a peaceful solution highly improbable. Even at the end of a long and very destructive cycle of violence, the conflict's complicated dynamics made it very difficult to find the pathway to a solution. The international community tried and failed on many occasions. Peace continually proved elusive. And the many failed peace attempts merely contributed to the conflict's perpetuation and to the people's hopelessness and increased resistance to new intervention. It was an impossible conflict.

While the polarized conflict system between FRELIMO and RENAMO became more entrenched, an unexpected group of actors began to explore alternatives. A young native, national bishop Monsignor Jaime Gonçalves, served as the catalyst. Gonçalves was linked to the Community of Sant'Egidio, a Catholic lay association that had already engaged with the FRELIMO government to facilitate religious freedoms in the second half of the 1970s. These efforts had been successful, and after the unexpected death of Mozambique's president, Machel Samora, the new leader, Joachim Chissano, sought the help of religious leaders to establish back-channel contacts with RENAMO.

Using its channels, Sant'Egidio arranged for a clandestine visit of Bishop Gonçalves to RENAMO headquarters deep in the jungle. This first meeting in 1988 became a turning point. At this meeting, Bishop Gonçalves and Alfonso Dlakama, the leader of RENAMO, were surprised to discover they were from the same ethnic tribe and spoke the same dialect. This was serendipitous. Their meeting was the beginning of an unpredictable series of events leading to an unorthodox journey to peace that included twenty-seven months of negotiations over eleven sessions. The journey lasted until the signing of the General Peace Agreement (GPA) on October 4, 1992, and beyond.

For over a decade, our team has systematically examined the Mozambique case, through participant observation, by conducting interviews with decision makers, and through various forms of archival research.[1] Having found it a particularly rich case for the study of the intractability of war, as well as the "impossible" emergence and sustainability of peace, here we illustrate some of the principles and practices of the 5 percent solution through its lens.

THE INTRACTABILITY OF MOZAMBIQUE

The civil war in Mozambique fits many of the criteria for intractable conflict, including the following:

- **The power of history.** Mozambicans' first sense of national identity began with their war of independence against Portuguese colonialism. Even after independence, war and struggle continued to shape their identities and social norms, and became deeply embedded in the society (e.g., the new national flag gave central prominence to a rifle). Then, when FRELIMO attempted to impose national unity in Mozambique by forcefully eradicating local traditions and authorities, it triggered a powerful backlash from RENAMO, which sought to protect the ancient histories and practices of its many tribal cultures. However, FRELIMO viewed RENAMO's resistance to changing the traditional ways as a form of loyalty to their former colonial past and so redoubled its efforts to destroy RENAMO. As the war raged on, the new struggle became internalized by members of both groups. And as atrocities mounted on both sides, the possibilities for peace diminished due to the debt owed to so many who had perished in the conflict. Both sides became imprisoned by the past.
- **Linked conflicts.** As the civil war in Mozambique escalated, it became clear that neighboring conflicts in apartheid South Africa and white supremacist Rhodesia, other struggles in Africa (e.g., Angola and Ethiopia), as well as challenges faced by the Soviet Union on the global stage were all closely linked with events in Mozambique. These dynamics fed the continuation of conflict.
- **Expense.** The cost of the civil war in Mozambique was estimated at $6 billion by 1986. The human cost, although incalculable, included a million deaths and 4.5 million refugees or "internally dis-

placed persons." It is estimated that at least one person was killed or wounded in every Mozambican family during the war.[2]

- **Endurance and unresponsiveness to conflict resolution.** The conflict had remained resistant to a number of peace initiatives and costly military actions for sixteen years, including attempts by many local, national, and international NGOs and agencies. It seemed impossible to solve.

THE ALM: COLLAPSE OF COMPLEXITY AND THE FORMATION OF A CLOSED, SELF-ORGANIZING SYSTEM

The Attractor Landscape Model suggests that beneath the characteristics of intractability described above, at a more basic level a few central mechanisms were at work perpetuating the conflict in Mozambique.

1. A collapse of subjective, social, and structural complexity in the system. The civil war in postcolonial Mozambique was influenced by myriad factors that included changes in global power dynamics (the rise and fall of the Soviet Union); regional political interests (particularly Rhodesia and South Africa); struggles over political, religious, and economic interests; a weak national identity; and a traumatized, militarized populace. Add to this the damage and atrocities committed by both sides as the conflict intensified, including the virtual decimation of the county's infrastructure, and you begin to see the chaos and complexity that was Mozambique in the 1980s.

However, by the early 1980s, a tightly coherent enmity system—RENAMO versus FRELIMO—was well established, which led to polarized and constrained thought, feeling, and action on both sides. This bipolar system of war forced people to join one or the other of the two groups, since "it may be safer and more profitable to join the ranks of armed exploiters rather than risk becoming one of the unarmed exploited."[3] The enemy was now clear. Social networks were limited to in-group members. Both psychological and physical movement between the camps was severely restricted by penalty of death; adaptation to changing circumstances was impossible. Coherence and consistency ruled.

2. A loss of balanced feedback leading to escalation and self-organization. The new political system in Mozambique was created in a top-down process. Consultations were limited to the governing party, and there was a strong disregard for local tradition. Because it had no mechanisms for corrective, bottom-up feedback, the system could not react to and embrace the needs of those excluded from the new order. The exclusion and consequent estrangement of considerable factions of the society created conditions for dissent.

The Marxist frame of FRELIMO took a very narrow view of dissent. Feedback was not welcomed unless it was supportive; nonsupportive responses were labeled "anti-revolutionary" and "anti-patriotic." This forced individuals and groups into a bind: either renounce their discontent and join the party line or harden the critique and be marginalized further. The escalation of conflict was the direct consequence of this exclusionary approach, which sharply reduced the opportunity for balance and self-correction within the system. The more the discontent hardened, the more those committed to FRELIMO's policies and RENAMO's counteractions became entrenched in their viewpoints.

3. Reinforcing feedback among psychological, social, and structural levels in the system. FRELIMO's local, regional, and national levels of operation became tightly coordinated to ensure full implementation of its centralized directives. This imposed top-down coordination. But other emergent processes instilled consistency from the bottom up. Over time, the fear, hatred, and trauma experienced by individuals was reinforced by FRELIMO's and RENAMO's violence and exclusionary social norms and networks—and were further institutionalized and reinforced by the two groups' laws and policies. These destructive dynamics were further strengthened by the regional investments of Rhodesia and South Africa in the continuation of the war. In time, it all lined up.

4. The emergence of attractor landscapes with strong attractors for destructiveness and weak, latent attractors for peace. The accumulation of negativity built up after the imposition of FRELIMO's policies, led to a catastrophic moment of transformation. The predisposition for violence, already present in the system at the levels of identity, symbol, and collective memory from prior wars, became redirected against either FRELIMO or RENAMO. A strong negative attractor then captured the dynamics of the system. At this point, the resolution of specific issues through peace attempts did little to quell the tide of hostility and suspicion.

5. A loss of adaptive, functional capacities. Over time, Mozambique's socioeconomic system lost its functionality and adaptive potential. Some of its basic functions—education, health, agriculture—were deliberately destroyed by the fighting parties; others were abused by the system to support the war (the pervasive spread of land mines made the people's legacy of farming a deadly choice). Preconflict social capital had been a hybrid of local traditions embedded within the colonial structure. When FRELIMO came to power, it destroyed the colonial legacy and attacked local traditions. When the new forms of social capital were again targeted in the civil war, many of the remaining adaptive functions of the social system, like trade and travel, were destroyed as well.

6. Self-organization and resistance to change. It all added up. The collapse of subjective complexity, polarization, the prevalence of reinforcing feedback, an emergent destructive landscape, and loss of adaptive capacities created the perfect storm we call the 5 percent.

INCREASING THE PROBABILITIES FOR PEACE IN MOZAMBIQUE

Peace cannot be made with the 5 percent. But it does happen. From the perspective of the ALM, peace, like intractability, is an emergent property, which means it is the result of many complex and unpredictable circumstances, events, and actions. In retrospect, we can see that numerous events and efforts were involved in creating the conditions contributing to the General Peace Agreement and subsequent durable peace in Mozambique. Some of these were the collapse of the Soviet Union, the emergence of a new South Africa under Mandela's leadership, the efforts of various religious and business leaders, the general contribution of churches, religious groups, NGOs, and civil society, the death of former President Samora Machel, and the utter exhaustion of the people.

But this does not mean that our attempts at conflict resolution and peacemaking are moot, buried under the rubble of so many complex interactions and factors. From the perspective of the ALM, *we can work to increase the probability that peace and other positive social states will emerge and be sustained.* This is what social psychologist Albert Bandura terms the *agentic management of fortuity.*[4] It involves probabilities. It entails working in a manner both locally informed and evidence based. It is responsive to changing circumstances, with the aim of decreasing the probability of destructiveness (deconstructing negative attractors) and increasing the probability of peace (fostering positive attractors). In particular, the ALM points to the catalytic functions of some people, actions, and events. These can play an important role in making other unfolding changes all the more relevant to the overall transformation of a conflict.

In Mozambique, we saw the emergence of peace made possible by seemingly insignificant connections and movements within the conflict system, started by a few key actors in the peace process. We view these actors as *catalysts* because their actions did not result in observable transformations of the enmity system but made it possible for the next steps to take place.[5] These catalytic effects probably took place only after certain other changes occurred that readied the system. However, we suggest that these catalytic functions are an essential component of the emergence of peace, as we hope to demonstrate through case of Mozambique.

THE THREE PRACTICES

Practice I: Complicate to Simplify

Zoom out before you focus in.

We begin our mapping of the Mozambique case by asking, What was the nature of the general patterns unfolding in Mozambique in the 1980s and 1990s relevant to conflict intractability and the emergence of peace? This shifts our analysis away from specific issues, actions, encounters, and outcomes toward an awareness of the internal dynamics and trends unfolding over time. It also situates events in Mozambique within the broader changes occurring regionally, within Africa, and the around the world.

Our high-level mapping of the story of the Mozambique civil war develops across nine temporal phases. At the top of the diagram on the next page you see the main elements of the war-system loops depicted in phases 1 and 2. These elements reinforced each other over many years, leading to polarization and stalemate between the camps. (This phase could be developed more fully to better understand the many loops contributing to intractability.) Then in phase 3 we see another loop forming: a small subsystem of constructive encounters that, importantly, begins to introduce some minor inhibiting feedback into the war system. This subsystem, initially protected by the major powers (RENAMO, FRELIMO, the Vatican), grows and spreads in phases 4 and 6, despite the inhibiting feedback introduced by phase 5: the disillusionment caused by so many previous failed attempts at peace. This suggests a readiness existed in the system for these types of dynamics, evidence of a latent attractor for peace. Over time, this subsystem of constructive engagement grew by forging new links in unpredictable ways, eventually challenging the full coherence of the war system and *contributing* to its destabilization. (A more complete mapping would indicate the role that macropolitical factors, such as the demise of the USSR, had on this as well.) In time, the peace agreement and the multiparty elections that ensued introduced considerable inhibitory feedback into the war system, keeping it in check to date.

Mapping is useful for a variety of reasons, including helping us to see the logic of a system and to understand the unfolding of events as part of a broader dynamic field of forces. For instance, the decolonization process in Mozambique was not, as in India, led by a nonviolent visionary like Mahatma Gandhi. On the contrary, the long and bloody war of independence was led by a small group of very committed militants who were constantly reminded of the power of arms by the violent repression

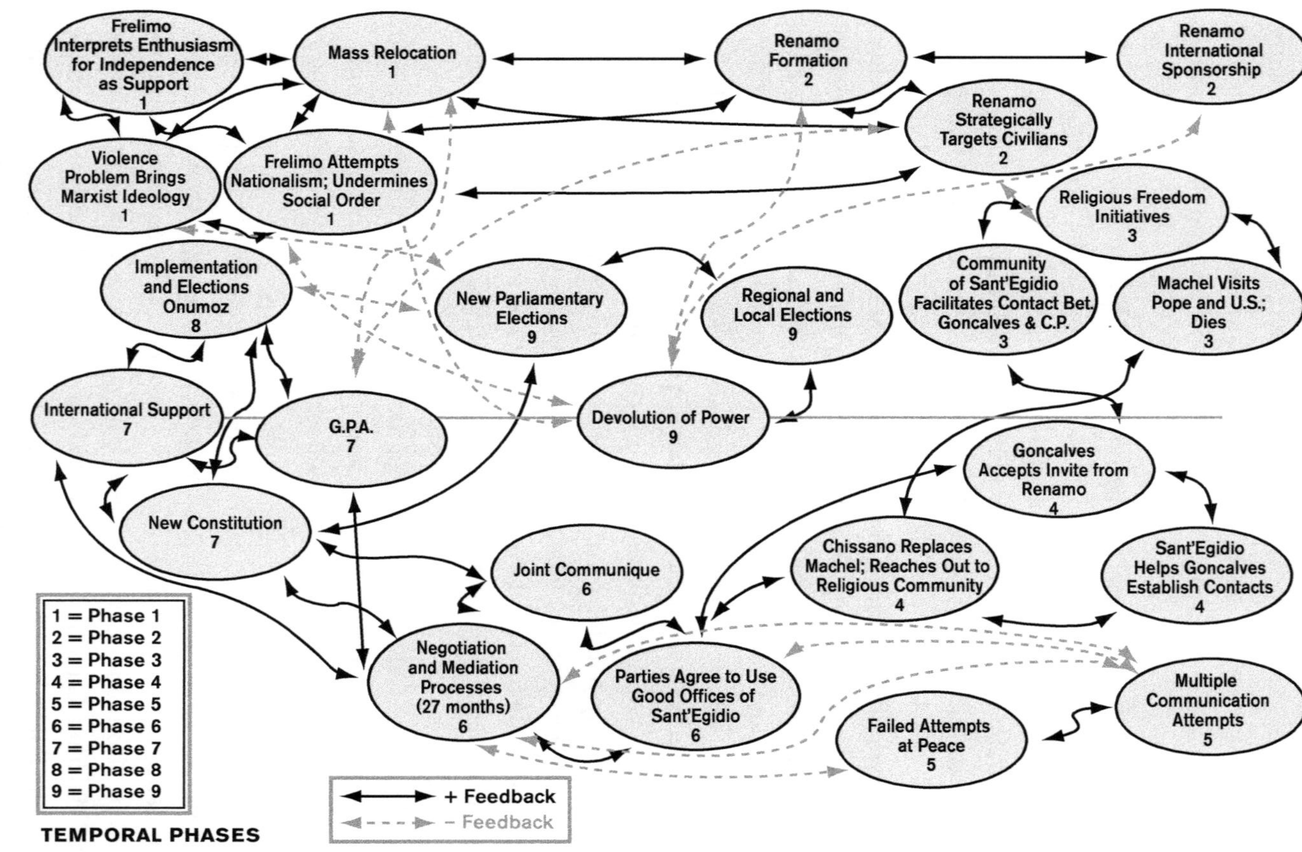

Feedback Loop Analysis of Mozambique's Conflict and Peace

of the Portuguese. Their Marxist-Leninist ideology also fueled the radicalized formation and growth of FRELIMO. Thus, violence was deeply rooted in the very formation of Mozambique as an independent country. It was also the legitimized framework for confrontation during the Cold War and in the regional context of white supremacist governments like those of Rhodesia and South Africa. This context is critical to understanding the logic of the trajectory of events in Mozambique.

Simplify

However, feedback loop–mapping is only useful if it leads to new insights about conflict dynamics, or helps identify critical hubs or links shaping the system.

Identify hubs, loops, and energy. Focusing in on the map of Mozambique, one would ask, Where are the significant feedback loops defining the patterns of the system? Where are the key hubs or energy centers within the network? Are these elements and links actionable? Where is there imbalance in the system between positive and negative feedback? Are there primary subsystems or clusters of loops that hang together?

In its early phases, the conflict was clearly driven by the intra- and intergroup dynamics of opposition and polarization between RENAMO and FRELIMO, although these dynamics played out in the context of important historical and regional-political events. After phase 3, a new dynamic, initially latent, began to emerge and eventually captured the main dynamics of the system. As these dynamics grew and spread, they first ruptured and then derailed the dynamics of the war attractor. This was critical. The minor inhibitory feedback introduced by the trust both sides had in the weak-power religious community Sant'Egidio, coupled with the bishop's visit with RENAMO (and relations with FRELIMO), helped to destabilize the coherent worldviews of both camps. These links did not have direct effects, but led to other links and so on, which in time helped decouple and then derail the war system.

Actionable leverage points in the system are often different for distinct stakeholders and are typically identified over time. When catalysts like Bishop Gonçalves initiate a constructive link in a closed war-system, they expose themselves to retaliation and can disappear, literally or politically. However, if the actor is able to choose his or her links carefully and appropriately, the new network grows. The more links the catalyst establishes, the more possible it is to restructure and reorient the whole system.

Identify integrative catalysts. Undoubtedly, the most important catalyst in the transition to peace was Bishop Gonçalves. He accepted a highly dangerous invitation to meet with RENAMO leader Alfonso Dhlakama, who at the time was isolated from other key figures in the conflict. Although the bishop was never a RENAMO supporter and stayed in direct contact with the FRELIMO government, he managed to establish a stable platform for communication outside the war system, because the two men happened to speak the same ethnic language, Ndau. Later, Gonçalves became one of the four mediators in the formal negotiations that ended the civil war.

Gonçalves internalized both sides of the conflict because he shared contradictory characteristics with the two opponents. Whereas at that time most bishops in Mozambique were white, he was one of the first native, black bishops. Despite being a Catholic (which the FRELIMO government associated with the colonialist Portuguese), he worked assiduously to have good working relations with the communist FRELIMO Party, helping to ease tensions between religious communities and the government. Educated in Mozambique and abroad, he had been exposed to various cultural settings; however, he maintained a strong sense of his local roots. He spoke many ethnic languages and could communicate easily with diverse communities in Beira, the second-largest city in Mozambique.

Gonçalves was invited into the role of catalyst by the Community of Sant'Egidio and other key figures. They had been communicating with him and valued his ability to listen to contradictory positions without taking sides and to imagine alternative solutions to the conflict. Being situated in a constant flow of information among various stakeholders allowed him to consider options that would not have occurred to others.

Most important, Gonçalves played a central role in the local society; many people shared with him their experience of the conflict, which made him a focal point, or in network terms, a *connector.*[6] This helped increase his desire for a solution; the more people he talked to, the more obliged he felt to act proactively to find peace. Yet his ties with friends outside Mozambique allowed him to maintain a certain distance, a space for consideration. Instead of becoming an advocate for an a priori solution, he was able to consider the possibility of peace emerging from the parties themselves and was willing to explore those possibilities fully. He welcomed new ideas and transmitted them, facilitating communication between the two parties and the others involved.

A catalyst like Gonçalves, who internalizes the contradictions inherent to the conflict, is better able to connect by positive links to each of the opposing groups. The existence of an individual linked to both opposing sides ruptures the system's coherence. In essence, the role of a catalyst is to decrease the strength of the forces that constrain the system by disrupting the closed dynamic of each system. Moreover, the catalyst provides a channel of communication. This opens up the system to both internal and external influences, which can pave the way for transformation and restoration of adaptive functions.

Practice II: Build Up and Tear Down

There were a variety of initiatives implemented in Mozambique to both build up positive potential in the system and to deconstruct the powerful pull of intergroup negativity and revenge. Here are a few illustrations.

Building Up

The identification and support of constructive actors and forces within the system was a primary strategy for increasing the probabilities for peace.

Supporting networks of effective action. During the first ten years after independence in Mozambique, the formation of the closed attractor landscape made it impossible to speak openly about peace. Any attempt to broach even remotely the possibility of direct contact with the "other side" was perceived as treason and treated accordingly. Yet actors like the churches, Bishop Gonçalves, and the Community of Sant'Egidio remained open to links with both the FRELIMO and RENAMO networks.

It is important to note that these relationships were not neutral or instrumental; rather, they were organic, growing out of genuine encounters. Cultivated over time, these relationships formed the backbone of the negotiation process.

Employing weak power. Initially, Sant'Egidio met enormous challenges in Mozambique. First, its power to exert influence was very limited, and so was its recognition by the international community. Second, communication with the leaders in Mozambique was so difficult that the main issue was to maintain the leaders' willingness to talk rather than achieve agreement.

During the conflict, the internal coherence of the two hostile systems was very high. Ideologically, militarily, and politically there was no way of communication and exchange between the systems. Change, however, emerged at the margins through nonthreatening communications allowing some key actors in the enmity system to consider alternatives to the status quo. This initial consideration was made possible by the "weaknesses" of the propositions and of the proponents (Sant'Egidio). The irony is that the party considering the alternative was then linked to it, not by virtue of the proponent's "strength" but by its own volition and the value of the proposition itself, thus creating a stronger commitment to it. It is known in psychology that attitude change is much more pronounced and permanent when it is perceived as coming from one's own experience rather than as a result of external pressure.[7] By applying little pressure, Sant'Egidio increased the perception that conciliatory views resulted from inside the individual parties.

Weak or soft power mediators, not perceived as a threat or source of pressure, also get attached to new social networks more easily and so can form positive connections with sides of a conflict. As a consequence, they too can significantly disrupt the coherence of the enmity system; the system can begin to "move" again and relax internal pressures. The main difference is that the catalyst comes from within the system, whereas many mediators come from the outside.

Serendipity. Perhaps the most important and remarkable event in this story of Mozambique happened by chance. When the Community of Sant'Egidio arranged, through the South African Secret Service, for

Bishop Gonçalves to meet secretly and illegally in the jungle with RENAMO leader Alfonso Dlakama, its members put their lives in jeopardy. But when, in this place of paranoia and fear, quite by coincidence Gonçalves and Dlakama discovered that they both spoke the rare ethnic dialect Ndau, something shifted. Trust bloomed. No one could have predicted this. But it was the beginning of something entirely new.

Acknowledging superordinate identities and goals. During the peace process in Mozambique, one fundamental step was the signing of the first Joint communiqué at the end of the first session of direct meetings between the government of Mozambique and RENAMO. It was held in Sant'Egidio headquarters in Rome, July 10–12, 1990. In that document the parties recognized themselves as part of the "larger Mozambican family," thus setting the stage for a unified identity beyond political and ideological differences. This was the first time the country became truly united under one vision of national identity. This common ground provided the future impetus for the remaining steps in the journey to peace.

Channeling conflict and dissent constructively. During the formation of the conflict attractor, disagreement became a punishable crime and the consequences were serious. As soon as the invitation to seek what unites and not what divides was welcomed by both parties, after the first direct meeting in Rome on July 1990, the possibility of disagreement and corrective feedback was paradoxically restored, making it possible for constructive tension to be recognized and welcomed back in the system. Today in Mozambique, it is clear that to say no to a policy is not treason and that dissent is not only permissible but also an effective tool for growth and development. Clearly, successful peace processes are less about agreements per se and more about *how disagreement is allowed and is managed.*

Tearing Down

Here are a few illustrations of how people worked actively to deconstruct and dismantle the negative attractors in Mozambique.

Identify discontinuities (carefully increase complexity). As the structure of conflict in Mozambique bound together perceptions of all the out-group members, the mere presence of Gonçalves and some of the Sant'Egidio members increased complexity, since a single negative judgment could no longer accommodate all the out-group members; Gonçalves was simultaneously an in-group and out-group member and Sant'Egidio was in contact with both. These discontinuities within the in-group–out-group divide widened slowly. The eventual acceptance of a peace agreement, a cooperative structure of interests, and a multiparty system was also inconsistent with the simplified view of overall incompatibility that had previously driven the conflict and so destabilized that attractor.

Decouple reinforcing feedback loops. After the signing of the GPA, the memory of the atrocities committed during the war constituted one of the major factors maintaining the now latent attractor for destructive relations. Although the decision not to impose punishment on those responsible was questioned ethically and legally, an old Mozambican belief helped the population address the issue. According to local tradition, people might not have been responsible for their actions during the war because they might have been influenced by an "evil wind" that blew in and consumed the society. Thus, a bad spirit was blamed for the atrocities committed. Externalizing the main source of the violence helped to restore adaptive relations and functions of the system by reducing the necessity for revenge. It is also interesting to note the parallels between the metaphor of a strong wind and strong attractors.

In addition, the demilitarization process in Mozambique proved similarly successful: guns and weapons were collected and piled in villages. RENAMO, the former contender and potential "spoiler" of the peace process, was transformed into the main opposing political party, becoming a staple of the multiparty system. These three actions helped to dismantle the considerable reinforcing loops that might have remained operative, even after the emergence of peace.

Introduce inhibiting feedback loops. (Early-warning systems, crosscutting structures, international monitoring, etc.) In Mozambique one of the greatest concerns of the parties, early in the peace negotiations, was the possibility of breaking the safety of the corridors negotiated during the first round of talks in Rome. Therefore, it was agreed that an independent commission would monitor military activity; as in many other peacekeeping operations, the positioning of independent monitors drastically reduced the mistrust between the parties and the chance of escalation at this most critical juncture.

Institutionalize more nuanced, alternative conflict narratives. (Through media, textbooks, official accounts, etc.) The first step toward peace in Mozambique emerged when the enemy was no longer described in derogatory terms as *macacos* (apes), and a new rhetoric was expressed throughout the system, from leadership to grassroots levels. It was also helpful that new narratives were allowed to form at local levels and not controlled at the central level, which had been a triggering issue at the start of the civil war.

Practice III: Change to Stabilize

The final practice highlights the importance of understanding and leveraging change and adapting effectively to changing circumstances in order to achieve sustainable solutions.

Shocks and instability. Several major political shocks contributed to the conditions that readied Mozambique for peace. Shock number one came when Mozambique's neighbor Rhodesia became the independent nation of The Republic of Zimbabwe in 1980, ending decades of white supremacist rule there. Destabilizing shock number two involved the end of the Cold War. It should come as no surprise that the demise of the Soviet Union had reverberations throughout Africa, particularly for FRELIMO, a Marxist government dependent on Moscow for funding. Shock number three happened when President Frederik de Klerk began negotiations in 1990 to end apartheid in South Africa. Even though the conflict in Mozambique had been well internalized by the late 1980s, these events shook the very foundation of events, providing sufficient instability and vulnerability in the system for change.

Identify the small things that change everything. The peace process essentially consisted of a series of small steps of increased communication between the parties, started by one small gesture from Bishop Gonçalves. The role these steps played in advancing any substantial solution was not initially visible; nonetheless, they helped constitute a platform for involving more stakeholders in communications and extending the scope of the issues that could be discussed. Only much later, during the final stages of the peace agreement, did concessions and integrative solutions start to appear; then the significant impact of earlier encounters could be understood.

Take time seriously. In Mozambique, the first contacts between the Community of Sant'Egidio and the FRELIMO government were established in the second half of the 1970s, almost fifteen years before the peace agreement. This began a slow, incremental process of trust building that established the conditions (an attractor) for later facilitating talks. Later, it took more than four years between the first meeting between Bishop Gonçalves and Alfonso Dlakama and the signing of the final General Peace Agreement. This illustrates how system states (like the level of conflict intensity) and attractors change at different time scales. Manifest conflicts can evidence dramatic changes in their states, from relatively peaceful to violent, or from intensely destructive to peaceful. Attractors tend to develop slowly and incrementally over time as a result of a host of relevant activities. Thus, changes, or the lack of changes, in the current state of a conflict should not be confused with changes in the underlying attractor landscape.

Adapting to change to foster stability. The General Peace Agreement was critical to ending the civil war in Mozambique. In fact, it directly contributed to the development of the new constitution, addressing and regulating many postwar issues. It is also critical to note that the "weak strength" of the peace process was robust enough to handle not only the reconciliation of the conflicting parties but also the reconstruction of the nation. The unity of the country was not superficial: not only did Mozambicans manage to handle the postwar reality, but also subsequent challenges involving floods, an AIDS epidemic, and extreme poverty. The agreement was followed by a remarkable demilitarization process, a peaceful resettlement of four million refugees, amazing economic growth, a successful reintegration of former soldiers into their communities, the rebuilding of the educational and health care systems, as well as new partnerships with international organizations and the effective use of foreign funds and support.

However, it must be acknowledged that after peace broke out in Mozambique, more people died of the HIV-AIDS virus than had died during the war. The virus, already circulating in the refugee camps, now spread widely among the general populace with the release of the refugees. Ironically, if war had continued, the virus would probably not have spread so rapidly and effectively. Had this growing epidemic been anticipated, antiretroviral drugs could have been distributed in the camps, and the problem would have been much less severe. It is clear that those who worked for peace in Mozambique are not responsible for the spread of the virus. But it is nevertheless essential to consider the consequences of human actions independent of initial intentions, and to stress the importance of remaining vigilant to the possibility of such unintended consequences of well-intended acts.

Mozambique did not develop an enmity system in a day, and the process that led to that system was fueled by good intentions and idealistic policies. The conflict was not the result of bad people doing bad things, but of humans trying to do their best, defending what they believed in and caring for what they held valuable.

As they did in Mozambique, solutions emerge over time through dedicated inquiry that recognizes latent attractors. Peace is possible even in the most difficult circumstances. But rather than try to impose interventions or be content with marginal change, it is essential to remain alert to the "next best move": the available option that presents the greatest chance of restructuring the system.

The Mozambique case also suggests the power of catalytic leadership. Such enemies rarely come together effectively when they are forced to, but rather when they accept the task of the shared exploration of what was once impossible, but now seems possible. It happened in Mozambique. It will happen elsewhere.

This is an abbreviated account of the attractor dynamics we consider central to understanding the intractability of conflict and the emergence and sustainability of peace in Mozambique. Their study has implications for similar transformations in other settings.

What We've Learned from Applying the ALM to Mozambique: Lessons for Israel-Palestine and Other Impossibilities

> One of the things that frustrates me about this conflict . . . thinking about this conflict is that people don't realize the complexity. I don't

> think people look at how many stakeholders there are in there and how much people are playing their angle . . . I think there's a whole element to this particular conflict to where you start the story, to where you begin the narrative, and clearly it's whose perspective you tell it from. Do you tell it from the perspective of the conquered Palestinian people who had their land taken away from them and have basically been pawns on the world chess board for decades upon decades, if not centuries; or do you take it from the perspective of the Jewish people, having survived a terrible genocide and looking for a home . . . One of the things that's always struck me is that there are very compelling narratives to this conflict and all are true, inasmuch as anything is true . . . I think the complexity is on so many levels . . . It's a complexity of geographic realities . . . the complexities are in the relationships . . . it has many different ethnic pockets . . . and I think it's fighting against a place, where particularly in the United States, in American culture, we want to simplify . . . we want easy answers. We want to synthesize it down to something that's . . . that people can wrap themselves around and take a side on . . . and sometimes I feel overwhelmed.
>
> —anonymous Palestinian, 2002

The Israeli-Palestinian conflict is today's default for intractable conflict. It is *the* problem that comes to mind for most people when we mention we are studying impossible conflicts. So it would be remiss for us not to address this ongoing tragedy. However, a comprehensive analysis and prescription for addressing this conflict would be both presumptuous and beyond the scope of this book. This conflict has been covered extensively by scholars and journalists for decades. Nevertheless, below we offer a few thoughts—provocations, perhaps—regarding the implications of the ALM model for addressing conflict and peace in Israel-Palestine and other areas of the world where peace seems illusive.

The 5 Percent Problem

1. It is complicated.[8] The Israel-Palestine conflict, as we know it in modern times, is a hundred-year-old conflict that involves a multitude of interrelated factors. They include the following:

- the demise and military defeat of the Ottoman Empire by Western powers at the end of WWI;
- the somewhat arbitrary imposition of international boundaries on the region after the war by the imperial powers of France and Britain;
- continued international interests in the region for purposes of geopolitical strategy and natural resources;
- unstable governance and underdevelopment in the region;
- the establishment and work of the Zionist movement to bring Jews to Palestine;
- the long-standing existence of traditional cultural and ethnic rivalries in the area;
- a long history of persecution of Jews, eventuating in the Holocaust in WWII, and the subsequent support of the international community in establishing a Jewish state in geographic Palestine;
- creation of a Jewish state by the international community;
- a long history of humiliation, displacement, wars, and subsequent occupation of Arab Palestinians by Israelis with the backing of imperialist power;
- contrasting identities, narratives, and national movements in Israel both *within* the Israeli community (for example, between the religious Shas Party and the Labor Party) and the Palestinian community (such as between the religious Hamas Party and Fatah Party) *and between* the Israelis and Palestinians;
- competition for scarce territory;
- a zero-sum competition for victim status in the eyes of the international community;
- the intransigence and political power of militant movements, including Palestinian Hamas and Israeli settlers;
- the existence of Jewish, Christian, and Islamic monotheists who compete for primacy in the eyes of their gods, and powerful subgroups within each who view reconciliation with other religious groups as sacrilegious;
- a multiplicity of failed attempts at intervention by the international community;

- very active lobbyist groups in America and Europe that fund, support, or otherwise intervene in the conflict;
- the spread of terrorism across the globe;
- concerns over important demographic shifts taking place in Israel;
- the export of Middle Eastern Christians to the West, which makes the issue of Jerusalem less tractable;
- the socialization of entire generations of youth in Israel into a perpetual state-of-war mind-set;
- the teaching of history and covering of events in the media in ways that contribute to oversimplification and polarization;
- emerging tensions over water rights in the region among Israel-Palestine, Jordan, Lebanon, Syria, and Turkey;
- a deep commitment by both sides to use violence to combat violence from the other side; and
- the obligation they feel to revenge those slain in the conflict.

Thus, today the conflict operates and is reinforced across a multitude of issues, time periods, stakeholders, and lands, as well as across three main levels: the intercommunal relationship between Israelis and Palestinians, a broader set of relationships between Israel and other Arab and Muslim countries in the Middle East, and the larger canvas of stakeholders operating in the international community.

2. It is simple. Despite the extraordinarily complex and evolving elements and dynamics constituting the conflict, and given that the broad parameters of a permanent two-state settlement are clear, for the most part, we suggest a few basic factors contribute most to its continued intractability:

- the tightly coupled nature of the psychological, political, communal, structural, religious, regional, and international dimensions to the conflict;
- the powerful accumulation of negativity and dissipation of positivity due to injustices, oppression, violence, loss, insecurity, and economic hardships experienced over decades;

- the considerable intracommunal divisions (dove-hawk-radical, religious-secular, etc.) that rage on and feed intercommunal divisions that are insufficiently addressed;
- the disproportional effects of small groups of extremists in establishing the dynamics of the conflict;
- the deep overt and covert investment of some external stakeholders (some members of the diasporas, autocratic leaders in the region, intelligence communities, corporations, etc.) in the continuation in the conflict;
- repeated attempts by some third parties to intervene on one of the levels of the conflict without a clear sense of the impact on the other levels;
- the paradox of instability and stability: how hardship and threats to security and stability reinforce a need to maintain the status quo;
- the logical but closed, nonadaptive, self-organizing nature of the system.
- In other words, the character of the attractor landscape for the conflict.

3. It is logical. Research conducted in Israel-Palestine documents how children, families, and communities construct pro-conflict, anti-peace process narratives and attitudes in order to cope with the violent circumstances of the conflict.[9] They suggest that this is one way communities adapt to the tragic loss of loved ones in an ongoing violent conflict—that it helps to believe their cause is noble, righteous, and good and these deaths are a necessary sacrifice and an important step toward a greater future.

Violent responses to fear and conflict also fit. High levels of threat, especially when they are normative, elicit a preventative orientation from people, where fight or flight are the most logical responses and long-term consequences are neglected.[10] In a situation where one cannot flee, fighting is considered *the* option. Research shows that, despite the inability of violence to achieve one's long-term goals, and despite its costs, it often feels right. It is a response that fits, both psychologically and politically, with how disputants are oriented to the world.[11]

In addition, holding on dearly to a coherent, stable attractor under conditions of threat and instability is a natural human survival instinct. Under such conditions, change, even in the direction of more constructive and less costly relations, feels too risky. It is better to hold on to what you know in order to ensure a stable platform for thought and action than to risk making matters worse.[12]

4. It is collapsed. This is evident across several levels. Research on integrative complexity, people's ability to think in both differentiated and integrated ways, shows that it tends to decrease substantially as conflict and war intensify. This is due to the effects of threat on information processing and also to a decrease in the amount of contradictory, nuanced information available during these periods.[13] In fact, simply labeling and discussing this complex, multilevel constellation of events as the "Israeli-Palestinian conflict" is evidence of this collapse.

In addition, the endurance of the Israeli-Palestinian community conflict has encouraged narrower self-definitions and mutually exclusive identities. In prior years, more people endorsed the "Arab Jews" identity, referring to the Jewish population who grew up and lived in Arab countries. By the same token, prior to the second intifada, more Palestinians from Israel were comfortable with their "Israeli Palestinian" identity. As the political situation deteriorates, you see more and more individuals adopting narrower identities.[14]

Contributing to collapse at the next level, research on communities in Israel-Palestine suggests it is common to find an alignment between individual-level beliefs, social identities, group narratives, and various societal institutions and mechanisms, such as education, media, politics, popular culture, holidays, etc., which culminates in a general *conflict ethos* for communities; that is, a general shared sense of the true story and rules for the conflict.[15] Of course, these perspectives differ to some degree in their level of alignment and coherence within groups (between more moderate and extreme subgroups) and are usually diametrically opposed between different communities (Jewish-Arab).

Beyond the internal dynamics of people and communities, scholars have also identified a strong linking between the intercommunal Israeli-

Palestinian conflict and other conflicts in the region and around the globe.[16] This results in what Stephen Cohen, founder of the Institute for Middle East Peace and Development, describes as "the crucible of multiple conflicts in the region and multiple grievances that feed upon one another and that produce reoccurring eruptions of violence."[17] When the psychological, communal, and environmental collapses of complexity combine, the probability of intractability grows exponentially.

5. It is an evolving human reality. The situation in Israel-Palestine is different today than it was yesterday. For instance, scholars who tracked changes in the communal narratives and collective memories of both sides report that the narratives change, often dynamically, in relation to one another, and typically move in opposite directions.[18] With these changes, we also see shifts in identities and identification with the conflict, international attention and support ebbing and flowing, and political leaders in Israel, Palestine, the United States, and elsewhere coming and going. Thus, the reality of the Israeli-Palestinian conflict is always in flux, which presents both challenges (what is relevant to peace now?) and opportunities (the conditions associated with previous failures at peacemaking have changed).

THE 5 PERCENT SOLUTION: INCREASING PROBABILITIES FOR PEACE

Peace cannot be brought to the Middle East. But it can happen. How?

Practice I. Complicate to Simplify

1. See the evolving system. As the quote at the beginning of this section suggests, the conflict would benefit greatly from stakeholders, third parties, and scholars of all types enhancing their capacity for seeing and comprehending the evolving system of the conflict. This includes understanding two dimensions of complex systems: complexity and time. Employing phase-stepped feedback loop–mapping and other visualization tools of the many interrelated elements, stakeholders, and levels of the conflict is one approach. However, the importance of understanding how different events unfold over time at different rates of change is also critical. For example, it is likely that a major political shock, like the assassination of Yitzhak Rabin, the death of Yasser Arafat, or even the war in Iraq or Iran's nuclear proliferation, could have a powerful impact on events in Israel-Palestine. However, as research has shown, these effects sometimes do not manifest for over a decade. The more we understand about complexity and temporal dynamics, the better our comprehension of peace.

2. Envision complex networks of peace. Peace, like intractability, is equifinal; there are many avenues to it. Franklin D. Roosevelt, when addressing the Great Depression, realized that it was far too complex to understand and know how to intervene effectively. So he decided to begin as many positive initiatives as possible, thinking that it would increase the odds that some of them would help. To some degree, this is how we should view the Israeli-Palestinian conflict. What would help is a vision of how a comprehensive set of initiatives can increase the probabilities for constructive dynamics and decrease the probabilities of destructive dynamics or war. These activities can come from many sources: from grassroots to national leaders to international powers and agencies.

3. Seed individual and societal complexity. Complexity matters. It is important to raise future populations with high levels of cognitive, emotional, and behavioral complexity. Combined with structural changes in the society that increase the complexity of social identities, networks, and institutions, this can help the probabilities for peace and ultimately increase options for constructive action.

4. Support what works. There are good works taking place all over Israel-Palestine and abroad. These include efforts by Search for Common Ground, Seeds for Peace, the International Rescue Committee, Ashoka, Gush-Shalom, Brit Shalom, Naamat, and Ta'ayush. These initiatives do not need to be tightly coordinated. However, establishing guidelines for employing good, evidence-based practices and monitoring long-term impact among NGOs and community-based organizations could mitigate some of the unintended consequences of these well-intentioned initiatives.

5. Identify and support integrative catalysts. The importance of identifying, supporting, and protecting integrative catalysts is critical. These, again, are multiethnic or multipolitical individuals and groups who have grown up and are operating inside the system; they internalize the key contradictions and controversies on which the conflict is based. Their capacity for forging ties where none exist and thereby rupturing ultracoherent beliefs and polarization is unique and vital.

Practice II. Build up and Tear down

1. Learn to see the invisible. Peace is always present, even in war. Today, peace and conflict are parallel realities in Israel-Palestine. They may operate as a figure-ground perceptual puzzle, where only one can be seen and felt at a time. But know they simultaneously coexist and that our actions with regard to one objective (containing violence in war) may have significant but unanticipated consequences on the other (jeopardizing conditions for stable peace).

2. Stop making peace. It is probably best for some peacemakers to not work directly on increasing the peace. In other words, it is critical that members of NGOs and community-based organizations do whatever possible to increase intercommunal positivity and decrease negativity and harm. However, it may be best to do so in a manner divorced from the "peace process" so as to avoid the polarization that can result from falling prey to the politics of that attractor.[19] One strategy for this is to work on negativity and positivity at the lowest possible levels, on the ground in communities, with little reference to conflict or peace; two examples are the Israeli-Palestinian Science organization and Green Action. Of course, officials should and must keep working for peace, but it may benefit community workers to see and frame their role in a different light.

3. Welcome weakness. In rebuilding their communities and exploring possibilities for addressing both intracommunal divisions and intercommunal peace, Israelis and Palestinians would do well to seek support from groups and organizations with weak power, or as Joseph Nye calls it, "soft power"; those that communities can trust, or those with moral authority, etc. Many churches and religious organizations played this role in Mozambique. This is a particularly useful approach for developing solutions toward which the parties ultimately feel greater commitment.[20]

4. Honor emotions. The histories of the conflict in Israel-Palestine have created a cauldron of emotion that permeates its network of relationships throughout the region and across the globe, and that serves to fuel and drive the conflict forward. The power of the mix of humiliation, rage, identification, loyalty, frustration, fatigue, guilt, shame, anger, and hopelessness cannot be overestimated. This experience must be acknowledged, respected, *honored,* and somehow integrated into the future of this region. Whether that is through compartmentalized channeling of emotion into progressive acts, or through local, traditional practices of healing and reconciliation such as occurred in Mozambique, it must be understood as the bedrock of sustainable peace.

5. Co-construct a new geographic superordinate identity. Work to co-construct a regional identity to stand side by side with the many ethnic and religious identities operating in the conflict.[21] As we learned in Mozambique, this cannot be imposed unilaterally. It must come from a relatively equal-power dialogue on the visions and challenges faced by the many communities and stakeholders who constitute the two states and the region.

6. Delink from other conflicts. The delinking of distinct conflicts that have become enmeshed is strongly associated with the termination phase of most enduring rivalries.[22] The fate of Israel-Palestine would improve considerably were it to delink from the many other regional and international conflicts with which it is associated. For instance, the Arab-Israeli conflict became less severe in the 1970s and 1980s as other rivalries began to delink, including Jordan's choice not to take part in the

1973 war and Egypt making peace with Israel. Even if delinking proves difficult, it must be recognized that most efforts regarding one conflict often have spillover effects in other, related conflicts.

7. Establish inhibiting feedback mechanisms. Once the intensity of the conflict dissipates, it is important to target specific links for the introduction of inhibiting feedback mechanisms, to help mitigate future surges in hostility and violence. Tactics such as establishing early-warning systems in neighborhoods to notify officials when intercommunal tensions heat up; increasing the presence of "neutral" monitors or observers in areas where conflicts tend to be triggered; and increasing the number of crosscutting structures like joint-sports teams, political clubs, and workgroups can help mitigate intergroup violence. Also, supporting feedback mechanisms that monitor and report on one-sided narratives in school history textbooks and popular media, like the Institute for Monitoring Peace and Cultural Tolerance in School Education, is essential for preventing future generations from returning to the same destructive patterns.

8. Limit the festering of negativity through movement. Experience and research tell us that attempts to ghettoize and constrain opponents during periods of open conflict establish ideal conditions for fostering the accumulation and spread of hostilities, which are more likely to fester when groups are constrained in one location.[23] These findings have direct implications for Israel's policies regarding refugee camps, checkpoints, and border walls. This is not to diminish Israel's very significant security concerns. It simply points out one consequence of such policies.

9. Identify, support, and develop indigenous repellers for violence. Communities around the world have well-established taboos against committing particular forms of violence and aggression. In particular, the major religions present in Israel-Palestine tend to promote actions reflecting moral values conducive to peaceful relations with other people. To varying degrees, they all emphasize impulse control, tolerance, nonviolence, and concern for the welfare of others. These features hold potential for the prevention of violence and the peaceful resolution of conflict. Efforts designed to emphasize these rules of interpersonal behavior can offset the intolerance associated with good-versus-evil categorization in the 5 percent. There are numerous instances in history when calls to a higher morality have defused conflicts and brought about interpersonal and intergroup harmony.

Practice III. Change to Stabilize

1. Capitalize on regional instability. One of the greatest challenges of the conflict in the Middle East presents perhaps one of the best hopes for peace. Instability in the region, brought on by tensions between the Middle East and the West, Shiites and Sunnis, secular and nonsecular groups, pro-settler and anti-settler groups, developed and developing countries, you name it, ironically reshuffles the deck. It can provide optimal conditions for dramatic changes and opportunities for a realignment of the system. A simple awareness of this can bring hope.

2. Delink the issues: break it down. Round-table negotiations, successful in the context of other intractable disputes, in particular within Eastern Bloc countries and the Soviet Union, are a useful starting point. They help to table the high-level power struggles over control and sovereignty inherent to these conflicts; instead, the focus is at a more concrete level, to move practical aspects of the society forward (functional health care, agriculture, transportation, tourism, etc.). Working at this lower level, while temporarily circumventing the global issues of power, control, and identity, can help to initiate an altogether new emergent dynamic.

3. Be (somewhat) patient. Sustainable, fundamental change takes time. Often it takes years, even decades. Nevertheless, it is incumbent on leaders to try to maintain a sufficient rate of progress toward their stated goals, and to actively communicate this progress, if they are to manage dissent among their constituents.

4. Throughout, make more decisions. As Dörner's research shows, leaders need to remain vigilant after they implement new decisions and actions in order to be prepared to address the unintended consequences of their policies. This is especially true when operating in tightly coupled, unpredictable systems like the 5 percent. Be vigilant about the unexpected consequences of peace.

5. Have humility. These perspectives and proposals for addressing the Israeli-Palestinian conflict are certainly not comprehensive or complete, and many build on previous recommendations and initiatives. But they illustrate how the ALM's approach can be applied to contemporary conflicts, big and small, and how it offers an integrative platform for understanding intractability and change, even in those conflicts that appear particularly dire.

THE ALM APPROACH PRESENTS a new way of seeing and thinking about old problems and solutions that is both provocative and promising. But it is still in its early stages of development. We invite you to join us in the further development, specification, testing, and implementation of the model and practices.

conclusion

It always seems impossible until it's done.
—***Nelson Mandela, 1994***

THIS BOOK CLAIMS THAT some conflicts are different. Many are troublesome, difficult, even painful, yet they can be managed or resolved in ways that either contain the damage or in fact make life better for the people involved. But some conflicts, approximately one out of twenty of the more serious ones we face, are different. Like some malignant forms of cancer, they are pathologies that grow and spread, unresponsive to most known forms of treatment. They can wreak havoc on the lives of those involved, instilling a great sense of despair. It is to these conflicts that we have turned our attention for over a decade, and discovered that they require us to *think different.*

Our new understanding of these problems is both complex and simple. It is complex because it is mindful of the facts that (1) all such conflicts are unique, (2) they usually involve a host of distinct subproblems that interact and influence each other in weird ways, and (3) they are always changing and therefore hard to nail down, diagnose, and resolve effectively. However, our view of the 5 percent is also simple because it suggests that no matter what the issues are, or how they got started, or who is involved, at some point they are really about how they *organize.* That they become very tightly coupled and closed self-perpetuating systems that spread, impervious to outside influence.

The Attractor Landscape Model offers a few basic principles and practices that can help us understand these conflicts differently and more accurately, and ultimately make a difference. However, using the ideas and practices outlined in this book is not without its challenges.

- First, because they swim against the tide of our own mental attractors: our prior understanding of conflict and peace. The ALM presents a new, unfamiliar, and therefore somewhat uncomfortable perspective and language; thus, it is likely to elicit resistance from those steeped in more standard approaches. As Nobel Prize physicist Murray Gell-Mann proclaimed at the Founding Workshops of the Santa Fe Institute, "Attractors might be connected with our human habit of getting stuck in a certain way of thinking and finding it extremely difficult to jump out of the rut into another way of thinking."[1] The ALM requires this jump.

- Second, the ALM is not a necessary approach in all conflicts (only in approximately 5 percent of them) and should be understood as such.
- Third, complex systems are always unpredictable; therefore, we can offer no guarantees that tactic A will lead to outcome B. However, our research suggests that a long-term commitment to applying the principles and practices outlined here is likely to lead to constructive changes in the *patterns* of the conflict over time.
- Fourth, the ALM approach and some of the tactics (like changing attractors) can take a long time to unfold and become evident and may feel too long in some situations to be useful; they might therefore meet with frustration and resistance from stakeholders.
- And fifth, because the *real* implementation of these tools in *real* conflicts requires a nuanced and informed understanding of each situation and its history. And it must be "local"—that is, grounded in the realities of the situation. This is the kind of intimate knowledge of conflicts that external third parties rarely possess. Local collaboration is vital.

Nevertheless, outlined below are a set of basic skills we can all build on to enhance our capacity for applying the ALM principles and practices effectively on the ground.

Understanding nonlinear networks of causation. Developing a basic understanding of how complex, nonlinear systems function, stabilize, and change, including becoming familiar with ideas of emergence, self-organization, attractors, repellers, feedback loops, networks, and unintended consequences.[2]

Enhancing complex thinking, feeling, acting, and identification. Learning the difference between divergent and convergent thinking and developing the skills for employing both in an iterative fashion when addressing complex, long-term problems. Also, enhancing our capacity for (1) *emotional complexity;* that is, increasing the degree to which we experience a broad range of emotional events and are able to make subtle distinctions within emotion categories; (2) *behavioral complexity,* defined as the array of differentiated and even competing behaviors people display; and (3) *social identity complexity,* or the capacity to identify with contradictory group memberships.[3]

Thinking globally and locally, and understanding how these viewpoints are connected. The theory of *action identification* holds that identities of action vary in level, from the low-level identities that tell how an action is done (such as chewing and swallowing) to higher-level identities that indicate the action's consequences (such as getting nutrition or gaining weight).[4] Understanding these differences is important for learning how to "work down below"; that is, how to identify and address the component parts of problems without their getting snarled in general principles. This is critical to altering attractor landscapes.

Understanding latent processes. Understanding how implicit (latent) processes (such as implicit intergroup attitudes and beliefs) operate psychologically and socially can provide important insight into how latent attractors develop and change over time.[5]

Managing the tensions between short-term and long-term thinking and action. Seeing how crisis intervention and long-term planning often work at cross-purposes and learning how to strike an effective balance are also critical for managing the long-term dynamics of intractable conflicts.[6]

Learning to see both the opportunities *and* the dangers ahead. The ALM suggests that conflict and peace often coexist. It is important to understand how our chronic prevention orientations (concerns with safety) versus promotion orientations (thinking about our hopes and dreams) affect our perceptions of social conflicts, and the importance of both for visualizing and attaining sustainable solutions. This can help us to appreciate the challenges and opportunities for working on both constructive and destructive attractors simultaneously.[7]

Leveraging multilevel strategies. Increasing probabilities for peace often requires thinking and working at different levels (psychological, social, structural, institutional, cultural) simultaneously. This necessitates an understanding of the activities and interventions possible at different levels, the differences in the time they take to unfold in a system, and a sense of the mechanisms that link these initiatives across levels.[8]

Together, these skills constitute a set of building blocks for developing the capacity to employ the ALM practices effectively. These are all learnable skills. Skills that many of us possess but that most of us would benefit from developing further.

ALMOST FIFTY YEARS AGO, John F. Kennedy made this appeal:

> Too many of us think [that peace] is impossible. Too many think it is unreal. But that is a dangerous, defeatist belief. It leads to the conclusion that war is inevitable, that mankind is doomed, that we are gripped by forces we cannot control. We need not accept that view . . . Let us focus instead on a more practical, more attainable peace, based not on a sudden revolution in human nature but on a gradual evolution in human institutions—on a series of concrete actions and effective agreements which are in the interest of all concerned. There is no single, simple key to this peace; no grand or magic formula to be adopted by one or two powers. Genuine peace must be the product of many nations, the sum of many acts. It must be dynamic, not static, changing to meet the challenge of each new generation. For peace is a process—a way of solving problems.[9]

This book presents the first systematic, integrated, evidence-based framework for understanding the 5 percent; it offers a coherent set of principles and practices for making peace at home, at work, and beyond. We have found that the closed, destructive, and coherent attractor dynamics operating in Kashmir, Cyprus, and Israel-Palestine are similar to those functioning in protracted disputes within families like Kasha and Anthony's, businesses like ExxonMobil and ChevronTexaco in Nigeria, and communities like Brookline and New York City. But, more important, even in the most hopeless and violent settings, like Mozambique, Liberia, and South Africa in the 1980s, we have also found that more positive latent attractors, "peace traps," quietly await their turn to capture the dynamics of the system. This is the moral of our story. Intractable conflicts can erupt anywhere, and so can peace.

The ALM allows us to build on and incorporate many of the important ideas and methods for peacekeeping, peace-making and peacebuilding developed by our predecessors and contemporaries, but to do so with a vision and approach that is comprehensive and mindful of the complex, long-term dynamics of systemic change. It allows for the merging of the old and the new, the preventative and the promotive, the complex and the simple, to make the impossible possible.

Returning finally to our ancient ancestors in the House of Atreus, it is important to note that the curse on the Tantalus's family was eventually broken, through the combination of a noble human act and a wise integrative catalyst.

A Parable of Human Progress

Generations after Tantalus, his great-grandson Agamemnon returned home from the Trojan War, only to be slaughtered by his own wife, Clytemnestra. (who was avenging Agamemnon's murder of their daughter Iphigenia). Agamemnon's only son, Orestes, was quite young at the time of his father's murder. But his sister, Electra, made him swear revenge. Orestes knew that it was his duty to avenge his father's death, but he also knew this meant killing his own mother. As Aeschylus wrote: "It was a son's duty to kill his father's murderers, a duty that came before all others. But a son who killed his mother was abhorrent to gods and to men."[10] So when Orestes was advised by the god Apollo to proceed with killing his mother, he knew he must work out the curse on his house by exacting revenge on his mother, paying with his own personal ruin. And so he did.

But Orestes' murderous act was met immediately by the constant torment of the Furies, the Female deities of vengeance. Eventually, after suffering from intolerable pain and guilt, Orestes pleaded for mercy from Apollo and Athene. Apollo represented everything the Furies were not: youth, masculinity, and enlightened intellect. He condemned the Furies, proclaiming Orestes should be set free from their wrath. But the Furies countered by arguing:

> There are times when fear is good.
> It must keep its watchful place
> at the heart's controls. There is
> advantage
> in the wisdom won from pain.
> Should the city, should the man
> rear a heart that nowhere goes
> in fear, how shall such a one
> any more respect the right?
> Refuse the life of anarchy;
> refuse the life devoted to one master.
> The in-between has the power
> by God's grant always . . .

Then Athena, the goddess of war and wisdom, who embodied the contradictions of masculinity and femininity, intellect and passion, transformed the scene. Because of the noble nature of his actions and his willingness to repent, she decided in favor of Orestes' freedom. This of course incensed the Furies, who threatened: "I, disinherited, suffering, heavy with anger / shall let loose on the land / the vindictive poison / dripping deadly out of my heart upon the ground . . ." But Athena reassured them, saying: "I will bear your angers. You are elder born than I / And in that you are wiser far than I. / Yet still Zeus gave me too intelligence not to be despised."

In her wisdom, Athena devised a means to honor the Furies. She offered to pay them tribute by *integrating* them, with their rage and passion, into the goodness and progress of society. The Furies accept this offer:

> This is my prayer: Civil war
> fattening on men's ruin shall
> not thunder in our city. Let

not the dry dust that drinks
the black blood of citizens
through passion for revenge
and bloodshed for bloodshed
be given our state to prey upon.
Let them render grace for grace.
Let love be their common will;
let them hate with single heart.
Much wrong in the world thereby is healed.

Through this act, Athene reconciled the need for fury and fear with the need for enlightened rational discourse. In so doing, she *transformed the tragedy inflicted on Tantalus's descendants into a parable of human progress.* In the end, Athena remarked that "neither he nor any descendant of his would ever again be driven into evil by the irresistible power of the past." And so ended the curse on the House of Atreus.

Even impossible problems can be brought to an end.

appendix a

THE ATTRACTOR SOFTWARE

The attractor software is essentially a visualization tool designed to help users see the three dimensions of conflict systems: current state, potential positive, and potential negative. It prompts the user to specify the key factors influencing the conflict (ideally generated from the mapping exercises) and the actions that can be undertaken, then to estimate the consequences of these actions with respect to three types of outcomes:

1. Their influence on the current state of the conflict
2. Their influence on the potential for future conflict or negative interactions
3. Their influence on the potential for positive social interactions and, ultimately, sustainable peace

The user, by evaluating each factor, estimates the strength and the direction of the influence of each factor on the *whole conflict system.* The software merely visualizes the understanding of the user; it is a tool for describing what parties and interveners have identified, based on their own expertise, experience, and mapping of a case.

The software does not estimate the importance of each factor by itself nor does it estimate its influences. It is up to the user:

1. To specify the case and the social relations to be analyzed (e.g., a marriage, an ethnic conflict)
2. To generate the factors most likely to influence the nature of the current and future relationship
3. To evaluate the importance and strength of each factor for the system and the direction of its influence for the three dimensions (see image on page 226)

The program provides a visualization of two attractors for any relationship: a positive attractor for favorable attitudes and positive actions, and a negative attractor for malignant or unfavorable attitudes and negative or violent actions (see image below). How the factors introduced by the user affect the overt thoughts and behaviors in the conflict will depend on the respective strength of the positive and negative attractors. If the current state of the relationship (the gray ball) is within the pull of a strong attractor, this state is unlikely to change despite the introduction of factors relevant to change. Conversely, if the state of the relationship is outside an attractor (such as in the image below), the relationship may display a dramatic, qualitative change (e.g., from positive to negative) with the addition of a single, seemingly unimportant factor.

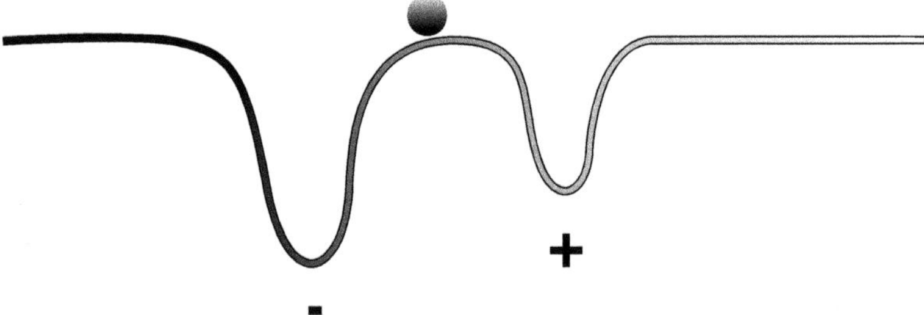

A conflict attractor landscape with two attractors, one for destructive interactions (left) and one for constructive interactions (right). The current state of conflict (gray ball) is at a tipping point between the two attractors, which is unstable and thus could be propelled into either attractor by relatively small, insignificant influences.

HOW TO USE THE PROGRAM

The attractor software program relies on the user's experience with the conflict or expertise in a particular area. It assumes that the user is somewhat knowledgeable about the factors relevant to the thoughts, feelings, and behaviors in the relationship, and that he or she can specify *his or her sense* of the relative importance of these factors. Someone who works with members of the Columbia University community, for example, may be in a position to identify the various conditions and triggers that affect each group. However, such analyses gain considerable depth and validity if they involve directly members of the various concerned groups. The users then type in the label for a factor and use a slider bar to specify its overall importance in affecting the relationships within the analyzed system.

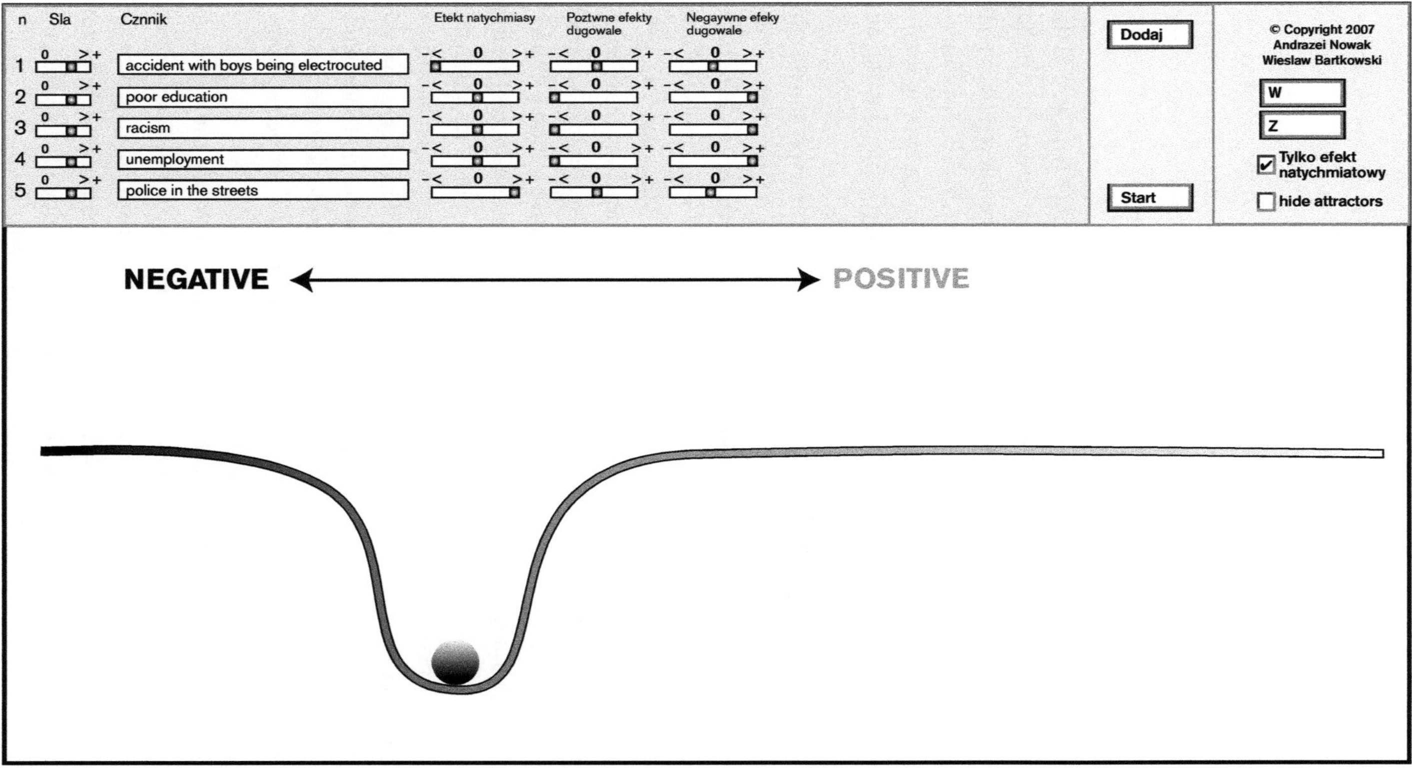

Input (list of factors on the top) and output (visualization of the attractor landscape and the momentary state represented by the moving ball toward the valley).

Despite the user's expertise and insight, the influence of specific factors introduced into the visualization software is often not obvious. In nonlinear systems, a minor provocation can push two groups into open warfare, while a major change in conditions might have little effect. This can be seen when the attractors characterizing the relationship are constructed and the resulting dynamics visualized. A momentary change in thought or behavior in response to a specific factor does not necessarily affect the long-term features of the relationship. However, strong potentials of systems (latent attractors) sometimes become manifest as qualitative shifts in the relationship unfold (such as radical shifts from peaceful relations to open conflict, or from violence to peace). If the state of a person or group is captured by an attractor, even strong forces that seem capable of changing thought and behavior may be countered by the attracting tendency of the prevailing thoughts and behaviors. But if a person or group's state is outside the pull of an attractor (as in the image above), even a minor force might be sufficient to move the person or group's thoughts and actions toward a different attractor.

In addition to allowing the user to employ his or her knowledge and insight to specify relevant factors and their respective importance, the program allows the user to specify the nature of their impact. Sometimes a factor can have both a positive and negative impact. In a marital relationship, for example, raising children can strengthen the bonds between the partners, but it can also produce considerable stress and thus challenge the relationship. To capture a factor's potential for both positive and negative effects, the user employs separate slider bars to indicate (1) how much the factor in question promotes (future) positive thoughts and behaviors and (2) how much the factor promotes (future) negative thoughts and behaviors in the relationship. It is worth emphasizing again that these two characteristics of relationships do not always act in opposition; in fact, they often prove to be somewhat independent. This means that the potential for positive interactions can grow or decrease somewhat independently from the potential for negative interactions. For example, fostering social contact between groups in conflict can increase the potential for both positive and negative interactions in the future.

The program also allows the user to specify, on a slider bar, the degree to which the factor in question contributes to momentary states of tension, open conflict, or violence. Again, the user's expertise and insights are critical here. In ethnic relations, for example, income disparity may be a very important factor in the long run, but it is unlikely to directly spark an episode of violence on a particular day. An act of humiliation, in contrast, may well provide the catalyst for momentary violence in such a relationship. A separate slider bar is provided to allow the user to specify the impact of each factor on the immediate versus long-term reactions of the system.

Finally, the program allows the user to reconfigure the attractor landscape directly. The preset configuration of positive and negative attractors may not capture the knowledge and insight of the user. It may be, for example, that the user feels that the positive attractor is relatively weak (a shallow valley) but has a wide basin of attraction (a wide valley), whereas the negative attractor is quite strong but has a narrow basin of attraction (a deep but narrow valley). By changing the attractor landscape, the user can observe whether the relevant factors and their specific effects (on positivity, negativity, and momentary conflict) begin to play a larger or smaller role in defining the overall quality of the relationship. The software can thus be employed in different ways to achieve different ends.

POTENTIAL APPLICATIONS OF THE PROGRAM

The attractor software can be useful in different ways. The benefits of working with the program include managing the complexity of the 5 percent, untangling the long- and short-term consequences of conditions and actions, and understanding that the same action can have conflicting effects on the positive and negative aspects of the conflict. Below we outline some of the possible applications and benefits of using the software.

1. Apply your general knowledge of conflict. The interactive nature of the program enables users to tap into their knowledge and insight regarding conflict, and to see how the factors they identify impact both the momentary and long-term potential states of the relationship among the conflicting parties. With the addition of each new factor, the momentary state of the relationship is changed, but whether and how this change affects the long-term relationship will depend on the attractor landscape. This should sensitize users to the distinction between interventions that have immediate but not long-lasting effects and interventions whose effects may not be immediately apparent but that change the attractor landscape and create more sustainable solutions and new possibilities for relationships.

2. Work with a specific case. Data can be collected on specific cases and used to identify relevant factors in particular conflicts, to specify the overall importance of these factors, and to define the impact of these factors on positivity, negativity, and momentary conflict. In this way, the program can be used to identify which factors should receive attention in real-world contexts.

3. Work in groups. Users can also interact with the software in small groups. This allows them to share insights and together identify relevant factors, specify the effects of these factors, and observe how the relationship responds in the short term (momentary state) and in the long term (attractor tendencies). Rather than arguing about the likely effects of different interventions, for example, the users can test their respective assumptions and intuitions through visualization, and in this way perhaps reach a common understanding with agreed-upon strategies for addressing the conflict.

4. Use as an intervention platform. The software can also be used as a platform for resolving conflicts among representatives of conflicting parties. The parties to a conflict often see the world in different terms, and this lack of a shared reality can contribute to a conflict's intractability. By working with this software in a collaborative venture, the representatives of the conflicting parties might discover what factors are most relevant to the maintenance of the conflict. More important, an initiative of this kind might promote an agreed-upon mode of intervention for resolving the conflict.

The software was developed to be easy to use, and our website has already had thousands of individual users go online to access and work with the program. So go to http://www.iccc.edu.pl/as/ to learn and play!

appendix b

ANALYTICAL CONTENTS

columbia university's international center for cooperation and conflict resolution (ICCCR)

http://www.tc.columbia.edu/icccr/

The ICCCR is an innovative center at Columbia University committed to developing knowledge and practice to promote constructive conflict resolution, effective cooperation, and social justice. **ICCCR's International Project on Conflict and Complexity (IPCC)** (http://www.tc.columbia.edu/icccr/index.asp?Id=Theory+and+Research&Info=International+Project+on+Conflict+and+Complexity) is an interdisciplinary consortium of peace and conflict scholars and practitioners from anthropology, psychology, international relations, physics, and complexity science, funded by the James S. McDonnell Foundation and the Community Foundation of Boulder, working to generate new insights and methods for addressing difficult intractable conflicts of all types. It generates and supports innovative, interdisciplinary, scholar-practitioner activities that address difficult, unresolved issues in the areas of conflict resolution and sustainable peace.

Peter T. Coleman, PhD, Social-Organizational Psychology is Director of the International Center for Cooperation and Conflict Resolution (ICCCR) at Teachers College, Columbia University, and Associate Professor of Psychology and Education at Teachers College, Columbia University, a member of the faculty of Columbia University's Earth Institute, Chair of the International Project on Conflict and Complexity (IPCC), Chair of the Advanced Consortium on Cooperation, Conflict, and Complexity (AC^4) at Columbia, and an affiliate of the International Center for Complexity and Conflict (ICCC) at the Warsaw School for Social Psychology in Warsaw, Poland. Dr. Coleman coedits *The Handbook of Conflict Resolution: Theory and Practice* (2000; 2nd ed., 2006) and has authored over sixty journal articles and chapters. He is also a New York State–certified mediator and experienced consultant.

Robin Vallacher, PhD, Social Psychology is Professor of Psychology, Florida Atlantic University, and Research Affiliate at Columbia University's ICCCR, IPCC and the Advanced Consortium on Cooperation, Conflict, and Complexity (AC^4) and the Center for Complex Systems, Warsaw University. In recent years, his work has centered on identifying the invariant properties underlying diverse social phenomena. Using experimentation and computer simulations, he and his colleagues are investigating the dynamism and complexity associated with such phenomena as self-regulation, social judgment, close relations, intergroup conflict, and the emergence of personality from social interaction. Dr. Vallacher has published five books, including two with Andrzej Nowak that develop the implications of dynamical systems for social psychology, and over a hundred articles and chapters.

Andrzej Nowak, PhD, Psychology is Professor of Psychology at the Warsaw School of Social Sciences and Humanities, where he is the Director of the Institute of Social Psychology of Informatics and Communications. He is also Professor of Psychology at University of Warsaw, where he directs the Center for Complex Systems at Institute for Social Studies, Associate Professor of Psychology, Florida Atlantic University, and Research Affiliate at Columbia University's ICCCR, IPCC and the Advanced Consortium on Cooperation, Conflict, and Complexity (AC^4). His primary focus is on the dynamical approach to social psychology. He has done research concerning social influence, social transitions, social dilemmas, emotions, and the self. His current research includes the use of coupled dynamical systems to simulate the emergence of personality through social coordination, attractor neural networks to model interpersonal and group dynamics, and cellular automata to simulate societal change. Dr. Nowak has published five books, including two with Robin Vallacher concerning dynamical social psychology, and over a hundred articles and chapters.

Andrea Bartoli, PhD, Anthropology holds the Drucie French Cumbie Chair at the Institute of Conflict Analysis and Resolution at George Mason University.

He works primarily on Peacemaking and Genocide Prevention. The Founding Director of Columbia University's Center for International Conflict Resolution (CICR), a Senior Research Scholar at the School of International and Public Affairs (SIPA), a Teaching Fellow at Georgetown University and at the University of Siena, and a Research Affiliate at Columbia University's ICCCR and the Advanced Consortium on Cooperation, Conflict, and Complexity (AC^4), Dr. Bartoli has taught in the United States since 1994. He is a board member of Search for Common Ground, has been involved in many conflict resolution activities as a member of the Community of Sant'Egidio (http://www.santegidio.org/en/), and has published books and articles on violence, migrations, and conflict resolution. He was coeditor of *Somalia, Rwanda and Beyond: The Role of International Media in Wars and International Crisis.*

Lan Bui-Wrzosinska, PhD, Psychology is a faculty member at the Warsaw School of Social Sciences and Humanities and a Research Affiliate at Columbia University's ICCCR, IPCC and the Advanced Consortium on Cooperation, Conflict, and Complexity (AC^4). Her interests are focused on the dynamical systems approach to intractable conflicts. She has cotaught courses in Poland, at Teachers College, Columbia University, and in Florida Atlantic University. She is currently developing a dynamical model of intractable conflicts and conducting experimental and qualitative studies on the dynamics of change in intractable conflicts. Lan Bui-Wrzosinska is also implementing conflict resolution programs in educational settings in Warsaw and New York City.

Larry Liebovitch, PhD, Astrophysics is Dean of Division of Mathematics and Natural Sciences and Professor in the Departments of Physics and Psychology at Queens College, City University of New York. Previously, he was Professor and Dean at Florida Atlantic University, Dr. Liebovitch earned a bachelor's degree in physics at City College of New York and a doctorate in astronomy from Harvard. He was a Postdoctoral Fellow at the Mount Sinai School of Medicine in New York and then served as Assistant Professor at the College of Physicians and Surgeons of Columbia University. He is formerly the Director of the Center for Complex Systems and Brain Sciences at Florida Atlantic University, where he also has appointments in the Departments of Psychology and Biomedical Science and at the Center for Molecular Biology and Biotechnology. He is a Research Affiliate at Columbia University's ICCCR and the Advanced Consortium on Cooperation, Conflict, and Complexity (AC^4).

Naira Musallam, PhD, Social-Organizational Psychologist received her BA in Psychology and Journalism from Tel Aviv University in 2000. She has held various positions in Israel-Palestine, including working with the Adler Research Center for Child Welfare and Protection, where she conducted research assessing the psychological impact of ethnopolitical conflict on various sects of the Palestinian and Israeli populations. She has worked with the Mar Elias Educational Institutions, dedicated to building peace through education, and also with Amnesty International. The U.S. Department of State awarded her the Israeli-Arab Scholarship to earn her master's degree in the United States. Ms. Musallam has completed her MA in Psychology and Education with a concentration in Conflict Resolution at Teachers College, Columbia University. Ms. Musallam served as the Vice President of the Educational Society for Middle East and North Africa at Columbia University and has interned with the International Center for Transitional Justice and the Institute for Mediation and Conflict Resolution.

Katharina Kugler, PhD, is a lecturer in psychology at the Ludwig-Maximilians-University, Munich, Germany. Previously, she held a Fellowship in Complexity and Conflict at the ICCCR to study at Teachers College and worked as a Research Assistant for Professor Coleman. She received her "Diplom" (combined BA and MA) in Psychology at the University of Munich, Germany. During her graduate studies she studied for one year at Teachers College, holding a Fulbright Scholarship. Her main research interest is in the role of emotions in conflicts. Ms. Kugler previously contributed to a series of studies that elaborated on how the experience of humiliation fuels intractable conflicts. Currently her research concentrates on conflicts within organizations, employing the dynamical systems theory approach.

notes

INTRODUCTION

1. Richard Lattimore, *Aeschylus 1: Oresteia* (Chicago: University of Chicago Press, 1953).

2. Paul F. Diehl and Gary Goertz, *War and Peace in International Rivalry* (Ann Arbor: University of Michigan Press, 2001).

3. John F. Burns, "British Military Expands Links to French Allies," *New York Times,* November 2, 2010, http://www.nytimes.com/2010/11/03/world/europe/03britain.html?ref=john_f_burns.

CHAPTER 1

1. Fox Butterfield, "Insanity Drove a Man to Kill at 2 Clinics, Jury Is Told," *New York Times,* February 15, 1996, http://www.nytimes.com/1996/02/15/us/insanity-drove-a-man-to-kill-at-2-clinics-jury-is-told.html.

2. Anne Fowler et al., "Talking with the Enemy," *Boston Globe,* January 28, 2001, F1–F3.

3. See Roger Fisher, William L. Ury, and Bruce Patton, *Getting to Yes: Negotiating Agreement Without Giving In* (New York: Penguin Books, 1981); Roy Lewicki, A. J. Literer, J. Minton, and D. M. Saundars. *Negotiation.* 3rd ed. (Boston: Irwin/McGraw-Hill, 2004); S. Coleman, E. Raider, and J. Gerson, "Teaching Conflict Resolution Skills in a Workshop" in Morton Deutsch and Peter T. Coleman, eds., *Handbook of Conflict Resolution: Theory and Practice* (San Francisco: Jossey-Bass, 2000), 499–545; International Center for Cooperation and Conflict Resolution Negotiation and Mediation Instruction Model, 2006, property of ICCCR, Teachers College, Columbia University; Morton Deutsch, *The Resolution of Conflict: Constructive and Destructive Processes* (New Haven, CT: Yale University Press, 1973); Morton Deutsch, "Constructive Conflict Resolution: Principles, Training, and Research," *Journal of Social Issues* 50, no. 1 (1994): 13–32; Deutsch and Coleman, "Cooperation and Competition," in *Handbook of Conflict Resolution,* 21–40.

4. Diehl and Goertz, *War and Peace.*

5. Roy Lewicki et al., "Individual Differences," in *Negotiation* (Boston: Irwin/McGraw-Hill, 1994), 324–48.

6. See Douglas P. Fry, *Beyond War: The Human Potential for Peace* (New York: Oxford University Press, 2007); Peter T. Coleman and Morton Deutsch, eds., *Psychology's Contributions to Sustainable Peace* (forthcoming from Springer Books in summer of 2011).

7. Bruce Barry and Richard L. Oliver, "Affect in Dyadic Negotiation: A Model and Propositions," *Organizational Behavior and Human Decision Processes* 70 (1996): 175–87; Peter T. Coleman, Jennifer S. Goldman, and Katharina Kugler, "Emotional Intractability: Gender, Anger, Aggression, and Rumination in Conflict," *International Journal of Conflict Management* 20 (2009): 113–31.

8. Ronald J. Fisher, *The Social Psychology of Intergroup and International Conflict Resolution* (New York: Springer-Verlag, 1990).

9. John Carey, "Online Extra: When More Medicine Is Less," *Bloomberg Businessweek,* May 29, 2006, http://www.businessweek.com/print/magazine/content/06_22/b3986016.htm?chan=gl (accessed December 7, 2010).

10. Christopher Honeyman, "Theory versus Practice in Dispute Resolution," 1977, http://www.convenor.com/madison/theory.htm.

11. Dietrich Dorner, *The Logic of Failure: Why Things Go Wrong and What We Can Do to Make Them Right* (New York: Holt and Co., 1996).

CHAPTER 2

1. Diehl and Goertz, *War and Peace.*

2. Jeremy M. Sharp, "U.S. Foreign Aid to Israel," Congressional Research Service, September 16, 2010, https://tcmail1.tc.columbia.edu/exchange/coleman/Inbox/RE:%20stats.EML/1_multipart_xF8FF_2_CRS_J.Sharp.pdf/C58EA28C-18C0-4a97-9AF2-036E93DDAFB3/CRS_J.Sharp.pdf?attach=1.

3. USAID, http://www.usaid.gov/policy/budget/money.

4. Amy Belasco, "The Cost of Iraq, Afghanistan, and Other Global War on Terror Operations Since 9/11," Congressional Research Service, September 2, 2010, http://www.fas.org/sgp/crs/natsec/RL33110.pdf (accessed December 7, 2010); USAID, http://www.usaid.gov/policy/budget/money.

5. Human Rights Watch, http://www.globalissues.org/article/86/nigeria-and-oil (accessed December 7, 2010).

6. John P. Lederach, *Building Peace: Reconciliation in Divided Societies* (Washington: USIP, 1997).

7. Marc H. Ross, *The Management of Conflict: Interpretations and Interests in Comparative Perspective* (New Haven, CT: Yale University Press, 1993).

8. Emda Orr, Shifra Sagi, and Dan Bar-On, "Social Representations in Use: Israeli and Palestinian High School Students' Collective Coping and Defense," *Papers on Social Representations* 9, no. 2 (2000): 1–20.

9. Adam Nossiter, "Bombs by Nigerian Insurgents Kill 8," *New York Times,* October 1, 2010, http://www.nytimes.com/2010/10/02/world/africa/02nigeria.html?ref=adam_nossiter (accessed December 7, 2010).

10. Adam Nossiter, "Far from Gulf, a Spill Scourge 5 Decades Old," *New York Times,* June 16, 2010, http://www.nytimes.com/2010/06/17/world/africa/17nigeria.html?th&emc=th (accessed December 7, 2010).

11. Human Rights Watch, http://www.hrw.org/en/node/87680.

12. John McCarthy and Patrick J. Hayes, "Some Philosophical Problems from the Standpoint of Artificial Intelligence," in B. Meltzer and D. Michie, eds., *Machine Intelligence* 4 (Edinburgh: Edinburgh University Press, 1969), 463–502; Jordan B. Peterson and Joseph L. Flanders, "Complexity Management Theory: Motivation for Ideological Rigidity and Social Conflict," *Cortex* 38 (2002): 429–58.

13. Peterson and Flanders, "Complexity Management Theory."

14. Also called metaphors. See Carol Dweck, *Mindset: The New Psychology of Success* (New York: Random House, 2007); Lewicki, Gray, and Elliot, *Making Sense;* George Lakoff and Mark Johnson, *Metaphors We Live By* (Chicago: University of Chicago Press, 2003); Gareth Morgan, *Images of Organization* (London: Sage Publications, 1997).

15. George A. Miller, "The Magical Number Seven, Plus or Minus Two: Some Limits on Our Capacity for Processing Information," *Psychological Review* 63 (1956): 81–97; Richard M. Shiffrin and Robert M. Nosofsky, "Seven Plus or Minus Two: A Commentary on Capacity Limitations," *Psychological Review* 101 (1994): 357–61.

16. See James G. March and Herbert A. Simon, *Organizations* (New York: Wiley, 1958).

17. Charles E. Osgood, *An Alternative to War or Surrender* (Urbana: University of Illinois Press, 1962).

18. See Kaiping Peng and Richard E. Nisbett, "Culture Dialectics, and Reasoning about Contradiction," *American Psychologist* 54 (1999): 741–54.

19. Peterson and Flanders, "Complexity Management Theory."

20. George A. Kelly, *The Psychology of Personal Constructs* (New York: Norton, 1955); Phillip E. Tetlock, "Cognitive Style and Political Ideology," *Journal*

of Personality and Social Psychology: Personality Processes and Individual Differences 45 (1983): 118–26; Lucian G. Conway, Peter Suedfeld, and Phillip E. Tetlock, "Integrative Complexity and Political Decisions That Lead to War or Peace," in Daniel J. Christie, Richard V. Wagner, and Deborah Du Nann Winter, eds., *Peace, Conflict, and Violence: Peace Psychology for the 21st Century* (Upper Saddle River, NJ: Prentice Hall, 2001), 66–75; Eshkol Rafaeli-Mor and Jennifer Steinberg, "Self-complexity and Well-being: A Research Synthesis," *Personality and Social Psychology Review* 6 (2002): 31–58.

21. See Peter Suedfeld and A. Dennis Rank, "Revolutionary Leaders: Long-term Success as a Function of Changes in Conceptual Complexity," *Journal of Personality and Social Psychology* 34 (1976): 169–78; P. Suedfeld, P. E. Tetlock, and S. Streufert, "Conceptual/Integrative Complexity: The Development and Current State of the Construct" (1992), in Charles P. Smith, ed., *Motivation and Personality: Handbook of Thematic Content Analysis* (New York: Cambridge University Press, 2008), 393–400.

CHAPTER 3

1. John M. Gottman and Nan Silver, *The Seven Principles for Making Marriage Work* (New York: Three Rivers Press, 1999).

2. Max Wertheimer, "Gestalt Theory" (1925), in Willis D. Ellis, ed. and trans., *A Source Book of Gestalt Psychology* (London: Routledge and Kegan Paul, 1938), 71–88.

3. Peng and Nisbett, "Culture Dialectics."

4. Kurt Lewin, *Principles of Topological Psychology* (New York: McGraw-Hill, 1936).

5. R. Poole. "Is It Healthy to Be Chaotic?" *Science* 243 (1989): 604–07.

6. A. L. Goldberger, D. R. Rigney, and J. B. West, "Chaos and Fractals in Human Physiology," *Scientific American* 262 (1990): 43–49.

7. G. Nicolis, *Introduction to Nonlinear Science* (Cambridge, UK: Cambridge University Press, 1995).

8. Ary L. Goldberger, "Fractal Variability versus Pathological Periodicity: Complexity Loss and Stereotypy in Disease," *Perspectives in Biology and Medicine,* 40 (1997): 543–61.

9. Daniel J. Siegel, *Mindsight: The New Science of Personal Transformation* (New York: Bantam, 2010).

10. Conway, Suedfeld, and Tetlock, "Integrative Complexity."

11. See Shawn W. Rosenberg, *Reason, Ideology and Politics* (Princeton, NJ: Princeton University Press, 1988); A. Golec and C. M. Federico, "Understanding Responses to Political Conflict: Interactive Effects of the Need for Closure and Salient Conflict Schemas," *Journal of Personality and Social Psychology* 87, no. 6 (2004): 750–62.

12. L. Bui-Wrzosinska et al., "Are They With Us or Against Us? The Effects of Need for Closure on Conflict Orientations and Catastrophic Escalatory Dynamics," working paper.

13. See Donna M. Webster and Arie W. Kruglanski, "Individual Differences in Need for Cognitive Closure," *Journal of Personality and Social Psychology* 67 (1994): 1049–62; Jeanne H. Fu et al., "Epistemic Motives and Cultural Conformity: Need for Closure, Culture, and Context as Determinants of Conflict Judgments," *Journal of Personality and Social Psychology* 92, no. 2 (2007): 191–207.

14. See Sun-Mee Kang and Phillip R. Shaver, "Individual Differences in Well-Differentiated Emotional Experience: Their Possible Psychological Implications," *Journal of Personality* 72 (2004): 687–726.

15. Katharina Kugler and Peter T. Coleman, "Moral Conflict and Complexity: The Dynamics of Constructive versus Destructive Discussions over Polarizing Issues," working paper.

16. See Katherine A. Lawrence, Peter Lenk, and Robert E. Quinn, "Behavioral Complexity in Leadership: The Psychometric Properties of a New Instrument to Measure Behavioral Repertoire," *Leadership Quarterly* 20 (2009): 87–102.

17. Marcial Losada, "The Complex Dynamics of High Performance Teams," *Mathematical and Computer Modeling* 30, nos. 9–10 (1999): 179–92; Kugler and Coleman, "Moral Conflict and Complexity."

18. See Sonia Roccas and Marilynn B. Brewer, "Social Identity Complexity," *Personality and Social Psychology Review* 6 (2002): 88–106.

19. George A. Quattrone, "On the Perception of a Group's Variability," in Stephen Worchel and William G. Austin, eds., *Psychology of Intergroup Relations* (Chicago: Nelson Hall, 1986); Natalie Hall and Richard J. Crisp, "Considering Multiple Criteria for Social Categorization Can Reduce Intergroup Bias," *Personality and Social Psychology Bulletin* 31 (2005): 1453–44; Marilynn B. Brewer, "The Social Psychology of Intergroup Relations: Social Categorization, Ingroup Bias, and Outgroup Prejudice," in Arie W. Kruglanski and E. Tory Higgins, eds., *Social Psychology: Handbook of Basic Principles,* 2nd ed. (New York: Guilford Publications, 2007), 695–715.

20. See Morton Deutsch, "Interdependence and Psychological Orientation," in V. Derlega and J. Gezelak, eds., *Cooperation and Helping Behavior* (Cambridge, UK: Cambridge University Press, 1982), 15–42; E. Tory Higgins, "Making a Good Decision: Value from Fit," *American Psychologist* 55 (2000): 1217–30.

21. See F. Heider, *The Psychology of Interpersonal Relations* (New York: Wiley, 1958).

22. See Solomon E. Asch, "Effects of Group Pressure upon the Modification and Distortion of Judgment," in Harold Guetzkow, ed., *Groups, Leadership and Men* (Pittsburgh: Carnegie Press, 1951); Solomon E. Asch, "Opinions and Social Pressure," *Scientific American* 193 (1955): 31–35.

23. See Marcial Losada and Emily Heaphy, "The Role of Positivity and Connectivity in the Performance of Business Teams: A Nonlinear Dynamics Model," *American Behavioral Scientist* 47, no. 6 (2004): 740–65; Losada, "Complex Dynamics."

24. Robert D. Putnam, *Bowling Alone: The Collapse and Revival of American Community* (New York: Simon & Schuster, 2000); Rochelle R. Côté and Bonnie H. Erickson, "Untangling the Roots of Tolerance: How Forms of Social Capital Shape Attitudes toward Ethnic Minorities and Immigrants," *American Behavioral Scientist* 52, no. 12 (2009): 1664–89.

25. See Peter T. Coleman and Christine T. Chung, *Surveying Attractor Landscapes for Conflict: Investigating the Relationship between Conflict, Culture, and Complexity,* unpublished manuscript (2010), Department of Organization and Leadership, Columbia University Teachers College, New York, NY.

26. See Peng and Nisbett, "Culture Dialectics."

27. See Michele J. Gelfand, Lisa Nishii, and Jana L, Raver, "On the Nature and Importance of Cultural Tightness-Looseness," *Journal of Applied Psychology* 91 (2006): 1225–44.

28. Richard E. Nisbett and Dov Cohen, *Culture of Honor: The Psychology of Violence in the South* (Boulder, CO: Westview, 1996).

29. See Robert A. LeVine and Donald T. Campbell, *Ethnocentrism: Theories of Conflict, Ethnic Attitudes, and Group Behavior* (New York: Wiley, 1972); Ashutosh Varshney, *Ethnic Conflict and Civic Life: Hindus and Muslims in India* (New Haven, CT: Yale University, 2002).

30. Diehl and Goertz, *War and Peace.*

31. Celia W. Dugger, "India's Leader Speaks of Reconciliation in Letter to Pakistan," *New York Times,* May 26, 2001.

32. Ibid.

CHAPTER 4

1. Summarized from Barbara W. Tuchman, *The Guns of August* (New York: Macmillan Co., 1962).

2. Evelin Lindner, *Making Enemies: Humiliation and International Conflict* (Westport, CT: Praeger Security International, 2006).

3. This is known technically as a deviation-amplifying process of mutual causation. See Magorah Maruyama, "The Second Cybernetics: Deviation-Amplifying Mutual Causal Processes," *American Scientist* 5 no. 2 (1863): 164–79.

4. Ibid.

5. Kugler and Coleman, "Moral Conflict and Complexity.

6. John Gottman, Catherine Swanson, and Kristin Swanson, "A General Systems Theory of Marriage: Nonlinear Difference Equation Modeling of Marital Interaction," *Personality and Social Psychology Review* 6, no. 4 (2002): 326–40.

7. Larry S. Liebovitch, et al., "Dynamics of Two-Actor Cooperation-Competition Conflict Models," *Physica A* 387, no. 25 (2008): 6360–78.

8. See http://www.hcz.org/home?gclid=CPqQspiS-6UCFQ915Qod6mSsqQ.

9. Gottman, Swanson, Swanson, "General Systems Theory"; Losada and Heaphy, "The Role of Positivity."

10. Lakoff and Johnson, *Metaphors;* George Lakoff and Mark Johnson, *Philosophy in the Flesh: The Embodied Mind and Its Challenge to Western Thought* (New York: Basic Books, 1999).

11. Irving L. Janis, *Victims of Groupthink* (Boston: Houghton Mifflin Co., 1972).

12. Peter T. Coleman and Krister Lowe, "Conflict, Identity, and Resilience: Negotiating Collective Identities within the Palestinian and Israeli Diasporas," *Conflict Resolution Quarterly* 24, no. 4 (2007): 377–412.

13. Andrea Bartoli, Lan Bui-Wrzosinska, and Andrzej Nowak, "Peace Is in Movement: A Dynamical Systems Perspective on the Emergence of Peace in Mozambique," *Peace and Conflict: Journal of Peace Psychology* 16, no. 2 (2010): 211–30; Andrzej Nowak et al., "From Crude Law to Civil Relations: The Dynamics and Potential Resolution of Intractable Conflict," *Peace and Conflict: Journal of Peace Psychology* 2 (2010): 189–209.

14. Andrzej Nowak, "Dynamical Minimalism: Why Less Is More in Psychology," *Personality and Social Psychology Review* 2 (2004): 183–93.

15. Mary Baron, "Reducing Angry Rhetoric Helped Abortion Dialogue," *National Catholic Reporter,* January 22, 2009, http://ncronline.org.

CHAPTER 5

1. See also Kaiping Peng, "Psychology of Dialectical Thinking," in Neil J. Smelser and Paul B. Baltes, eds., *International Encyclopedia of the Social and Behavioral Sciences* (Oxford, UK: Elsevier Science, 1999); Peng and Nisbett, "Culture Dialectics."

2. See Morgan, *Images of Organization;* Siegel, *Mindsight.*

3. N. R. Kleinfield, "Mideast Tensions Are Getting Personal on Campus at Columbia," *New York Times,* January 18, 2005, http://query.nytimes.com/gst/fullpage.html?res=9C01E2D81238F93BA25752C0A9639C8B63 (accessed December 10, 2010).

4. Wendell Jones and Scott Hughes, "Complexity, Conflict Resolution and How the Mind Works," *Conflict Resolution Quarterly* 20 (2003): 4–20.

5. Stephen J. Stedman, "Spoiler Problems in Peace Processes," in Paul C. Stern and Daniel Druckman, eds., *International Conflict Resolution after the Cold War* (Washington, DC: National Academies Press, 2000).

6. Maruyama, "Second Cybernetics" and "Mindscapes, Management, Business Policy, and Public Policy," *Academy of Management Review* 7 (1982): 612–19.

7. See Lukasz Jochemczyk and Andrzej Nowak, "Dynamical Negotiation Networks: A Dynamical Model of Negotiation Process," paper presented at the 2009 Annual Conference of the International Association for Conflict Management, http://ssrn.com/abstract=1484899 (accessed December 10, 2010).

8. Scott Sherman, "The Mideast Comes to Columbia," *Nation,* April 4, 2005; Lisa Hirschmann, "Middle East Studies: Film Sparks Debate among Students, Bringing National Attention to Middle East Studies at Columbia," *Columbia Spectator,* May 9, 2005, and "MEALAC Controversy Lies Low for Fall Semester," *Columbia Spectator,* November 10, 2005; James Romoser, "Middle East Studies: University Response to Controversy Focuses on Systemic Failures," http://www.columbiaspectator.com/2005/05/09/middle-east-studies-university-response-controversy-focuses-systemic-failures; Kleinfield, "Mideast Tensions"; Joseph Massad, "Response to the Ad hoc Committee Grievance Report," http://www.columbia.edu/cu/mealac/faculty/massad/; Alix Pianin, "Professors Protest Massad's Tenure," *Columbia Spectator,* September 22, 2009, http://www.columbiaspectator.com/2009/09/22/professors-protest-massads-tenure; Kim Kirschenbaum and Alix Pianin, "Administration Quiet about Massad," *Columbia Spectator,* September 8, 2009, http://www.columbiaspectator.com/2009/09/08/administration-quiet-about-massad.

9. Kleinfield, "Mideast Tensions."

10. Romoser, "Middle East Studies."

11. Ibid.

12. "Intimidation at Columbia," *New York Times* editorial page, April 7, 2005, http://www.nytimes.com/2005/04/07/opinion/07thu1.html?_r=1&pagewanted=print&position.

13. Kleinfield, "Mideast Tensions."

14. Hirschmann, "Middle East Studies" and "MEALAC Controversy."

15. Elisabeth Bumiller, "We Have Met the Enemy and He Is PowerPoint," *New York Times,* April 26, 2006, http://www.nytimes.com/2010/04/27/world/27powerpoint.html?_r=2 (accessed December 7, 2010).

16. Nowak, "Dynamical Minimalism."

17. Stanley Wasserman and Katherine Faust, *Social Network Analysis: Methods and Applications* (Cambridge, UK: Cambridge University Press, 1994); Jochemczyk and Nowak, "Dynamical Negotiation Networks."

18. See related TED Video at http://www.ted.com/talks/eric_berlow_how_complexity_leads_to_simplicity.html.

19. International Center for Cooperation and Conflict Resolution and the Center for International Conflict Resolution.

20. Andrzej Nowak et al., "Seeking Sustainable Solutions: Using an Attractor Simulation Platform for Teaching Multi-Stakeholder Negotiation," *Negotiation Journal* 26, no. 1 (2010): 49–68.

21. Craig A. Smith and Phoebe C. Ellsworth, "Patterns of Cognitive Appraisal in Emotion," *Journal of Personality and Social Psychology* 48 (1985): 813–38.

22. Losada and Heaphy, "The Role of Positivity."

23. Gottman and Silver, *Seven Principles.*

24. Ryszard Praszkier, Andrzej Nowak, and Peter T. Coleman, "Social Entrepreneurs and Constructive Change: The Wisdom of Circumventing Conflict," *Peace and Conflict: Journal of Peace Psychology* 16, no. 2 (2010): 153–74.

25. Bartoli, Bui-Wrzosinska, and Nowak, "Peace Is in Movement."

26. Joseph S. Nye Jr., *Soft Power: The Means to Success in World Politics* (Cambridge, MA: Public Affairs, 2008).

27. See the documentary *Pray the Devil Back to Hell* at http://www.praythedevilbacktohell.com.

28. Dean G. Pruitt, "Readiness Theory and the Northern Ireland Conflict," *American Behavioral Scientist* 50 (2007): 1520–41.

29. Louise Diamond, "Multi-track Diplomacy in the 21st Century," in European Centre for Conflict Prevention, eds., *People Building Peace: 35 Inspiring Stories from Around the World* (Utrecht, Netherlands: International Books, 1999), 77–86.

30. Morgan, *Images of Organization.*

31. Daniel M. Wegner, "Ironic Processes of Mental Control," *Psychological Review* 101 (1994): 34–52; Daniel M. Wegner and Ralph Erber, "The Hyperaccessibility of Suppressed Thoughts," *Journal of Personality and Social Psychology* 63 (1992): 903–12.

32. C. Neil Macrae et al., "Out of Mind but Back in Sight: Stereotypes on the Rebound," *Journal of Personality and Social Psychology* 67 (1994): 808–17.

33. Robin R. Vallacher and Daniel M. Wegner, "Action Identification Theory," in P. Van Lange, A. W. Kruglanski, and E. T. Higgins, eds., *Handbook of Theories in Social Psychology* (London: Sage).

34. Coleman and Lowe, "Conflict, Identity, and Resilience."

35. Go to http://www.nifi.org.

36. S. Chaiken, R. Giner-Sorolla, and S. Chen, "Beyond Accuracy: Defense and Impression Motives in Heuristic and Systematic Information Processing," in Peter M. Goldwitzer and John A. Bargh, eds., *The Psychology of Action: Linking Cognition and Motivation to Behavior* (New York: Guilford, 1996), 553–87.

37. Ronald A. Fisher, *Interactive Conflict Resolution* (Syracuse, NY: Syracuse University Press, 1997).

38. Harold H. Saunders, *A Public Peace Process: Sustained Dialogue to Transform Racial and Ethnic Conflicts* (New York: St. Martin's Press, 1999).

39. Roccas and Brewer, "Social Identity Complexity."

40. Elise Boulding, "Enlivening Our Social Imagination," in Don Carlson and Craig Comstock, eds., *Citizen Summitry: Keeping the Peace When It Matters Too Much to Be Left to Politicians* (Los Angeles: Tarcher, 1986), 309–28.

41. Varshney, *Ethnic Conflict.*

42. Diehl and Goertz, *War and Peace.*

43. William Ury, *The Third Side: Why We Fight and How We Can Stop* (New York: Penguin, 2000), http://www.thirdside.org.

44. http://www.imtd.org.

45. Unpublished interview. See Peter T. Coleman et al., "Reconstructing Ripeness I: A Study of Constructive Engagement in Protracted Social Conflicts," *Conflict Resolution Quarterly* 26, no. 1 (2008): 3–42; Peter T. Coleman

et al., "Reconstructing Ripeness II: Models and Methods for Fostering Constructive Stakeholder Engagement Across Protracted Divides," *Conflict Resolution Quarterly* 26 no. 1 (2008): 43–69.

46. Naira Musallam, Peter T. Coleman, and Andrzej Nowak, "Understanding the Spread of Malignant Conflict: A Dynamical-Systems Perspective," *Peace and Conflict: Journal of Peace Psychology* 16, no. 2 (2010): 127–51; Andrzej Nowak et al., "From Crude Law."

47. Fry, *Beyond War.*

48. Morgan, *Images of Organization.*

49. Diehl and Goertz, *War and Peace.*

50. Ibid.

51. I. William Zartman, "Ripeness: The Hurting Stalemate and Beyond," in Stern and Druckman, *International Conflict Resolution,* 225–50.

52. See Coleman et al., "Reconstructing Ripeness I"; Coleman et al., "Reconstructing Ripeness II.

53. Peter T. Coleman, "Conflict, Complexity, and Change: A Meta-Framework for Addressing Protracted, Intractable Conflicts–III," *Peace and Conflict: Journal of Peace Psychology* 12, no. 4 (2006): 325–48.

54. Maire A. Dugan, "A Nested Theory of Conflict," *A Leadership Journal: Women in Leadership–Sharing the Vision* 1, no. 1 (1996): 9–20.

55. Quy N. H. Insead, "Time, Temporal Capability, and Planned Change," *Academy of Management Review* 26 (2001): 601–23.

56. Ibid.

57. See Herbert C. Kelman, "Interactive Problem Solving: A Social-Psychological Approach to Conflict Resolution," in W. Klassen, ed., *Dialogue toward Inter-Faith Understanding* (Jerusalem: Ecumenical Institute for Theological Research, 1986), 293–314; Fisher, *Interactive Conflict Resolution.*

58. Connie J. G. Gersick, "Revolutionary Change Theories: A Multilevel Exploration of the Punctuated Equilibrium Paradigm," *Academy of Management Review* 16 (1991): 10–36.

59. Ibid.

CHAPTER 6

1. See Bartoli, Bui-Wrzosinska, and Nowak, "Peace Is in Movement."

2. Andrea Bartoli, Aldo Civico, and Leone Gianturco, "From Violence to Political Engagement: Ending Violence, Expanding Political Incorporation," in

Bruce W. Dayton and Louis Kriesberg, eds., *Conflict Transformation and Peacebuilding: Moving from Violence to Sustainable Peace* (New York: Routledge, 2009).

3. David Keen, *The Economic Functions of Violence in Civil Wars* (New York: Routledge, 2005).

4. A. Bandura, "Social Cognitive Theory: An Agentic Perspective," *Asian Journal of Social Psychology* 2 (1999): 21–41.

5. Bartoli, Bui-Wrzosinska, and Nowak, "Peace Is in Movement."

6. Albert-László Barabási, *Linked: How Everything Is Connected to Everything Else and What It Means for Business, Science, and Everyday Life* (New York: Basic Books, 2002).

7. Kurt Lewin, Ronald Lippitt, and Ralph K. White, "Patterns of Aggressive Behavior in Experimentally Created Social Climates," *Journal of Social Psychology* 10 (1939): 271–301; M. Banaji and L. Heiphetz, "Attitudes," in Susan T. Fiske, Daniel T. Glibert, and Gardner Lindzey, eds., *Handbook of Social Psychology* (New York: Wiley, 2010), 353–93.

8. Summarized from Stephen Cohen, "Intractability and the Palestinian-Israeli Conflict," in Chester A. Crocker, Fen O. Hampson, and Pamela Aall, eds., *Grasping the Nettle: Analyzing Cases of Intractable Conflict* (Washington, DC: U.S. Institute of Peace Press, 2005), 343–56; Shibley Telhami, "Beyond Resolution? The Palestinian-Israeli Conflict," in Crocker, Hampson, and Aall, *Grasping the Nettle,* 357–74.

9. Nadim N. Rouhana and Daniel Bar-Tal, "Psychological Dynamics of Intractable Conflicts: The Israeli-Palestinian Case," *American Psychologist* 53 (1998): 761–70.

10. E. Tory Higgins, "Beyond Pleasure and Pain," *American Psychologist* 52 (1997): 1280–1300; Jack S. Levy, "Contending Theories of International Conflict: A Levels-of-Analysis Approach," in Chester A. Crocker, Fen O. Hampson, and Pamela Aall, eds., *Managing Global Chaos: Sources of and Responses to International Conflict* (Washington, DC: U.S. Institute of Peace Press, 1996).

11. E. Tory Higgins et al, "Transfer of Value from Fit," *Journal of Personality and Social Psychology* 84, no. 6 (2003): 1140–53.

12. Robin R. Vallacher et al., "Rethinking Intractable Conflict: The Perspective of Dynamical Systems," *American Psychologist* 65, no. 4 (2010): 262–78.

13. Carol A. Porter and Peter Suedfeld, "Integrative Complexity in the Correspondence of Literary Figures: Effects of Personal and Societal Stress," *Journal of Personality and Social Psychology* 40 (1981): 321–30.

14. Coleman and Lowe, "Conflict, Identity, and Resilience."

15. Rouhana and Bar-Tal, "Psychological Dynamics"; Daniel Bar-Tal, "Social-Psychological Foundations of Intractable Conflict," *American Behavioral Scientist* 50, no. 11 (2007): 1430–53.

16. Diehl and Goertz, *War and Peace;* Cohen, "Intractability."

17. Cohen, "Intractability."

18. Rafi Nets-Zehngut, "Mapping the Israeli Collective Memory of the Israeli-Arab/Palestinian Conflict," unpublished doctoral dissertation, 2009, Tel-Aviv University; Telhami, "Beyond Resolution?"

19. Praszkier, Nowak, and Coleman, "Social Entrepreneurs."

20. Lewin, Lippitt, and White, "Patterns of Aggressive Behavior"; Lester Coch and John R. P. French Jr., "Overcoming Resistance to Change," *Human Relations* 1 (1948): 512–32.

21. Herbert C. Kelman, "The Interdependence of Israeli and Palestinian National Identities: The Role of the Other in Existential Conflicts," *Journal of Social Issues* 55, no. 3, (1999): 581–600; Herbert C. Kelman, "Reconciliation as Identity Change: A Social-Psychological Perspective," paper presented at the Conference on Reconciliation, Hebrew University of Jerusalem, June 13, 2001.

22. Diehl and Goertz, *War and Peace.*

23. Nowak et al, "From Crude Law."

CONCLUSION

1. Murray Gell-Mann, "The Concept of the Institute," in David Pines, ed., *Emerging Syntheses in Science* (Redwood City, CA: Addison-Wesley, 1988), 1–15.

2. See Dorner, *The Logic of Failure;* Fritjof Capra, *The Hidden Connections: Integrating the Biological, Cognitive, and Social Dimensions of Life into a Science of Sustainability* (New York: Doubleday, 2002); Steven Johnson, *Emergence: The Connected Lives of Ants, Brains, Cities, and Software* (New York: Scribner, 2001); Barabási, *Linked;* Jones and Hughes, "Complexity"; Malcolm Gladwell, *The Tipping Point: How Little Things Can Make a Big Difference* (Boston: Little, Brown, 2000); Gersick, "Revolutionary Change Theories"; Maruyama, "Mindscapes"; Morgan, *Images of Organization;* Andrzej Nowak and Robin R. Vallacher, *Dynamical Social Psychology* (New York: Guilford Press, 1998).

3. See Conway, Suedfeld, and Tetlock, "Integrative Complexity"; Rafaeli-Mor and Steinberg, "Self-Complexity and Well-Being"; Suedfeld and Rank, "Revolutionary Leaders"; Suedfeld, Tetlock, and Streufert, *Conceptual/*

Integrative Complexity; Peterson and Flanders, "Complexity Management Theory," *Cortex* 38 (2002): 429–58; Siegel, *Mindsight;* Golec and Federico, "Understanding Responses"; Fu et al., "Epistemic Motives"; Kang and Shaver, "Individual Differences"; Lawrence, Lenk, and Quinn, "Behavioral Complexity in Leadership"; Roccas and Brewer, "Social Identity Complexity"; Losada and Heaphy, "Role of Positivity"; Losada, "Complex Dynamics."

4. D. M. Wegner et al., "The Emergence of Action," *Journal of Personality and Social Psychology* 46, no. 2 (1984): 269–79; Robin R. Vallacher and Daniel M. Wegner, "What Do People Think They're Doing? Action Identification and Human Behavior," *Psychological Review* 94 no. 1 (1987): 3–15; Vallacher and Wegner, "Action Identification Theory."

5. Wegner, "Ironic Processes"; Wegner and Erber, "Hyperaccessibility"; Macrae et al., "Out of Mind"; E. Tory Higgins, William S. Rholes, and Carl R. Jones, "Category Accessibility and Impression Formation," *Journal of Experimental Social Psychology* 13 (1977): 141–54; Mahzarin R. Banaji, Curtis Hardin, and Alexander J. Rothman, "Implicit Stereotyping in Person Judgment," *Journal of Personality and Social Psychology* 65, no. 2 (1993): 272–81; Dweck, *Mindset;* Peter T. Coleman, "A Tale of Two Theories: Implicit Theories of Power and Power-Sharing in Organizations," in Dean Tjosvold and Barbara Wisse, eds., *Power and Interdependence in Organizations* (Cambridge, UK: Cambridge University Press, 2009).

6. Lederach, *Building Peace;* E. Allison Holman and Roxane C. Silver, "Getting Stuck in the Past: Temporal Orientation and Coping with Trauma," *Journal of Personality and Social Psychology* 74 (1998): 1146–63; I. Boniwell and P. G. Zimbardo, "Balancing One's Time Perspective in Pursuit of Optimal Functioning," in P. Alex Linley and Stephen Joseph, eds., *Positive Psychology in Practice* (New York: Wiley, 2003).

7. Higgins, "Beyond Pleasure and Pain"; Higgins et al., "Transfer of Value."

8. S. W. J. Kozlowski and K. J. Klein, "A Multilevel Approach to Theory and Research in Organizations: Contextual, Temporal, and Emergent Processes," in Katherine J. Klein and Steve W. J. Kozlowski, eds., *Multilevel Theory, Research, and Methods in Organizations* (San Francisco: Jossey-Bass), 1–32; Levy, "Contending Theories"; Dennis J. Sandole, *Capturing the Complexity of Conflict: Dealing with Violent Ethnic Conflicts in the Post-Cold War Era* (New York: Pinter, 1999); Varshney, *Ethnic Conflict.*

9. John F. Kennedy's American University Commencement Address, June 10, 1963.

10. Lattimore, *Aeschylus I.*

index

ABOUT THE AUTHOR

PETER T. COLEMAN is associate professor of psychology and education at Columbia University, director of the International Center for Cooperation and Conflict Resolution, and on the faculty of Teachers College and The Earth Institute at Columbia. In 2003, he received the Early Career Award from the American Psychological Association, Division 48: Society for the Study of Peace, Conflict, and Violence. He lives in New York.

PublicAffairs is a publishing house founded in 1997. It is a tribute to the standards, values, and flair of three persons who have served as mentors to countless reporters, writers, editors, and book people of all kinds, including me.

I. F. Stone, proprietor of *I. F. Stone's Weekly*, combined a commitment to the First Amendment with entrepreneurial zeal and reporting skill and became one of the great independent journalists in American history. At the age of eighty, Izzy published *The Trial of Socrates*, which was a national bestseller. He wrote the book after he taught himself ancient Greek.

Benjamin C. Bradlee was for nearly thirty years the charismatic editorial leader of *The Washington Post*. It was Ben who gave the *Post* the range and courage to pursue such historic issues as Watergate. He supported his reporters with a tenacity that made them fearless and it is no accident that so many became authors of influential, best-selling books.

Robert L. Bernstein, the chief executive of Random House for more than a quarter century, guided one of the nation's premier publishing houses. Bob was personally responsible for many books of political dissent and argument that challenged tyranny around the globe. He is also the founder and longtime chair of Human Rights Watch, one of the most respected human rights organizations in the world.

• • •

For fifty years, the banner of Public Affairs Press was carried by its owner Morris B. Schnapper, who published Gandhi, Nasser, Toynbee, Truman, and about 1,500 other authors. In 1983, Schnapper was described by *The Washington Post* as "a redoubtable gadfly." His legacy will endure in the books to come.

Peter Osnos, *Founder and Editor-at-Large*

www.ingramcontent.com/pod-product-compliance
Ingram Content Group UK Ltd.
Pitfield, Milton Keynes, MK11 3LW, UK
UKHW041040180625
459791UK00012B/76/J

9 781586 489212